Inspiring, informative books for thoughtful readers
wanting to make changes and realize their potential.

Other titles in the series include:

Dating, Mating and Relating
The complete guide to finding and keeping your ideal partner

Deliver Outstanding Customer Service
Gain and retain customers and stay ahead of the competition

Let's Split the Difference
Tips, tools and techniques for MBTI® practitioners to
help clarify best-fit type with clients

Starting and Running a Successful Consultancy
How to build and market your own consulting business

Teamwork from the Inside Out Field Book
Exercises and Tools for Turning Team Performance Inside Out

Turning Team Performance Inside Out
Team Types and Temperament for High-Impact Results

Type Trilogy Guidebook and Card set

FLAWLESS FACILITATION

LEARN to Maximize Engagement and Retention for All

SUSAN NASH

Flawless Facilitation
LEARN to Maximize Engagement and Retention for All

ISBN 978-1-7338225-0-3

Published by:
EM-Power Inc.
1074 Morgan Hill Drive,
Chula Vista, CA 91913
Tel: +1 619 990 6811

Contents

Introduction

Welcome to FLAWLESS FACILITATION!

This publication is designed as a practical "How To" book for any professional in the Training and Development field and/or any individual responsible for helping people learn effectively. It represents a unique combination of practical course design principles, detailed skills and techniques for facilitating active learning, and knowledge about how different personality types learn.

In the Introduction...

We will describe how to use this book to raise your effectiveness in facilitating impactful individual development and learning events. We will provide background information on the origins of the T.E.A.C.H. to L.E.A.R.N. approach and describe the role of the Facilitator and Learner in this context. Finally, we will provide high-level information about the structure and purpose of each section of the book.

GAME PLAN

You will learn about:

- What Makes a Great Facilitator?
- The origins of the T.E.A.C.H. to L.E.A.R.N. Approach
- Who is the audience for this book?
- How to use this book.
- What is in this book?

What Makes a Great Facilitator?

In this book, we will focus on crystallizing knowledge, skills and techniques to help Facilitators design and deliver memorable global learning events. We will combine theoretical principles with specific, detailed skills analysis and descriptions.

So what makes a Great Facilitator?

EXERCISE 1-1: THINK ABOUT A GREAT FACILITATOR.

- Think about a great Facilitator who created a **positive learning experience** for you. What did they say or do that made this a fun, interesting, relevant or meaningful experience for you?
- Think about a poor Facilitator who created a **negative learning experience** for you. What did they say or do that made this irrelevant, unengaging, or disinteresting for you?
- Then look at the themes that emerge from this analysis.

TRY IT ON: WRITE YOUR IDEAS HERE...

Positive Learning Experience

_____

_____

_____

Negative Learning Experience

_____

_____

_____

CASE STUDIES

In research from a global company, over 900 participants were asked, "What makes a Great Facilitator?" The answers were surprising. The responses included good facilitation skills, engaging, good examples, high energy and a positive environment. There were no direct references to the Facilitator's Presentation Skills.

- **Good facilitation skills** included adapting to the needs of the group, keeping the flow of the session, guiding group discussion, answering questions, providing instructions and providing direction.
- **Engaging** was defined as the degree to which the Facilitator made the session interactive.
- **Good examples** were defined as real-life, relevant, fun and to the point.
- A positive environment was when participants felt "at ease" and that the learning was inclusive, and safe.

FOUL!

Too often **presenting** is confused with **facilitating**. Our premise is that for learning to be effective, participants (whether children or adults) need to be actively engaged throughout the learning journey. Therefore, we need to facilitate – not just present data!

Themes

The positive themes that normally emerge about great Facilitators relate to:

- Social engagement
- Time for reflection
- Feeling "safe" and validated in the training session
- Opportunities to get hands-on with any content or approach
- Resilience of content
- Accuracy of, and interest in, course content
- Connection to past experience, solving a problem or growing expertise
- Expertise/knowledge of the Facilitator

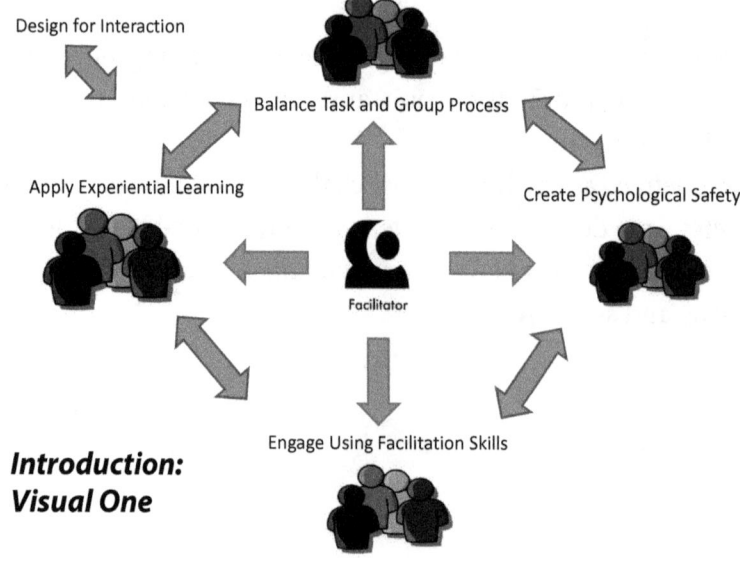

Introduction:
Visual One

These themes relate to a complex combination of:

- Balancing Task and Group Process in any learning event (see Chapter One for the definition of these terms)
- Ensuring participants are actively involved in learning
- Protecting individual's needs in terms of self esteem
- Catering to differing thinking styles in terms of preferences and Type
- Contrasting energy and approach for different content areas in terms of pace and movement

By understanding each of these individual facets, it is possible to build a "toolkit" of techniques that can help make learning relevant for all types.

TIMEOUT!

- A key learning point is that when a Facilitator engages the group and the audience is actively learning, these techniques are often transparent to participants.
- As a result, the more involved the participants, the more likely they are to say, "This person was a Great Facilitator".

FOUL!

Many of these ideas may seem quite simple and detailed. However, it is only by defining the specific aspects of skills and behaviors that it is possible to understand exactly "How" positive learning can take place.

Origins of the T.E.A.C.H. to L.E.A.R.N. Approach

> "A good teacher can inspire hope, ignite the imagination, and instill a love learning."
>
> *Brad Henry*

This book and methodology evolved from over thirty years of designing effective learning events, developing and delivering workshops around the world, writing Training/Facilitator Guides, and running in-depth Train-the-Trainer sessions to enable consistent delivery of content with multiple trainers, languages and countries. Up to this date, hundreds of Facilitators have rolled out customized soft skills programs to thousands of participants in subjects ranging from retail sales, technical customer support, management and leadership, to teaching, facilitation and learning. The culmination of this corporate-focused work for such clients as Google, Oracle, PUMA, Gucci, Kipling and North Sails was developing and rolling out globally a teaching/learning program to a substantial Shia Muslim community for improving the effectiveness of teachers and reducing drop out of students from their Madrasah – or Sunday Schools. This project enabled me to understand that a Flawless Facilitator possesses the ability to design and deliver effective learning events that appealed to all types, no matter what personality, culture or generation. This talent requires a combination of:

- Targeted design using active learning principles.
- Practical application of best practices in facilitation techniques.
- Use of a variety of customized activities.
- In-depth understanding of what each type needs to learn effectively (normally assessed by the Myers Briggs Type Indicator – MBTI®).

Who is the Audience for this Book?

For this book, the audience could be anyone who is trying to stimulate behavior change through learning and development of others. This could include:

- Leaders
- Teachers
- Professional Facilitators
- Coaches
- Managers
- Preachers

How to Use this Book

This is a hands-on book. Throughout it, you will find the material organized into different categories designed to create a learning experience that is interactive, inspiring, informative, and clear. The information types include:

GAME PLAN

An overview of what you will achieve within each chapter.

EXERCISES

Instructions for activities you can use to try on material and put concepts to work. These actions focus on developing facilitation expertise.

For each exercise there will be a section labeled **Try It On!** You can use this section to write your ideas.

FOUL!

To clear up a perception that may not be accurate.

COACHING POINT

A note or reminder about what to do or look for as you apply the facilitation practices. Coaching points often contain recommendations about how to act and suggest behaviors to build competency.

TIMEOUT!

A clarification or side note about useful information to build facilitation knowledge. This may include definitions, statistics and facts.

CASE STUDIES

Examples of how principles have been applied in real-life case studies.

SCORECARD

A series of questions to help you review the outcomes from each section.

What is in this Book?

TIMEOUT!

T.E.A.C.H. to L.E.A.R.N.

We have used the acronym T.E.A.C.H. as the "anchoring" course/program development methodology. If any program design follows these core principles, the facilitator will be more successful in teaching skills, knowledge and techniques in an interactive way that "sticks".

We have used the acronym L.E.A.R.N. to explain in more detail why and how the T.E.A.C.H. methodology tends to work with multiple types, generations and cultures.

This book is comprised of this introduction and six main sections:

- **Chapter One** – In the first chapter, we will introduce **The T.E.A.C.H. Methodology** as a way of helping the Facilitator incorporate the Task and Group Process elements of a learning experience into course design. As part of the detailed description for how to design an effective workshop, we will use The T.E.A.C.H. Methodology within each module to combine practical application with sharing of knowledge, skills or techniques in a dynamic way. We will also review how to prioritize content so that there is time to incorporate learner engagement. The purpose of this section is to provide the design principles that underlie any learning event.

- **Chapter Two – L: Leverage Active Learning Principles.** In this chapter, we will review the principles of Andragogy and Pedagogy, define Active Learning and highlight some of the benefits of using this more engaging approach. In addition, we will review some of the current research about neuroscience and learning to show how this knowledge supports the T.E.A.C.H. Methodology. We will specifically introduce the Development Process as a model to understand how the brain operates when trying to implement a new skill or habit. The purpose of this section is to provide the Facilitator with some key background knowledge about the importance and relevance of Active Learning. This chapter will provide the theoretical foundation for the rest of the skills and techniques presented in this book.

- **Chapter Three – E: Engage the Audience.** As we have discussed, the ability to engage the audience has a direct influence on how we are perceived as a Facilitator. In this chapter, we will review the communication process between one and many. We will describe in detail Involving Facilitation skills and techniques that can build connection to create a safe learning environment. When we use facilitation skills effectively, they are often transparent to the learner. We will spend time describing the attributes of Directive Facilitation and contrast the attributes of Involving and Directive styles as we evaluate the Spectrum of Collaborative Facilitation. Using Visual Aids can stimulate auditory, visual and kinesthetic learners so we will review how to use these tools effectively. We will also outline how to handle challenging situations, which can occur with the most experienced Facilitator. Finally, we will summarize how these skills integrate with The T.E.A.C.H. Methodology. The overall purpose of this chapter is to define and describe the skills that create a conversational learning climate.

- **Chapter Four – A: Apply Experiential Learning.** Participants tend to remember effective activities. In this chapter, we will describe many of those that a Facilitator can use to cement learning, build involvement and apply the content introduced. We will describe the general principles for using any activity, as well as provide detailed guidelines for how and when to use each activity to provide a learning benefit. We will evaluate which activities we could use at different stages of the Learning Cycle and review some simple guidelines for designing effective activities. Finally, we will summarize how activities can fit within The T.E.A.C.H. Methodology. The purpose of this section is to help the Facilitator to select and use a wide variety of learning activities based on the context to achieve learning objectives.

- **Chapter Five – R: Recognize Different Learning Styles.** In this chapter, we will begin to look at learning through the lens of personality differences. First, we will look at what might motivate different types to learn, using the theory of Temperament originally articulated for the modern world by David Keirsey. We will introduce how to vary our language to appeal to different Temperaments, and which learning approaches tend to work for each type. We will also look at the different energies associated with facilitating learning using the Linda Berens Interaction Styles framework. We will discuss the importance of adapting energy and approach to different content areas in order to maximize engagement and retention. Finally, we will review how Temperament and Interaction style integrate with The T.E.A.C.H. Methodology. The purpose of this section is to help clarify general and specific principles for appealing to all types. Understanding these frameworks will help you become a more versatile Facilitator.

- **Chapter Six – N: Nurture Different Thinking Styles.** In this chapter, we will review the eight "Cognitive Processes" originally articulated by Carl Jung. This knowledge is helpful to understand, both in terms of program design, as well as in understanding Facilitator and participants' innate mental habits around learning. We will integrate Temperament, Interaction Style and Cognitive Processes within the concept called Whole Type. We will provide high-level descriptions for each Whole Type profile, associated with some specific techniques for teaching each Type. The purpose of this section is to demonstrate how we can appeal to different Thinking Styles by including a diversity of data gathering approaches and catering to different judging criteria. This can increase the Facilitator's success in connecting with varying types of students.

- **Summary and Action Plan –** In this chapter we will review the key principles covered and capture key action ideas to help you become a Flawless Facilitator.

- **Appendix** – In the Appendix we will show how the four preferences associated with the Myers Briggs Type Indicator® approach integrate with Whole Type and a "four-letter" code.

As described above, there will be case studies, individual exercises, activities and coaching points to enhance learning.

What Else?

Feel free to make the book your own: write in the spaces provided, complete the exercises, and make notes about your learning. Remember, any behavior change needs constant reinforcement: use this book as one of the tools in your toolkit for achieving facilitation excellence!

THE T.E.A.C.H. METHODOLOGY

Chapter Overview

The first step in becoming a Flawless Facilitator is to design any learning intervention in order to optimize engagement and learning. In this chapter, we will first outline the Task and Group Process elements involved in learning. Then we will spend some time reviewing how to design an effective learning session by understanding the audience, being clear about the purpose of any intervention, defining key outcomes and then structuring the program to maximize retention. Within this structure, we will describe The T.E.A.C.H. Methodology and show how it helps to balance the Task and Group Process elements to maximize learning. Finally, we will provide some simple techniques to help prioritize content to be included in any program.

GAME PLAN

You will learn about:

- The Task and Group Process Elements in Learning
- Overall Design Structure
- The T.E.A.C.H. Methodology
- Prioritizing Content

Task and Group Process Elements in Learning

> "Learning is not attained by chance, it must be sought for with ardor and attended to with diligence."
>
> *Abigail Adams*

In any learning experience, the Facilitator's responsibility is to balance the Task (**What** is to be learned) and Group Process (**How** the group is learning). If the two become out of balance, participants pick up the incoherence and tend to make judgments unconsciously about the Facilitator's expertise.

TIMEOUT!

The **Task Element** in Learning will include any knowledge or information shared, relevant statistics or data, key skills to be taught or techniques to be introduced. It is **What** participants are there to learn.

The **Group Process Element** in Learning will include how interaction is managed within the group including large group discussions, questions and answers, Ice-breakers and experiential activities such as role-plays, case studies, etc. It is **How** participants internalize and personalize the learning.

(This approach has been modified from the work of Bales on Task and Socioemotional Distinctions.)

If the Facilitator focuses only on teaching the content (the Task element), without engaging the audience (Group Process), learning will not occur for all participants. In the same way, if the Facilitator manages the group dynamic without covering the content to be taught, the session might be harmonious – yet without any tangible outcome.

Below are some typical examples of Task and Group Process.

Task ⟷ Group Process

TASK/WHAT	GROUP PROCESS/HOW
Introduction • Objectives • Agenda • Parking Lot • Context Setting	**Introduction** • Roles: Facilitator and Prisoner/Vacationer/Learner • Using an Ice-Breaker • Gathering Participant Expectations • Establishing Ground Rules

TASK/WHAT	GROUP PROCESS/HOW
Main Content • Themes • Theories • Techniques • Concepts/Models • Skill Definition • Examples • Staying on track • Educating: Directive Facilitation	**Main Content** • Asking questions • Getting group feedback • Monitoring energy • Having fun • Guiding group discussions • Processing participants' reactions • Dealing with challenging participants • Involving: Inclusive Facilitation
Activities • Exercise set up • Instructions • "Facilitator moments" • Prioritizing activities	**Activities** • Observing exercises • Checking for understanding • Clarifying learning points • Thinking creatively
Summary • Making decisions • Pushing for closure	**Summary** • Processing insights/emotions • Probing for learning

What can make the Facilitator's role complex is that there is a constant need to monitor and manage task progress with positive group dynamics. If the balance is lost between the Task and Group Process elements, participants may become dissatisfied with the Facilitator and learning experience.

EXERCISE 1-1:
THINK ABOUT YOUR ROLE AS A FACILITATOR

- Look at the previous list related to Task and Group Process.
- On which element do you think you tend to focus more attention? Why?
- How could you make sure you consider both elements?

TRY IT ON: YOUR ROLE AS A FACILITATOR

Write your ideas here...

Which Element – Task or Group Process?

_____

_____

Why?

_____

_____

How to Adapt?

_____

_____

FOUL!

It can be easy as a Facilitator to fall into the "Expert Trap" of becoming the person who answers all questions and owns key data. This can mean a lack of focus on Group Process with the result that learning may pause and participants may feel disempowered.

If a Facilitator can constantly monitor Task and Group Process elements for cohesion, then the group will learn more.

COACHING POINT

Underpinning the ability to balance Task and Group Process is the Facilitator's belief and trust that the group will be able to provide many of the important content elements (What), as long as the design of the session is effective, and the associated Group Process is positive.

Overall Design Structure

The following information is provided to help describe the design principles underlying any learning event.

Chapter One:
Visual One

Design: Who, Why, and What?

TIMEOUT!

Before designing any content, it is important to identify:

- **Who** will be participating – what is the audience analysis?
- **Why** are you holding this learning event – what is the purpose?
- **What** is the main outcome you are trying to achieve?

Who – Audience Analysis

The more we can learn about the potential audience, the more we are able to tailor program design to match participant needs.

Factors to consider might include:

- What is the audience's existing level of knowledge of the topic?
- What do you think is the participant's level of interest in the topic?
- What is the audience's attitude towards the topic, the organization, and you?
- What hidden agendas might there be? (A hidden agenda is like an ulterior motive someone in the audience might have separately from learning the content.)
- Which participants do you know as you begin?

Why – Purpose of Learning Event

There can be many different purposes for learning events. For instance, the purpose can be to:

- Inform e.g. Product knowledge training
- Entertain e.g. Company meetings
- Teach e.g. Sales training
- Motivate e.g. Team Building sessions

Having a clear purpose can help in designing both the content and the flow of any session.

What – Outcome of Event

It is important to think about the outcome of any learning event in order to prioritize the content to include in the session. The outcome statement will articulate clearly what you want the audience to know, think, feel, or be able to do, as a result of participating in the session. For instance from a sales training program, "Participants will be able to sell more products that meet consumer needs using an approach that is in alignment with Brand Identity." Being clear about the outcome can also help to prioritize important content (see notes at the end of this Chapter).

What – Learning Objectives

Objectives are statements that describe what the learner is expected to achieve as a result of instruction. Because they direct attention to the participants and the types of behaviors we want them to exhibit, sometimes these statements are called "behavioral" objectives.

TIMEOUT!

A learning objective is much more specific than an Outcome Statement. According to Robert Mager (author of *Performance-Based Learning Objectives*), the ideal learning objective has three parts:

1. A measurable verb.
2. The important condition (if any) under which performance is to occur.
3. The criterion of acceptable performance.

(Frequently you will not see the criterion or the condition specified if they are obvious. However, sometimes adding the condition(s) and/or the criterion gives more clarity to a learning objective.)

EXERCISE 1-2: THINK ABOUT A SESSION YOU HAVE DESIGNED

1. Who – To what extent did you conduct an audience analysis? What else could you have done?
2. Why – What was the purpose of the session you designed?
3. What – To what extent could you define the outcome in one sentence? How did the learning objectives relate to the overall outcome?

TRY IT ON: DESIGN – WHO? WHY? WHAT?

Write your ideas here…

   1. **Who – Audience Analysis**

_____

_____

_____

   2. **Why – Purpose**

_____

_____

_____

   3. **What – Outcome and Objectives**

_____

_____

_____

CASE STUDY: INTERVIEWING SKILLS WORKSHOP

Who? The target audience was Retail Store Managers many of whom had not received formal interviewing skills training.

Why? To teach Behavioral Interviewing Skills and Process.

What – Outcome? To reduce staff turnover from poor hiring decisions.

What – Behavioral Objectives (Samples)

- To define target job competencies for an open job role.
- To ask candidates effective behavioral interviewing questions.
- To recognize Moments of Truth and the consequent need to ask for more detailed information from the candidate.
- To evaluate the candidate using appropriate, specific data.

Design Structure

The overall design structure normally includes an element of "Tell them what you are going to tell them, tell them, and then tell them you told them."

- Preview – Introduction
- View – For each Subject
  - Include a Hook
  - Include Information following the T.E.A.C.H. Process
- Review – Summary and Action Plan

TIMEOUT!

Repetition of key content elements can help to raise learning and retention levels.

Introduction

The key aims in a training program Introduction are to:

- Define the role of the Facilitator and the role of the participants.
- Establish a safe yet stimulating learning environment.
- Engage the audience in the learning event by using activities such as Ice-Breakers.
- Set clear objectives and expectations for the session.
- Clarify agenda, ground rules and Parking Lot.

TIME OUT!

The Introduction plays an important role in establishing a successful event by establishing the Group Process for learning as well as defining the key Task elements included in the training program.

Many learning events start by outlining the agenda and objectives. The challenge with this approach is that individuals may not be in a place to hear and internalize this content because they are in a new social context. According to research conducted by Google, for teams to work well, people need to feel safe psychologically. A safe environment is where participants feel comfortable enough to acknowledge their own weaknesses, voice their gaps in knowledge, and ask for help when they need it. The key question individuals are trying to answer is, "Can I take risks as part of learning in this workshop without feeling insecure or embarrassed?" The safer participants feel, the more they will appreciate the Facilitator's expertise.

One way to answer this question is to start the workshop with an Ice-Breaker to help the team get to know each other, begin to build relationships, and to demonstrate that expression of ideas and diversity of thought are encouraged and supported.

TIMEOUT!

The following flow for the Introduction can help to establish a positive Task and Group Process (see later notes for more detail):

- Introduction of Facilitator
- Define Roles of the Facilitator and Participant
- Ice-Breaker
- Expectations
- Objectives
- Agenda
- Ground Rules
- Parking Lot
- Context Setting

Let's review each of these elements in more detail.

Introduction of Facilitator

There is debate on how much data the Facilitator could/should present about their background at the beginning of the session. I advocate providing less data because the priority at the beginning of the session should be to establish Group Process and build Psychological Safety. My name is, "_____" is probably sufficient!

COACHING POINT

To meet the needs of those who believe the Facilitator needs to share more information to build credibility, you can distribute a Facilitator bio as pre-work, as a handout, or ask the program sponsor to do a **brief** introduction. **Facilitator's build credibility by facilitating!**

Define Roles: Facilitator Role

It can be important to state almost immediately that your role is to act as a Facilitator and then ask the group, "What does a Facilitator do?" (Make sure to wait for the answer and repeat answers!) In this way, there is alignment between your words ("My role is as a Facilitator") and your actions (facilitating by asking questions, listening and repeating.)

FOUL!

There is irony in a Facilitator who begins a session saying, "This program will be highly interactive", followed by a 15 + minute one-way introduction of his/her background and skills!

Define Roles: Participant Role

A fun and effective way to set the scene and define roles is to use the "Prisoner, Vacationer, Learner" script as shown below.

TIMEOUT! SCRIPT FOR PRISONER, VACATIONER, LEARNER

"I have observed that there are often three types of students in the room, Prisoners, Vacationers and Learners. (Pause for laughter!)

- What might Prisoners be thinking? (Don't want to be here.)
- What might be Prisoners' body language? (Arms folded, no eye contact, flipping through materials.)
- What might Vacationers be thinking? (I don't care what we are doing – at least I am not at work!)
- What might be Vacationers' body language? (Relaxed, eating lots of snacks.) Could be called Club Ed.
- What are Learners thinking? (What will I walk away with?)
- What might be Learners' body language? (Leaning forward, answering questions, eye contact.)
- Who has the most fun? Prisoners, Vacationers or Learners (Learners)

Using this script accomplishes several things:

- It highlights that you are observing participants' behavior.
- It raises the issue of "Prisoners" in a lively and non-confrontational way.
- It indirectly describes the behaviors you expect from participants – a key element in defining Group Process.
- It names behaviors that might be perceived as negative in a non-judgmental way, thereby building Psychological Safety. (Many participants tend to be overloaded with work and/or the project owner may not have clearly explained the reasons for learning, so they may be entitled to feel defensive initially or non-engaged.)
- It is funny so creates a connection between the Facilitator and the group.

Ice-Breaker

Ice- Breakers can be an effective way to start a training session or team-building event. In their ideal form, they start to get people engaged with each other and the topic of the session. (Group Process and Task)

FOUL!

Ice-breakers don't work if they seem to focus merely on getting people talking and have no other point.

So when considering which Ice-Breaker to use, consider the following criteria:

- How can it include an element of personal introductions so that you and the other participants can get a feel for who is in the room?
- How can it "set the context" for the topic? For instance, if the subject is coaching, could you ask for their initial thoughts on the definition of coaching?
- How can you use it to identify the audience's current level of knowledge about the topic? The suggestion in the question above would serve this purpose.
- How can it raise the interest in the topic? For instance, if the subject were coaching, how could the group share positive coaching examples? Could you share any relevant coaching statistics?
- How can you use the Ice-Breaker to build trust? For instance, in the question above, this asks individuals to share personal judgments that could help to build trust.
- How can you use the Ice-Breaker to build alignment behind the topic? For instance, sharing the definition of coaching after individuals have shared their thoughts would begin to align the group around the subject.

COACHING POINT

Make sure any Ice-Breaker is set up so that everybody "wins". An ice-breaker with "Losers", any degree of embarrassment or negative feedback, can shut down rather than build the group process.

It is important to pick or design the best Ice-Breaker to create an effective learning environment. (More detail on learning activities that can be used as Ice-Breakers are described in Chapter Four.)

Participant Expectations

As we discussed earlier, participants may walk into your classroom with plenty of reservations (e.g. I already know this stuff, I have to be here because my manager told me to be here). As a Facilitator, it is important to be prepared and realize the participants' mind-set may not be 100% focused on learning. If participants can actively spend time defining their expectations from the session, this can help to overcome these reservations. In addition, if Learners create personal learning objectives, you can help the Learner buy in to the content and flow. As a Facilitator, this information can also help you see where you might need to customize your content and flex the agenda.

COACHING POINT

If the Facilitator has a clear idea of the problem participants are trying to solve, this can help focus expectations, build credibility and target learning more effectively.

Objectives

Here you can review the learning objectives that you (or others) created in the design and development process. Objectives relate to "What" will be covered – the first specific Task element in the Introduction.

COACHING POINT

It is preferable to review the objectives after participants have identified their expectations for a number of reasons:

- It enables you to link course objectives directly with participant aims.
- It starts with participants' knowledge and experience and builds on it – a key principle in Andragogy (see notes in Chapter Two).
- It enables you to reset expectations if individuals want to achieve something that is not directly included in the content.
- It reinforces trust and builds psychological safety.

Agenda

The agenda sets the structure for the session, shows the sequence of subjects to be covered and represents the second main Task element in the introduction. Some types, specifically Stabilizers (see Chapter Five) – might get frustrated if a lot of time is invested in the Introduction before covering the Agenda.

COACHING POINT

To overcome any concerns about the delay in covering the Agenda and Objectives, include this information as a handout or as pre-reading with the Joining Instructions.

Ground Rules

| TIMEOUT! | |

Ground rules articulate a set of expected behaviors for workshop conduct. Ideally, the audience should be involved in setting the Ground Rules so that these guidelines appear as "owned by the group", dynamic, relevant and less of a cliché.

Ground rules are set in the Introduction with the explanation of their purpose – for example, to ensure that everyone is heard, to ensure that participants work together toward greater understanding, rather than contribute disjointed pieces. It is important for Facilitators to hold participants accountable to these guidelines during the session. Sample Ground Rules could include:

- Listen actively and attentively.
- Ask for clarification if you are confused.
- Do not interrupt one another.
- Challenge one another respectfully.
- Critique ideas, not people.
- Avoid put-downs (even humorous ones).
- Take responsibility for the quality of the discussion.
- Do not monopolize discussion.

| COACHING POINT | |

When the Prisoner, Vacationer, Learner Story is used to define the role of the Participant (see earlier notes), it could mean that time does not need to be invested in Ground Rules in the Introduction.

In addition, if the Facilitator follows the flow of the Introduction as shown, this will mean that many of these Ground Rules have already been demonstrated in establishing the Group Process. It is always an option to introduce the Ground Rules later in the session should the Group Process deteriorate.

Parking Lot

TIMEOUT!

Paste a piece of Flip Chart paper – headed Parking Lot – on the wall.

If items arise that are outside the scope of current discussion, the Facilitator lists these ideas on the Parking Lot.

The Parking Lot helps to track important items, ideas and issues that may not be directly relevant at a time in the agenda. The principle is to return to them later while also validating the participants who raised them.

The benefits of using a Parking Lot are considerable and include:

- It shows the person raising the question/issue that he/she has been heard.
- It provides the Facilitator with an opportunity to review the items later in order to either discuss or send follow-up materials.
- When reviewed, it can sometimes show that the issue may not have been relevant.
- It can also show that an item has been addressed later in the program.

Context Setting

TIMEOUT!

Occasionally there is a need, beyond the Ice-Breaker and Expectations to spend additional time positioning the content of the program and/or the benefits of learning more about the subject. We call this process "Context Setting".

For instance, in a Leadership development workshop, there may be a need to look at the broader subject of Leadership before beginning to introduce specific leadership tools, skills and strategies. This Context Setting can be part of the Introduction or in a section all on its own.

CASE STUDY:
INTRODUCTION TO "MANAGING CONFLICT"

Below is an example for the flow of the Introduction for a Managing Conflict Workshop:

Facilitator Introduction: "My name is _____ and I will be the Facilitator for today's workshop."

Facilitator Role and Participant Role (Prisoner, Vacationer, Learner).

Ice-Breaker/Expectations – Table group discussion on program expectations.

Program Objectives and Agenda – Facilitator reviews objectives and agenda.

Context Setting: Open Space Exercise (see Chapter Four for definition of Open Space).

- How would you define Conflict?
- What are the causes of Conflict?

- What are the positive aspects of Conflict?
- What could be the negative consequences of Conflict?

This activity was used to surface participants' existing knowledge about Conflict and to highlight that Conflict has a positive as well as a negative side.

EXERCISE 1-3: YOUR INTRODUCTION

Think of a Training Session that you have designed and/or delivered.

1. Which of the elements that we have reviewed did you include in your Introduction? (Facilitator Introduction, Role of Facilitator, Participant Role, Ice-Breaker, Expectations, Objectives, Agenda, Ground Rules, Parking Lot, Context Setting)
2. How did you sequence your Introduction differently from the suggested flow above?
3. How will you design your Introduction differently as a result of this information?

TRY IT ON: YOUR INTRODUCTION

Write your ideas here...

1. **Elements Included?**

_____

_____

_____

2. **Sequence Similar or Different?**

_____

_____

_____

3. **Design your Introduction Differently?**

_____

_____

_____

Main Content of the Session: Use of Hooks

TIMEOUT!

A Hook is designed to raise the audience's interest in a specific topic. You can use a Hook in the Introduction, at the beginning of each module, or at important learning points throughout the content.

The definition of a Hook is, _"An umbrella statement, activity or question that provides a conceptual link between the learner's existing knowledge and the new learning."_ (Ausubel, 1968.) By using a Hook, the Facilitator gives participants the opportunity to use their brains immediately-which engages their thought processes!

FOUL!

Great Hooks are not "fluff." When you use a Hook, the aim is more than to get an easy laugh. A good Hook:

- Has clear relevance to the topic.
- Elicits past knowledge, emotions, and/or experiences of most people in your audience.

Examples of Hooks can include:

Question

Questions are perhaps the easiest type of Hook to create, particularly if they imbed both of the criteria above. Examples:

- "Would you be willing to…"
- "Raise your hand if you've ever…"
- "How many of you have ever…"

Provocative Fact or Statistic

An effective Hook often combines a question with a follow-up piece of data that shocks or moves participants in some way. Example:

- "Raise your hand if you hate cancer."
- "It's shocking to think that, statistically, (%) of the (#) of us in this room today will die from cancer in the next five years."

Think-Back

Ask the participants to recall an experience that had emotional meaning for them that is relevant to the topic. You can request that they close their eyes for an even more evocative experience.

Story/Illustration or analogy

Human beings learn the complex through stories. Facts and figures activate two parts of our brain, and by contrast, stories activate seven parts of our brain. In addition, stories stimulate emotion-releasing cortisol and oxytocin – both of which can increase retention.

COACHING POINT

Make sure you script your story carefully –a well-written story enhances learning and engagement of students. A poorly written story can detract from the message and switch off the audience.

TIMEOUT! STRUCTURE FOR STORIES

- Be clear on the "Why?"
- Make sure the story supports your key learning point.
- Pick the subject; you or someone else.
- Begin with some sort of trigger; something happens to someone.
- Define the complication; something that forces a choice.
- Expand your plot; someone overcoming an obstacle or an instance of creativity.
- Incorporate emotional elements to enhance the impact.
- Finish with the transformation or learning point.

CASE STUDY: WINNER/LOSER TAPE STORY

Why: A story was selected to demonstrate how to change mental attitude using the concept of Winner/Loser Tapes. The concept called Winner and Loser Tapes can be used as a tool to help overcome presentation nerves.

Subject: How individuals can change internal dialog from a Loser Tape to a Winner Tape, which can help to reframe a challenging situation.

The overall context is established by;

1. Define attitude, "Attitude can be defined as the way you might mentally approach a situation.
2. Provide a simple example of a Winner Tape – "I like to facilitate workshops – every time I am due to facilitate, I tend to say internally, "I am going to enjoy this and we will all learn something.""
3. Provide a simple example of a Loser Tape – "I am not good with technology. When faced with new technology I tend to say internally, "I am not going to be able to manage this – something will go wrong." And something then does!"
4. Highlight: "As a result of playing the Winner Tape I am more likely to enjoy facilitating, Conversely, as a result, of playing the Loser Tape I am more likely to have issues with technology."

Trigger: Personal challenging situation

Here we incorporate the more intense personal situation to raise emotions and stimulate behavior change. I share a particularly challenging year, "In this year, my father died, my son was really ill and then I was involved in a nasty car accident."

Complication: Forcing a Choice

In this context, I could choose to say, "What did I do to deserve this?" (Loser Tape) which would have negatively impacted my attitude. Alternatively "How can I see the positives in this situation?" (Winner Tape).

Expand the Plot:

"The positives were that my son and I survived, and that my father lived long enough to know and love my son. Although I did not find much to laugh about that year, adopting the Winner Tape helped to get through this difficult situation."

Transformation/Learning Point

So conclude with, "We have seen how the concept of Winner and Loser Tape can help in a serious personal situation. How could this idea help in managing nerves when presenting?" The discussion tends to surface ideas such as there are more challenging situations than presenting! Changing our attitude – inserting a Winner Tape – can help us to overcome presentation nerves.

Audience involvement activity

You can use an activity related to the subject you are introducing – see Chapter Four for more ideas about the various experiential exercises you can use.

Video/Music

You can use an alternative media such as a Video clip or music to "pull in" the audience to the subject material.

COACHING POINT

Any video clip needs to be short, relevant and targeted specifically to the message you are trying to deliver. Ideally, you want it to stimulate the correct emotions, send the correct message and appeal to all.

Pictures/Products

For some content areas, you can use a picture or a sample product as a Hook – e.g. product training.

FOUL!

Hooks normally take no longer than 2-3 minutes!

EXERCISE 1-4: HOOKS

1. What Hooks have you used?
2. What will you do differently in terms of the Hooks you use to engage the audience?

TRY IT ON: HOOKS

Write your ideas here...

   1. **Hooks you have used**

_____

_____

   2. **What will you do differently?**

_____

_____

The T.E.A.C.H. Methodology

Within each module, applying the T.E.A.C.H. Methodology can help to:

- Balance the Task and Group Process Elements in Training.
- Provide a structure to guide Active Learning.
- Increase implementation and retention.

Within each subject, TEACH can be used to structure content to optimize learning and create a conversational tone. We have used an acronym related to the content to make the approach easy to remember.

TIMEOUT! T.E.A.C.H.	
T	**Topic and Hook:** State the subject
E	**Engage the Audience:** Conduct an activity in order to enlist the group in learning and/or identify what they already know
A	**Abstract Information:** Introduce concepts, theories, models, information, techniques, and skills
C	**Concrete Application:** Use examples, exercises and activities to cement learning
H	**How to Apply:** Encourage learners to take responsibility for implementing learning

Let's review each of these steps in a little more detail.

T: State the Topic

The Facilitator can say the Topic or could use a Hook to lead the group into the Topic.

FOUL!

In this step of TEACH we are NOT defining the topic – or providing much information on the subject. We are merely naming the content to be covered. For instance: Managing Nerves.

E: Engage the Audience

You can either engage the audience by using some type of large group discussion (see Chapter Three for more details) or by using some type of Experiential Learning activity (see Chapter Four for more details).

TIMEOUT! ENGAGE BEFORE SHARING CONTENT

There are many reasons to engage participants before sharing knowledge, skills or expertise.

- It gives you a way to assess the audience's current level of knowledge/interest/skills in the subject.
- It raises energy, motivation and buy-in to the topic.
- It encourages individuals to begin the learning journey by referring to their own experience (See Chapter Two for more information on adult learning theory).
- It establishes a positive group process that can smooth the introduction of the Task element of learning.

- It meets individuals' need for social engagement when learning (See Chapter Two for more information).
- It contributes to Psychological Safety.
- It validates participants and increases the connection between the Facilitator and the Group.

Taking time to design a relevant engagement activity or process can increase overall learning and retention. More information on a range of learning activities is in Chapter Four.

A: Share Abstract Information

This is the Task/Content area that the Facilitator wishes to introduce, and which the group is there to learn. This can include:

- Information
- Knowledge
- Theories
- Concepts
- Models
- Skills
- Techniques

This element is traditionally the focus of design and development activity.

C: Provide a Concrete Application

For participants to internalize content, create their own meaning from subjects, and for learning to take place, it is essential that individuals have the opportunity to apply the knowledge, practice a skill or try out a technique. The more customized the activity to the learning objective, the better. For instance, you could set a quiz on knowledge shared. You could use a role-play to develop proficiency in a skill that has been introduced. More detail is included in Chapter Four.

H: Ask How individuals Plan to Implement Learning

At the end of each module, it is helpful to give individuals time to reflect on their key learning points, and explore what they are going to do differently as a result of this knowledge. Individuals may not internalize the content without taking the time for personal reflection. The need for this reflection time is explained more in Chapter Two describing Active Learning.

FOUL!

Often we miss the reflection and planning stage because of the amount of content and/or lack of understanding of the importance of establishing some type of action planning steps.

COACHING POINT

The How to Apply can be facilitated through a pair's discussion or by providing a simple worksheet on which to capture key action ideas.

Applying the T.E.A.C.H. Methodology enables the energy to move between the Facilitator and the Group, thereby balancing the Task and Group Process elements of learning in following way.

Energy with Facilitator   **Energy with the Group**

TIMEOUT!		
T	**Topic and Hook:** State the subject	
E	**Engage the Audience:** Conduct an activity in order to enlist the group in learning and to identify what they already know	
A	**Abstract Information:** Introduce concepts, theories, models, information, techniques, and skills	
C	**Concrete Application:** Use examples, exercises and activities to cement learning	
H	**How to: apply** Encourage learners to take responsibility to implement learning.	

COACHING POINT

Therefore, the energy anchors with the **Facilitator** when they state the **Topic**.

The energy moves to the **group** during **Engage**.

The energy moves back to the **Facilitator** for **Abstract** data: teaching of knowledge, skills, techniques, etc.

The energy moves back to the **group** for **Concrete Application**.

Finally, the energy moves to the **individual** on **How to Apply** the knowledge/skills.

CASE STUDY

Let's review an example of TEACH in action.

T: Topic
The Topic is – **How to Manage Nerves when Presenting**

E: Engage the Audience
An Open Space exercise answering three questions (see Chapter Four for the explanation of Open Space Exercises):

- What types of things make you stressed or nervous when presenting?
- What are the signals that indicate whether you are stressed or nervous?
- What techniques do you use to help you manage your nerves?

A: Abstract Data
A model is shared to help change attitude around nerves when presenting (See earlier Story on Winner/Loser Tapes).

C: Concrete Application
In pairs, review some typical Loser Tapes when presenting.
Replace the Loser Tapes with Winner Tapes.
Identify your "favorite" Loser Tape and explore how to change it to a Winner Tape.

H: How to Apply
Individuals write down what they will do differently when managing nerves when presenting.

EXERCISE 1-5: THE T.E.A.C.H. METHODOLOGY

T: Topic
E: Engage
A: Abstract
C: Concrete
H: How to Apply

1. Looking at the stages in TEACH – which steps do you tend to naturally incorporate?
2. Which stages might get missed?
3. How can you ensure that you cover all the stages in TEACH in future sessions?

TRY IT ON: THE T.E.A.C.H. METHODOLOGY

Write your ideas here…

1. **Stages in TEACH that you incorporate?**

_____

_____

2. **Stages in TEACH that you might miss?**

_____

_____

3. **How to cover all the stages in TEACH?**

_____

_____

FOUL!

The most common objection to The T.E.A.C.H. Methodology is that it takes too long! Remember, learning will be drastically reduced without interaction, experiential activities and implementation planning.

COACHING POINT

The most common steps missed are Engage, Concrete Application and How to Apply. So then, you can say TA-TA to any learning! (T and A – no E, C and no H)

Alternatively, E and H are missed making any training TAC (y) – (no E and No H.)

So the question remains – how do we maintain the interaction when there is so much content to cover? The answer is, "You don't!" The key is to prioritize content as described in the next section.

Summary and Action Plan

The purpose for the conclusion of any training program is to summarize key learning points and define implementation planning for the entire session. The length of the summary can depend on the length of the overall event – and should be minimally 15-20 minutes. Failing to invest time in this area can mean that you will reduce retention.

Prioritize Content

One of the main reasons that Facilitators do not use The T.E.A.C.H. Methodology is that they try to include too much content – the Task element. Then, they drop activities, lose participant engagement and, as a result, implementation and retention. They drop the Group Process element in order to include all the Task components.

Must, Could and Should Know

TIMEOUT!

A simple way to prioritize content is to differentiate between:

- Must Know
- Should Know
- Could Know

- The Must Know content is at the top of the iceberg — what participants actually hear and see in the course content and objectives.
- The rest is content you know, but it stays below the surface and you do not overwhelm the learners with it.
- Elements in Should Know can be incorporated if the Facilitator has time and/or discovers that the group is more knowledgeable than anticipated.

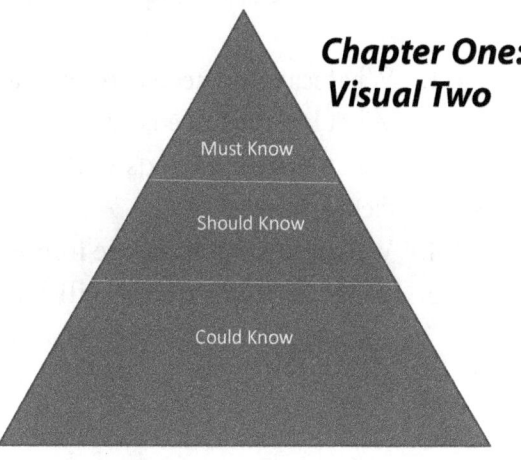

Chapter One: Visual Two

- Content in Could Know can be left to follow-up programs, activities or projects.
- From this analysis, it is possible to create learning objectives for each of the content/skills areas.

As Facilitators, we often have the "burden of knowledge"; we know so much that we are tempted to explain it all and overload our learners.

COACHING POINT

The following list identifies some criteria to help in prioritizing between Must, Should and Could:

- The student should already possess the knowledge, skill or ability/attitude.
- The task will be trained later after foundation is provided.
- The task is accomplished infrequently.
- There isn't enough time.
- The return on the investment is not adequate to justify the time.

In addition, what makes this prioritization difficult is that each group may be different in terms of learning needs.

Below are a few additional questions to aid in prioritizing content:

1. What learning needs are the most urgent or imperative?
2. What learning needs are critical to reducing important risks? (safety, legal, etc.)
3. What learning needs will have the most impact on performance? (quality, efficiency, etc.)
4. What learning needs are important for succession planning?
5. What learning needs will have the greatest impact on morale, retention, and engagement?

CASE STUDIES

In teaching Temperament theory (see Chapter Five), it is possible to teach a complex range of subjects.

The content can be prioritized in the following way:

Must know – Individual's accurate self-assessment of their Temperament for self-awareness.

Should know – Clues to recognize other Temperaments.

Could know – Temperament Targets with in-depth analytical knowledge.

It is then possible to simplify the course design to focus on the first aspect, and leave the other two elements for later workshops.

COACHING POINT

For the items that are in the Should Know and Could Know category, explore how this content could be covered using alternative media: written handout, Webinar, one-on-one discussion, follow-up sessions, etc.

The Stairs Technique

Another tool to help in planning the sequence of modules is to use The Stairs Technique. Once the Facilitator has prioritized the Content into three to five key learning objectives, these elements have to be sequenced for delivery. The way to sequence content is important because it influences what information is processed and retained.

TIMEOUT!

One design technique suggests a simple-to-complex sequence, a cumulative strategy. Other designs allow the learners the freedom to choose their own learning sequence based upon mastery of prerequisite lessons or the instructional components available.

Two methodologies called chunking and sequencing come into play with The Stairs Technique.

Chunking

The experimental psychologist George A. Miller found that "The Magic Number 7, Plus or Minus 2" described the maximum quantity of ideas, facts, or issues that people are able to actively attend to at any one time. This is called the Rule of 7. As more and more complex concepts are delivered, the recall capabilities significantly decrease. While there is increased debate about the accuracy of this rule, the underlying principle remains sound. To enhance and maximize learning potential, instructors should chunk/divide content into manageable units of information. This phenomenon is called the chunking limit.

TIMEOUT!

Chunking allows students to focus their attention on key concepts that are presented, thereby enhancing the power of retention and recall.

Sequencing

Sequencing allows for the thoughtful release of content that encourages motivation during learning and raises retention. Facilitators need to present Content systematically if learners are to meet goals and objectives.

TIMEOUT!

Content can be sequenced using approaches such as:

- Easy to hard
- Each skill individually before skills are combined
- Time sequence of an event – such as a sales meeting

COACHING POINT

To summarize

Step One: Introduce the initial content to your audience. Once you've taken that step up and introduced the content, you need to give the audience time to process the information. So stay on this step for a while by using one of the activities from Chapter Four to increase retention.

Step Two: Then, once you've given the audience enough time to process, move on to the second block of information you need to cover. Give your participants time again to process this information through active experimentation, concrete application, reflection, etc.

Step Three: Finally, you move on to the third step and yet another block of information. Again, with time to process, question, clarify, and practice some sort of learning activity, to help internalize the information.

CASE STUDIES

Reviewing the Temperament example earlier, here is how the Facilitator used the Stairs technique:

Introduce high-level flip-chart activity for awareness of core needs and values.

Review animals activity – to begin to describe some of the possible behaviors associated with each Temperament.

Present Case Studies – to provide more in-depth examples of Temperament behaviors in a work context.

Use Cards activity for further defining key Temperament attributes.

Ask each person to **self-select best fit.**

EXERCISE 1-6: PRIORITIZING CONTENT

1. How will you prioritize your content using the Must Know, Should Know, Could Know model?
2. How could you utilize chunking and sequencing with The Stairs Technique?

TRY IT ON: PRIORITIZING CONTENT

Write your ideas here…

Must Know, Should Know, Could Know

_____

_____

_____

The Stairs Technique

_____

_____

_____

Chapter Summary

In this Chapter, we have explored how to design an interactive workshop or learning event so that the Facilitator can be as successful as possible. We defined the Task and Group Process elements that a Facilitator needs to balance at all times to achieve learning. Designing and developing a workshop to balance these elements can make the Facilitator's role more impactful. Therefore, in designing a workshop, the course developer needs to consider Who will be attending (the audience), Why (the purpose of the event) and What the group needs to achieve (both in one overall outcome statement and in more specific behavioral objectives). The overall course structure, designed to achieve these learning objectives, has three main elements, the Introduction (Preview), the main content (View) and the Summary and Action Plan (Review). The purpose of the Introduction is to establish the Group Process element of productive learning and then define the Task elements to be covered. Within the main body of the program, we advocate using Hooks to engage the audience and applying The T.E.A.C.H. methodology to help maximize engagement and retention. Finally, it is important to review the content in the summary and action plan to specify key implementation ideas and close out the Group Process. Effective Facilitators prioritize content by using the Must Know, Should Know, Could Know methodology so as not to overwhelm participants. They also organize the content using The Stairs Technique to ensure that participants do not get frustrated by a lack of structure and the Group Process is not lost in pursuit of including too much content (Task).

The key principles we have described are:

- The Facilitator must constantly manage the Task and Group Process.
- The first step in designing learning events is to Identify the Who, Why and What.
- Structure the Introduction to balance Group Process and Task to establish a positive and safe learning environment.
- Use Hooks and The T.E.A.C.H. Methodology to make learning relevant and active.
- Summarize key learning and action ideas in an application section.
- Prioritize content using Must/Could/Should to balance Task and Group Process.
- Use The Stairs Technique to Chunk and Sequence the content to reduce participant overload and improve retention.

SCORECARD

- What were your key learning points about Task and Group Process? What will you do differently as a result?
- To what extent do you ask the Who? Why? and What? questions when undertaking program design? What would be the benefit of asking these questions?
- What will you do differently in planning the Introduction in your learning sessions? Why?
- What Hooks will you introduce and why?
- How will you ensure you follow the steps in TEACH? How will you manage the content so that there is time to use this methodology?
- How will you make sure there is time and attention spent on action planning?
- How will you organize and sequence your content differently using the Stairs and Chunking Techniques?

L: LEVERAGE ACTIVE LEARNING PRINCIPLES

Chapter Overview

A Flawless Facilitator needs to understand why and how Active Learning works, both in order to explain to some more skeptical participants, and to know how and when to flex style to achieve success. This chapter will provide the theoretical background for the design principles we have discussed in Chapter One and will establish the relevance for the rest of the knowledge, skills and techniques we will describe in the rest of this book. We will begin by describing Active Learning and contrast the two approaches of Andragogy and Pedagogy. Then we will review some recent research on Neuroscience and the Learning Cycle to discuss its relevance to facilitators and to explore teaching methodologies that can help in all stages in the Learning Cycle. We will also demonstrate how The T.E.A.C.H. Methodology facilitates all the elements of the Learning Cycle. Additionally, we will explore the importance of social learning. This includes how mirror neurons help learning, the role of emotions, and how to maintain participants' attention in the learning journey. Finally, we will share an adaptation of the Conscious Competence framework, which we call the Development

Process, to show the stages and provide a high-level timeline for either learning a new skill or enhancing existing habits.

GAME PLAN

You will learn about:

- Active Learning Principles
- Andragogy and Pedagogy
- Neuroscience and the Learning Cycle
- Learning Cycle and TEACH
- Social Learning
- Development Process

Active Learning

> "Learning is an active process. We learn by doing. Only knowledge that is used sticks in the mind"
>
> *Dale Carnegie*

Active learning is constructivist learning.

TIMEOUT!

According to the University of Minnesota's Center for Teaching and Learning, Active Learning is an instructional approach in which participants engage with the material they study through reading, writing, talking, listening and reflecting. Passive Learning is a traditional instructional style that involves teachers lecturing and students taking notes.

Below are some examples of Passive and Active Learning associated with typical behavioral objectives.

TYPE OF LEARNING	FORMATS	PEOPLE ARE ABLE TO... BEHAVIORAL OBJECTIVES
Passive Learning	Verbal receiving: **Read**	• Define • Describe • List • Explain
	Verbal receiving: **Hear**	
	View images: **See**	• Demonstrate • Apply • Practice
	Visual receiving: **See and Hear** Watching an example or demonstration	
Active Learning	Receiving/participating: **Say and Write** Being involved in hands on workshops	• Analyze • Define • Create • Evaluate
	Doing: **Say and Do** Doing real life activities	

FOUL!

There is some debate about the Retention statistics for each type of learning. Dales' Cone of Learning is often quoted with the following retention rates.

Read = 10%	Hear and See = 50%
Hear = 20%	Say = 70%
See = 30%	Say and Do = 90%

These are not accurately quoted, as retention can vary depending on different personality types. However, the general principle that Active Learning produces higher engagement and retention than Passive Learning appears to be consistent.

Andragogy and Pedagogy

"Pedagogy" literally means "leading children". "Andragogy" is a term coined to refer to the art/science of teaching adults. Originally used by Alexander Kapp (a German educator) in 1833, Eugen Rosenstock-Huessy developed Andragogy into a theory of adult education. American educator Malcolm Knowles popularized the theory and approach in the States in the publication The Modern Practice of Adult Education (1970).

TIMEOUT!

Knowles defined **Andragogy** as "an emerging technology for adult learning which is learner-centered/directed approach for people of all ages."

Pedagogy can be thought of as "teacher-centered" or "directive learning"

Chapter Two: Visual One

Pedagogy/Teacher Centered

Introduction: Visual One

Andragogy: Learner Centered

Design

Teacher

Design for Interaction

Balance Task and Group Process

Apply Experiential Learning

Create Psychological Safety

Facilitator

Engage Using Facilitation Skills

Assumptions

The five assumptions underlying Andragogy describe the Active Learner as someone who:

- Has an independent self-concept and who can direct his or her own learning.
- Has accumulated a reservoir of life experiences that is a rich resource for learning.
- Has learning needs closely related to changing social roles.
- Is problem-centered and interested in immediate application of knowledge.
- Is motivated to learn by internal rather than external factors (Merriam, 2001, p.5).

Knowles used these principles to propose a program for the design, implementation and evaluation of adult learning. Since the development of his theory, Knowles has acknowledged that the principles he outlined did not apply solely to adult education. The development of the theory simply illustrates that the designer "should involve Learners in as many aspects of their education as possible and in the creation of a climate in which they can most fruitfully learn" (Merriam, 2001, p.7). Knowles' focus with the development of Andragogy was the notion of the material being learner centered and the learner being self-directed.

> "In its broadest meaning, 'self-directed learning' describes a process by which individuals take the initiative, with our without the assistance of others, in diagnosing their learning needs, formulating learning goals, identifying human and material resources for learning, choosing and implementing appropriate learning strategies, and evaluating learning outcomes."
>
> *Malcolm Knowles*

COACHING POINT

Below are some examples of how to make learning more participant-centered.

CONTENT	STUDENT CENTERED
What, How and When to Learn	High level of student choice
Past experiences	Participant past experience is a learning resource
Attitude	Participant active and participative
Orientation	Relevant to participant context
Dependency	Empowers participant to be self- directed learners
Motivation	Internally driven and curious
Outcome	Independence
Process	Facilitation with Active Learning
Power	Primarily with students
Energy direction	Multi-directional

If we follow the following adult learning principles, we can help to ensure any program is Learner-Centered. **The more we are Learner-Centered, the more successful we will appear as a Facilitator.**

TIMEOUT!

Adult Learning Principles:

- Adults need to be involved in the planning and evaluation of their instruction.
- Experience (including mistakes) provides the basis for learning activities.
- Adults are most interested in learning about subjects that have immediate relevance to their job or personal life.
- Adult learning is problem-centered rather than content-oriented.

CASE STUDY: NEURO-PSYCHOLOGY OF LEARNING I

EM-Power rolled out globally a two-day workshop using the knowledge of Temperament and Interaction Style to Madrasah teachers. We followed the Andragogy Principles as described below.

- A cross-section of Madrasah teachers and Faith Subject Matter Experts were involved in the design and delivery of the original Pilot program.
- The program was customized to link to cultural values and incorporated a wide range of learning activities so that participants could learn by doing.
- All the teachers were voluntary so they had a deep commitment to using the knowledge in the most practical and time-effective way.
- The problem the team was trying to solve was to retain children and young adults within the Madrasah and Faith Community. Only content that was directly relevant to that end goal was incorporated into the program.

EXERCISE 2-1: ACTIVE LEARNING

Look at the previous list related to Active Learning Principles.

- How could you involve your participants in the planning and evaluation of instruction?
- How could you use your audience's past experience as the basis for learning activities?
- How can you make sure learning is relevant to the participants' current context?
- What problem will your workshop help them to solve?

TRY IT ON: ACTIVE LEARNING

Write your ideas here...

Involvement in planning and evaluation?

_____
_____
_____

Use of past experience?

_____
_____
_____

How to make relevant for their current context

_____
_____
_____

What problem are you trying to help them solve?

_____
_____
_____

Asking these questions can help to make your program design more practical and relevant, at the same time it can contribute to improved learning and retention.

Neuroscience and the Learning Cycle

An important way to become more effective in facilitating learning is to develop ways to engage several regions of the cerebral cortex in the process. Educator and biologist Zull (2002) proposed a Learning Cycle that links the breakthrough work of Kolb (1981) on experiential learning with neuroscientific research. The Learning Cycle begins with gathering information, followed by reflection, creation and active testing. Each step of the cycle is associated with a different region of the brain—those areas associated with sensory, associative and motor functions (Zull, 2002). While this alignment with parts of the brain is somewhat oversimplified (as these functions are more networked and less hierarchal than this picture would suggest) it provides a useful way to understand the overall workings of the brain as it relates to learning.

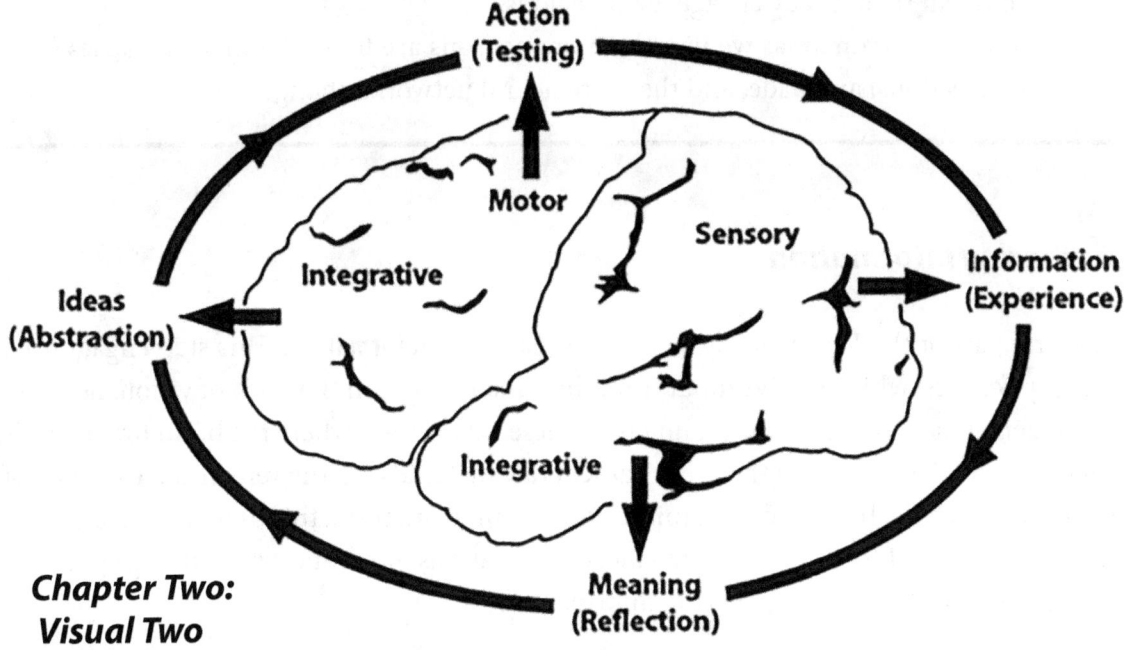

Chapter Two:
Visual Two

Source: The Experiential Learning Cycle and Regions of the Cerebral Cortex Zull 2002

TIMEOUT!

The cerebral cortex can be divided into four major regions with different functions (see above):

- Sensory cortex (gathering information)
- Integrative cortex near the sensory cortex (reflecting and making meaning of information)
- Integrative cortex in the front (creating new ideas from these meanings)
- Motor cortex (testing and acting on those ideas).

COACHING POINT

- If Facilitators provide experiences and assignments that engage all four areas of the cerebral cortex, they can expect deeper learning and greater participant commitment than if they engage fewer regions.
- The more brain areas we use, the more neurons are fired, the more synapses (or connections) are made, and the more neural networks change.

Gathering Information

The first part of the Learning Cycle involves **Gathering Information**. This step engages the sensory cortices, which receive input from the outside world in the form of vision, hearing, movement, touch, position, smell and taste. These cortices are where the brain first records concrete experience – where the brain gathers raw materials for the remaining elements of the Learning Cycle. In a typical organizational-learning program, this part of the cycle tends to receive the most focus and energy – most explanations, presentations and large portions of courses focus heavily on gathering information.

Excerpt from Key Aspects of How the Brain Learns James E. Zull

Getting information is essential for learning. It is so fundamental that the other pillars are sometimes neglected. One demonstration of this is found in schools or other learning situations where getting information becomes the only goal. This can lead to the assumption that learning is better if courses are crammed with content. It is important to realize that sensing (that is, gathering data) does not immediately lead to understanding. The data fed into the sensory neocortex are just that: data. A computer analogy has some value here. The data collected by the sensory neocortex are like bits that, by themselves, have no useful meaning. Learning is not equal to data collection. Nevertheless, it is essential to gather data.

Gathering Data means encouraging our students to use as many senses as possible – not just listening to a presentation.

TIMEOUT!

Each sensory aspect has its own value.

- **Vision** is arguably the most powerful, giving us precise spatial input on objects in the world, and mapping those objects on the neocortex. These maps become the stuff of images that then, along with language, underlie cognition and thought.
- **Auditory data** is the core of language, which has both cognitive and emotional content. It also gives us crude mapping information about location.
- **Touch** substitutes for vision in that we can use it to create maps of anything within our reach, and it can also provide data about texture, hardness, and so forth.
- **Smell and Taste** yield qualitative information that is sensed through our emotion system. Sweet, sour, fragrant, and putrid all trigger experiences in our body that we then interpret as feelings. These feelings become part of the sensory data and enrich it, engendering emotional responses.
- **Movement** accesses different regions of the brain. Simply by getting students out of their seats, new levels of self-discovery and self-expression are encouraged. In

addition, by letting participants experience the curriculum through their bodies, we help them make deeper emotional, interpersonal, and kinesthetic connections to workshop subjects.

Using different learning approaches can facilitate more effective gathering of information (See Chapter Four for more detail on each of the Activities described below.)

COACHING POINT

Games are designed to help people to learn about certain subjects, expand concepts, reinforce development, understand an historical event or culture, or assist them in learning a skill as they play. They can involve physical activity, board, card or video games.

Open Space Activities invite participants to take responsibility for what they care about. They establish a marketplace of inquiry, reflection and learning, bringing out the best in both individuals and the group.

Brainstorming is a group process that collects as many ideas as possible in a short time, without concern for quality. Ideas do not have to be practical or original. Brainstorming could be when an entire group answers a question or explores ideas around a subject. Brainstorming can also be part of pairs or team exercises.

Case Studies are student-centered activities based on topics that demonstrate theoretical concepts in an applied setting and provide an opportunity to raise awareness or discuss a specific subject.

Problem Solving Activities encourage students to learn about a subject through the experience of solving an open-ended problem. Students learn both thinking strategies and domain knowledge.

EXERCISE 2-2: GATHERING DATA

- What learning approaches do you currently use to help students gather data?
- To what extent do you engage all the senses in gathering data? Vision? Sound? Touch? Smell? Taste? Movement?
- What additional learning approaches could you use to improve data gathering through multiple senses?

TRY IT ON: DATA GATHERING

Write your ideas here...

Current approaches in gathering data?

_____

_____

Engaging all the senses? Vision? Sound? Touch? Smell? Taste? Movement?

_____

_____

Other Learning Approaches?

_____

_____

Reflection

TIMEOUT!

- **Reflection**, the second part of the cycle, engages the temporal lobe.

- During reflection, the brain integrates the sensory information received during the gathering stage.
- Reflection is inherently private—it happens within the Learner and requires time and space for Learners to pause and digest.

Even the quickest Learner needs reflection time. Without reflection, learning will be disconnected and shallow—sufficient to pass a test after a night of cramming—but otherwise transitory. Reflection is ultimately a search for connections—conscious and subconscious—and it works better when sensory inputs are shut out. Eliminating distractions allows the brain to focus attention on integrating information already received.

COACHING POINT

Reflection is necessary for insight formulation—the somewhat mysterious process that occurs when a solution comes to mind suddenly, often after an impasse, and seems obviously correct. Insights fuel the creativity and innovation that are prerequisites for success in today's competitive marketplace. ("Understanding What Makes People Tick," 2009).

Excerpt from Key Aspects of How the Brain Learns James E. Zull

New data flows from the sensory neocortex toward the association regions in the back of the brain. As it flows, bits of data are merged into combinations that begin to produce a larger, more meaningful image. There is a natural hierarchy in these regions of cortex, with the lower ones providing the smaller bits that, together, become the higher ones. It is through these associations that we categorize and label objects and actions and identify the spatial relationships inherent in them. ...... Associations occur between memories as well as between elements of sensory data. Thus, comprehension depends on the associations between new events and past events. The more past events are available to draw on, the more powerful the meaning. Our ability to comprehend new information is also deeply based on assembly of images in the back association cortex. These images are remembered and used as tools in thought. Ultimately, physical images give us the metaphors we use in language. When we understand, we say, "I see."

..... All this assembly and association of bits of data, memories, and images might be considered the slowest part of learning. It takes time and involves rerunning our data over and over. It takes reflection. Such reflection is often missing in workshops.

In our fast-paced, "talk out loud" culture, building in time and space for reflection is not always easy. **Using different learning approaches** can facilitate Reflection that is more effective. (See Chapter Four for more detail on each of the Activities described below.)

COACHING POINT

Individual Reflection/Writing – can be helpful for those with an Introverting preference (those who like to reflect before speaking) and for helping groups to reflect after a data gathering experience.

A Learning Journal – can also be helpful to review key insights and capture individual reflections.

Quizzes/Knowledge Checks – can stimulate thought on key learning points and begin the Reflection process.

Coffee/Stretch Breaks – allow individuals the opportunity to step back in addition to helping protect physical energy.

Learning Modules – Dividing content into spaced-out Learning Modules (rather than eight-hour sessions) can build reflection time into learning process. The disadvantage of course is ensuring participants attend all sessions (if not in a school environment).

CASE STUDY: NEURO-PSYCHOLOGY OF LEARNING II

- Pre-work was used to begin reflection on course content with specific assignments related to gathering prior experience.
- Reflection is built into the learning journey in many of the programs developed for this Shia Muslim community.
- Day One begins with quiet time for participants to focus on expectations and learning goals.
- Each learning day incudes reflection time in the morning, often associated with a reading related to content from the Quran.
- Modules are paced so that there was time to integrate learning between in-person events.
- Webinars are held to explore questions and share additional knowledge.

EXERCISE 2-3: REFLECTION

- To what extent do you create the space for participants to reflect on any learning?
- What additional approaches could you use to facilitate reflection time?

TRY IT ON: REFLECTION

Write your ideas here...

Current approaches in Reflection?

_____

_____

_____

Other Learning Approaches?

_____

_____

_____

Creation

As connections are being made by reflective thinking, learners start the process of creating new ideas and solving problems. "We change from being receivers of knowledge to creators of knowledge." (Zull, 2002, p. 18). **Creation** is the point in the Learning Cycle at which the learner shifts from receiving and absorbing information to creating knowledge in the form of abstractions such as ideas, plans, concepts and symbolic representations.

TIMEOUT!

- The prefrontal cortex is fully engaged in this executive brain process.
- Creation involves the manipulation of information in working memory to create new relationships and new meaning. Data is organized into new arrangements and that data is attached to the networks that represent prior knowledge.
- Through this process, learners create their own understandings.

What works for one person is not necessarily what works for another. To that end, learners need to have the opportunity to make meaning in their own ways.

FOUL!

Attempts to save time by explaining things, more often than not result in the loss of meaning creation. Until learners actively create their own ideas, learning has little chance of enduring.

By definition, creation requires giving control to the learner. This conscious rearranging and manipulation of items…comes closest to what we call thinking. (Zull, 2002, p. 185)

Excerpt from Key Aspects of How the Brain Learns James E. Zull

The flow of specific meanings or even bits of sensory data from the back associa-tion cortex to the front association cortex becomes the basis for conscious thought and planning. It engages what has been called working memory. A small number of relevant individual concepts, facts, or meanings are intentionally inserted into working memory. Determining "relevance" is part of the work. For example, when planning to change a tire, data about tires and cars must be used, not data about horses (or even roads). The chosen information is then manipulated such that a solution to the problem arises. Use of the tire, jack, and car must be organized in sequence. First get the jack, then lift the car, then remove the tire. However, this plan is not just a list of steps; taken as a whole it is a theory, hence an abstraction.

Such plans, theories, and abstractions consist of a combination of images and language. They are the result of intentional associations, selected and manipulated for a purpose. This is the function of the front association cortex, and it represents perhaps the most elevated aspect of learning. It involves intent, recall, feelings, deci-sions, and judgments. They are all required for development of deep understanding.

Using different learning approaches can help participants to create their own understanding. (More information on these differing Activities is in Chapter Four).

COACHING POINT

Project-based Learning requires participants to use diverse skills—such as researching, writing, interviewing, collaborating, or public speaking—to produce various work products. This can give a more "integrated" understanding of the concepts and knowledge learned, while also equipping Learners with practical skills to apply at work.

Observational Learning helps the process of creation through watching others, retaining the information, providing feedback and then later replicating the behaviors that were observed.

Jigsaw Learning is a cooperative learning technique where the participants take an active part in their learning. In becoming a teacher of sorts, each student becomes a valuable resource for the others while at the same time creating their individual understanding of the subject they are presenting.

Lecture: The Facilitator introduces new models, theories, techniques, data or skills. The aim is to provide an opportunity for participants to enhance their existing knowledge and build new understanding by integrating new frameworks.

Read and Teach is a learning technique where participants have to read and digest some specific information, data or theories. As they present the key learning points to other students, they are unconsciously creating their individual meaning from the subject material.

EXERCISE 2-4: CREATION

- What current approaches do you use to enable participants to create their own meaning?
- What additional learning approaches could you use to facilitate Creation?

TRY IT ON: CREATION

Write your ideas here…

Current approaches in Creation?

_____

_____

Other Learning Approaches?

_____

_____

Active Testing

Active Testing differs from most people's typical understanding of testing.

TIMEOUT!

- **Active Testing** is a physical process that engages the motor cortex.
- It allows the brain to make the abstract concrete by converting mental ideas into action.

- Any action inspired by ideas qualifies as active testing: reading another book on the topic; talking to someone about the book; explaining and talking about what was learned; hearing what someone else thinks; researching the topic on the web; seeking out people who live the topic and talking to them; setting up experiments to test, answering probing questions.

Acting upon ideas is important because taking action biologically completes the cycle and the brain gets ideas so the body can act. At the same time, the action of the body provides sensory feedback to the brain. "It is through action that the biological wholeness of learning becomes apparent" (Zull, 2002, p.104).

Using different learning approaches can help participants to test their learning. (For more complete information about each of the Activities below, check out Chapter Four.)

COACHING POINT

Role-Plays provide an opportunity to practice in real time specific ideas and skills in a non-threatening environment, emulate behavior from the real world, and obtain feedback.

Simulations provide an advanced opportunity to test out skills, knowledge and techniques, in immersive experiences that replicate and amplify real life situations and problems. They enable practicing of behavior while avoiding unnecessary risk.

Fieldwork represents a consciously planned set of experiences occurring in a practice setting designed to move students from their initial level of understanding, skills and attitudes to more advanced levels of comprehension.

Problem-Based Learning can help students develop flexible knowledge, effective problem solving skills, self-directed learning and effective collaboration skills.

Demonstration: In specific contexts, for instance presentation/facilitation skills, participants can apply all the knowledge skills and techniques by demonstrating their skills. This provides an opportunity to discover what is working for them and what is not.

EXERCISE 2-5: ACTIVE TESTING

- What current approaches do you use to enable participants to test their learning?
- What additional learning approaches could you use to facilitate Active Testing?

TRY IT ON: ACTIVE TESTING

Write your ideas here…

Current approaches in Active Testing?

_____

_____

_____

Other Learning Approaches?

_____

_____

_____

FOUL!

Participants will have preferences for different elements of the Learning Cycle. Therefore, these stages are not always sequential!

CASE STUDY: RETAIL SALES TRAINING

A customized retail sales training program incorporated all four stages in the Learning Cycle in the following way.

Data Gathering: videos, products, activities and a game were used to build brand awareness and clarify product positioning.

Reflection: at the end of each section, participants completed a Learning Log and then shared their input with a "buddy".

Creation: specific areas of the program explored how to develop a more proactive, customer-focused sales experience – combining skills and knowledge introduced in the session with existing experience.

Active Testing: role-plays and fieldwork were used to cement knowledge and assess development.

If Facilitators can ensure that different learning approaches are used to cater to differing stages of the Learning Cycle, this will help to ensure more effective learning no matter what an individual's unique learning style might be. In Chapter Four, we will review in detail the range of different activities and provide additional suggestions as to which stage in the Learning Cycle each might support and why.

Learning Cycle and TEACH

Using The T.E.A.C.H. Methodology helps to cover all stages in the Learning Cycle as shown below.

Topic and Hook	• Hook can provide information for Gathering Data (e.g. by looking at past experience.) • Hook can help in Internal Reflection (e.g. by stimulating thought around a specific question.) • Hook can help in Creating Ideas (e.g. by debriefing a learning point.)
Engage the Audience	An activity or group discussion can stimulate: • Data Gathering because it can involve multiple senses. • Internal Reflection because a question and pausing can stimulate thought. • Creating Ideas because engagement contributes to learning. • Active Testing because any engagement activity encourages an element of safe exploration.
Abstract Information:	Abstract Information can help: • Data Gathering because this reflects new content. • Internal Reflection by providing new data to be connected with existing knowledge.
Concrete Application:	An activity or group discussion can stimulate: • Further Data Gathering because it can involve multiple senses. • Internal Reflection because a question and pausing can stimulate thought. • Creating Ideas because application contributes to learning. • Active Testing because any application process encourages an element of safe exploration.
How to Apply	This stage focuses on Internal Reflection, Creation and a decision about Active Testing.

Social Learning

In this section we will review the principles around:

- The Social Brain
- Emotions in Learning
- The Importance of Attention and Learning.

The Social Brain

> *"Like every living system, from single neurons to complex ecosystems, the brain depends on interactions with others for its survival. Each brain is dependent on the scaffolding of caretakers and loved ones for its survival, growth and well-being . . . The brain is an organ of adaptation that builds its structure through interactions with others (Cozolino, 2006, p. 15).".*

In the 1980s, Giacomo Rizzolatti and several colleagues at the University of Parma, Italy, were doing neuroscientific research with monkeys, studying how different neurons were specifically associated with particular actions. During the course of their work they accidentally discovered that some of the neurons they recorded would respond when the monkey saw a researcher pick up a piece of food as well as when the monkey picked up the food. Later, in the 1990s, Rizzolatti and his colleagues published a seminal paper coining the mirror neuron system, describing its role in action recognition, and suggesting that humans, too, have a mirror neuron system. Much work has been done since on this topic, including *Functional magnetic resonance imaging* (fMRI) studies demonstrating a human mirror neuron system. This is truly one of the most exciting areas of neuroscientific research with profound implications.

TIMEOUT!

People learn from one another, sometimes without even realizing that they are doing so.

We are wired to need social interactions and to make real connections with others.

There is great power in the interactions among Learners and between Facilitators and Learners.

With the increasing shift from face-to-face meetings and events to virtual and digital formats, careful thought must be given to how we build human interaction into learning solutions.

FOUL!

While there are excellent reasons and effective ways to deploy virtual and digital learning solutions, it is important to recognize that these tend to provide only part of the answer. We need to continue to find ways to nurture the connections between learners in person—even in an increasingly digital workplace!

COACHING POINT

By using The T.E.A.C.H. Methodology, we naturally incorporate a social learning environment by combining back and forth energy, with facilitation skills and experiential learning activities.

Emotions and Learning

More and more literature in psychology, Neuroscience and economics is revealing the very critical role that emotion plays in our lives. Neuroscientific research has revealed that emotion and cognition are not neatly divided in the brain.

TIMEOUT!

- Virtually all mental activities involve both emotion and cognition (LeDoux, 2000).
- Not surprisingly, emotion plays a powerful and complex role in the learning process.
- The existence of neural wiring between the thinking and emotional centers of the brain suggest that emotions can either enhance or inhibit the brain's ability to learn.

Understanding the right balance requires taking a closer look at the Neuroscience around emotion and learning.

Emotion is the fuel and foundation of learning: emotion is required to engage the Learning Cycle as well as to move through it (Zull, 2002). However, the right amount of emotion is needed for learning—not too much and not too little. In the early twentieth century, psychologists discovered that learning is maximized in a moderate state of arousal—what we could call "relaxed alertness."

COACHING POINT

- If learners are not aroused at all, they will not engage.
- If they are too aroused, they will be unable to stay focused.
- By combining back and forth energy, facilitation skills and experiential learning a Facilitator can help to orchestrate this state of "moderate arousal".

More recently, Neuroscience has provided a biological basis for these psychological findings, adding further support for Zull's understanding of the emotional chemicals of the brain as the fuel for learning. It turns out that a moderate level of arousal triggers neural plasticity by increasing production of neurotransmitters and neural growth hormones, enhancing neural connections and cortical reorganization (Cozolino, 2006). Cozolino calls the ideal emotional state for learning one of "safe emergency"—in other words, there is a high level of attention, without the negative impact of anxiety.

TIMEOUT!

Similarly, research has shown that stress in the learning environment, negative memories from prior learning, or stress in the broader environment can negatively affect the potential for learning.

These stressors can operate at both conscious and subconscious levels.

In addition, as findings in cognitive psychology and Neuroscience indicate, the brain is geared to minimizing threat and maximizing reward (Gordon, 2000).

Upon encountering a stimulus, the brain tags it either as good or bad: if good, the brain engages with or approaches it; if bad, the brain disengages, or avoids it. Some studies have found that it is easier to trigger an avoid response and harder to create an approach response because the avoid response creates far more arousal in the emotional networks of the brain (Baumeister, Bratslavsky & Vohs, 2001).

The implications for learning are powerful. Learners are constantly and subconsciously monitoring their learning environments and are naturally wary of lurking threats. Openness to learn is greatly diminished when there is a lack of psychological safety or when learners sense a potential for loss of control.

If a Facilitator has unconsciously contributed to these negative events, they may be judged poorly by participants.

COACHING POINT

By using The T.E.A.C.H. Methodology, we are naturally stimulating a "move towards" versus "move away from" learning environment that can result in higher learning and retention.

The Importance of Attention and Learning

Because of the brain structure and the fast-paced, stimulus-rich environment, that characterizes our lives, engaging and maintaining attention when learning can present a significant challenge.

Grab the Attention

The brain is designed to immediately filter all incoming sensory stimuli and select only those that are relevant at that moment so as to encode them. There is actually no such thing as a learner who is not paying attention: the brain is always paying attention to something, although it may not focus on relevant information or on what the instructor intends (Wolfe, 1998). It drops information that does not fit easily into an existing network. It "forgets" information that it does not find useful and important. By necessity, the vast majority of sensory data is not encoded—the brain simply cannot pay attention to all the incoming stimuli.

COACHING POINT

- In designing learning experiences, it is important to discover ways to quickly, effectively and powerfully grab the learner's attention.
- The brain will ignore data that, in terms of existing neural networks, is meaningless.
- Therefore the more we use relevant "Hooks", link context to past experience, and engage the learner actively, the more data will be sorted by the brain as relevant.

Keep the Attention

Throughout the Learning Cycle, it is important to manage attention largely due to the severe constraints of working memory.

TIMEOUT!

- The term working memory describes a "limited capacity system that is capable of storing and manipulating temporary information involved in the performance of complex cognitive tasks such as reasoning, comprehension and certain types of learning" (Baddely, 2009).
- In other words, working memory is where conscious thinking happens.
- Working memory has a smaller capacity than long-term memory and takes more energy.
- Sustained use of working memory, even within its constraints, can deplete working memory effectiveness.

Designing learning experiences so as to minimize the load placed on working memory and enable effective processing is perhaps the key to attention management. Cognitive overload can result from the asking learners to do too much at once. The more we can keep the group's attention, the more satisfied learners will be.

COACHING POINT

- Following good course design and reducing the amount of content to be covered using the Should, Could, and Would Approach can help to optimize working memory.
- In addition, The T.E.A.C.H. Methodology can help to reduce information overload by integrating content with consistent participant engagement.

Multi-Tasking and Attention

The brain cannot attend to two or more attention-rich stimuli simultaneously—simply put, multitasking does not work ("Understanding What Makes People Tick," 2009). A 2000 study by Naveh-Benjamin and colleagues provides a deeper of understanding of what this means for learning.

TIMEOUT!

- The authors discovered that there were significant differences between encoding and retrieval activities involved in processing information created through multitasking.
- The researchers demonstrated that encoding requires more attention than retrieval.
- Divided attention during the encoding phase of learning significantly reduced memory.

Since encoding is the first of three memory stages (storage and retrieval are the other two), the implication is that the quantity and quality of memory is profoundly influenced by multitasking.

Continuous Partial Attention

Linda Stone, a former Microsoft vice president turned educator and speaker, coined the term "Continuous Partial Attention" to describe how many people use attention today (Stone, 2008).

TIMEOUT!

- The term "Continuous Partial Attention" goes beyond mere multitasking.
- It refers to the desire to connect and be connected at all times and to the way that people scan the environment for the best place to be connected at any given moment.

While Stone notes that this technique can be useful in small doses, it ultimately adds to stress and compromises a person's ability to reflect, to make decisions and to learn effectively.

COACHING POINT

Using Ground Rules to establish the learning context and then reinforcing this context using facilitation skills (to be reviewed in the next chapter) can help to manage Continuous Partial Attention Syndrome to improve the learning environment.

EXERCISE 2-6: SOCIAL LEARNING ENVIRONMENT

- To what extent do you create a Social Learning Environment? What else can you do to help people learn from each other?
- How can you create a relaxed and yet stimulating atmosphere – one of moderate arousal? How can you manage negative emotions so they do not detract from learning?
- How can you grab and keep attention? How can you manage multi-tasking and Continuous Partial Attention?

TRY IT ON: DATA GATHERING

Write your ideas here…

Social Learning Environment?

_____

_____

Create positive emotions? Manage negative emotions?

_____

_____

Manage Attention?

_____

_____

Development Process

> "Progress is impossible without change, and those who cannot change their minds cannot change anything."
>
> *George Bernard Shaw*

Often, there can be the assumption that the aim for any learning and development activity is to build new skills. In fact, workshops can teach new frameworks, techniques and models, as well as help individuals recognize the skills they possess and explore how they might enhance these. In this section, we will share an updated version of the Conscious Competence model, which we call the Development Process. This is the focus of another book called **Contextual Coaching.**

DEVELOPMENT PROCESS			
Capability: Areas for Enhancement		**Incapability: Areas for Learning**	
Acquired Strengths	Innate Talents	Skills to Learn	Innate Weaknesses

TIME OUT!: DEVELOPMENT PROCESS

- As you can see above, there are two main performance areas: Capability, things we do well that we can enhance, and Incapability, things we could improve by learning new knowledge, skills or techniques.
- There are two different types of Capability. First, there are acquired strengths – skills we have learned to perform at a high level. Examples could include keyboard skills, driving, being assertive, and negotiation skills. Second, there are innate talents that are unique to an individual; areas of proficiency that they have not been taught, they

are simply able to demonstrate certain abilities. Examples could include showing empathy, constantly seeing possibilities, systematic organization, being tuned in to the here and now, etc.

- There are two different types of Incapability. First, there are new skills, knowledge, or techniques to learn. Examples could be learning a process when you join a new department, start a new job, introduce a new system, etc. Second, there are innate "blind spots" or weaknesses that are unique to an individual and are not related to experience or learning. Examples could include being oblivious to people's reactions, not recognizing social norms, showing emotions on the face, etc.
- The Development Process is similar for Acquired Strengths and Innate Talents so we will describe one process for these.
- In the same way the process for Learning New Skills and Overcoming Weaknesses is similar, so we will describe one process for this.
- As society mainly tends to focus on "bad news" or areas for learning, let's begin here.

Development Process: Skills to Learn/Innate Weaknesses

Let's first review the development process that is required for an individual to either learn a new skill or overcome an innate weakness.

CASE STUDY: LEARNING A NEW SKILL

Peter is a Merchandiser responsible for introducing a new inventory management system. When he reviewed this system as part of the screening process, it looked pretty straightforward.

When he first started to try to use the new system it felt awkward and different from the previous system he had used. Using the new system required much more investment of energy on his part.

Over the next three weeks he began to get used to the system and, although he still had to think about it, at least he was able to access the data in a more efficient way.

Three months later, he is really comfortable with the system and is able to use it, without thinking, with the same proficiency that he used the original system. He is able to reap the rewards of the efficiencies offered by the new system.

EXERCISE 2.7: WHEN YOU HAD TO LEARN A NEW SKILL....

Think of a time when you had to learn a new skill in sport, work or home life]

How long did it take?

What stages did you experience as you developed the new skill?

TRY IT ON! LEARNING A NEW SKILL

What skill did you learn?

_____

_____

_____

What were the stages that you experienced in learning the new skill?

_____

_____

_____

EXERCISE 2.8: WHEN YOU HAD TO OVERCOME A WEAKNESS....

Think of a time when you received feedback on a personal area for improvement.

What stages did you experience as you tried to overcome that weakness?

TRY IT ON! OVERCOMING A WEAKNESS

What was your personal area for improvement?

_____

_____

_____

What stages did you experience as you tried to overcome that weakness?

_____

_____

_____

Chapter Two:
Visual Three

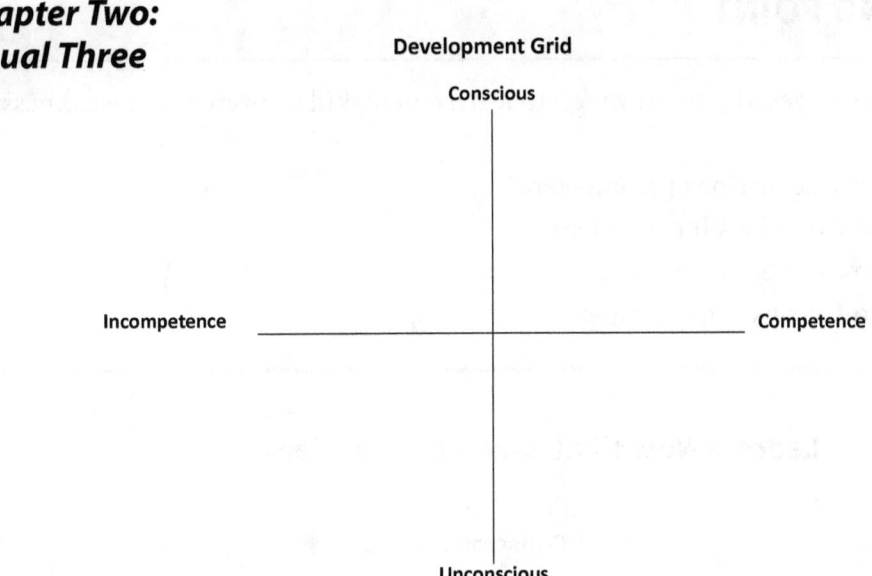

TIME OUT!: DEVELOPMENT GRID

As you can see this performance grid has two axes: Competence–Incompetence, and Conscious–Unconscious.

- Competence and Incompetence relate to Ability or Proficiency in a task.
- Incompetent means that the person hasn't developed that ability. Competent means that the person has that ability.
- Conscious and Unconscious relate to an individual's awareness of their performance level.
- Conscious means that the person is aware. Unconscious means that the person is not aware.
- This produces four quadrants involved in the process of either overcoming a weakness or in learning a new skill: Unconscious Incompetence, Conscious Incompetence, Conscious Competence and Unconscious Competence.

Credit to Gordon Training International

COACHING POINT

There are four stages to move through to learn a new skill or overcome a weakness.

1. Begin in Unconscious Incompetence.
2. Move to Conscious Incompetence.
3. Move to Conscious Competence.
4. Move to Unconscious Competence.

Learn a New Skill/Overcome a Weakness

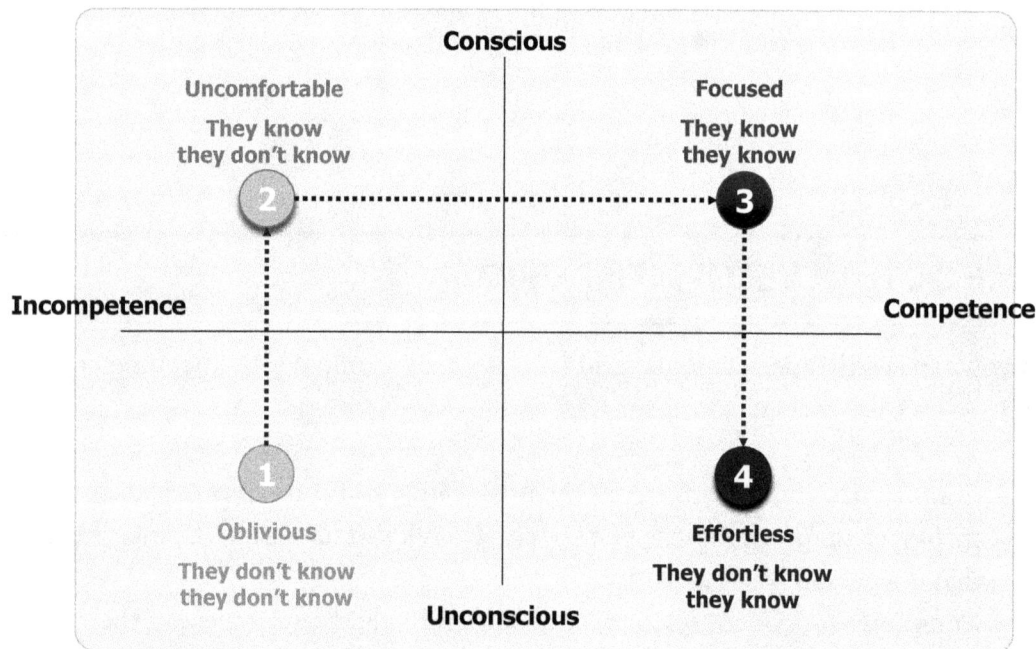

Chapter Two:
Visual Four

Let's define this Development Process in more detail.

LEVEL OF PROFICIENCY	DESCRIPTION
1. **Unconscious Incompetence**	**The mental state experienced is Oblivious** • The person is not aware of the existence or relevance of a specific skill: **they don't know that they don't know!** • The person is not aware that they have a particular deficiency in the area concerned. • The person might deny the relevance or usefulness of the new skill. • This can be the mental state prior to attending a learning event.

To move from Step One to Step Two, an individual needs to become aware.

2. **Conscious Incompetence**	**The mental state experienced is Uncomfortable** • The person becomes aware of a skill to learn often when attending a workshop. • As a result, they may move to Conscious Incompetence: **they now know that they don't know!** • The person realizes that applying a skill or ability in this area will improve performance. • The person cannot perform the skill or behavior without assistance. • The person has a sense of the extent of their capacity in the relevant skill or behavior, and a measure of what level of performance is required to be competent. • Occasionally individuals fall back into Unconscious Incompetence through denial: they don't think the data they received is accurate, they don't believe the skill or behavior is relevant or useful, etc. **Credit to Psycho-cybernetics**

EXERCISE 2.9: EXPERIENCING CONSCIOUS INCOMPETENCE

Fold your arms in the way that is most comfortable for you.

Have a look and see which arm is uppermost.

Now fold your arms the other way with the other arm on top.

How does that feel?

COACHING POINT

Most of you probably found this uncomfortable or awkward. You just experienced Conscious Incompetence. The challenge is that when development feels uncomfortable, we may decide that we're physically or mentally incapable of completing the task, stop practicing a new behavior, and return to our comfort zone (Unconscious Incompetence).

To move from Step Two to Step Three the individual needs to commit to the skill or behavior, and practice it for 21-30 days – hence the importance of the action planning in the summary of any workshop.

LEVEL OF PROFICIENCY	DESCRIPTION
3. Conscious Competence	**The mental state experienced is Focused** • The person achieves Conscious Competence in a skill or behavior when they can perform it reliably at will. **They know they know.** • The person will need to concentrate and think in order to perform the skill or demonstrate the behavior. • The person can perform the skill or demonstrate the behavior without assistance. • The person will not reliably perform the skill or show the behavior without consciously thinking about it – the skill or behavior is not yet "second nature" or "automatic." • The person can probably demonstrate the skill or behavior to another, but is unlikely to be able to teach it well to another person.

To move from Step Three to Step Four the individual needs to continue to practice for three months or longer.

4. Unconscious Competence	**The mental state experienced is Effortless** • The skill or behavior becomes so practiced that it enters the unconscious parts of the mind – it becomes "second nature." **They don't know they know.** • Common examples are driving, sports activities, typing, manual dexterity tasks, listening, and paraphrasing. • It becomes possible for certain skills to be performed while doing something else, for example, talking while driving a car. • The person might now be able to teach others the skill concerned, although after some time of being unconsciously competent the person might actually have difficulty in explaining exactly how they do it – the skill has become largely instinctual. • The ability to teach or coach skills lies in the second Development Process, which we will review later.

TIME OUT!: LEARNING A NEW SKILL / OVERCOMING AN INNATE WEAKNESS

- To learn a new specific task, technique, or behavior you have to move through the stages: you can't jump a stage.
- As individuals progress through each stage, there seems to be a "tipping point" when the skill or behavior "clicks."

COACHING POINT

Remember when you first started learning to drive.

1. Before you got in the car the whole process may have looked easy. You were **Oblivious:** you did not know you did not know. You were in **Unconscious Incompetence**.
2. Then you got behind the wheel for the first time, stalled the car, found it difficult to change gears, watch the traffic, and check your speed all at the same time, and you knew how difficult driving could be. You were **Uncomfortable**: you knew you did not know. You were in **Conscious Incompetence**.
3. Then you had lessons, and after about three weeks you were doing better – doing the right things, but still having to concentrate on it. You were **Focused:** you knew that you knew. You were in **Conscious Competence**.
4. Finally after about three months it all seemed to "click." You were able to drive without thinking about it. Driving became **Effortless**: you did not know that you knew. You were in **Unconscious Competence**.

> "Too many people die with their music still inside them."
>
> *Oscar Wilde*

Development Process: Innate Talents/Acquired Strengths

In addition to areas for improvement, participants also possess certain innate talents and acquired strengths. These are areas either they either possess a natural gift such as spatial awareness, physical aptitude, interpersonal effectiveness, tactile ability, or strategic thinking, etc., or certain skills and techniques that they have learned but now use without thinking. Innate talents differ from acquired strengths because they are natural to us – things we know how to do but have never been taught. We may not be aware of these abilities because we were never told about them or it never occurred to us that they were valued or important. Because they are inborn, we tend to assume everyone else can perform as we do.

CASE STUDY: LEARNING ABOUT STRENGTHS

A few weeks ago Jean attended a sales training program. During the session she recognized that she naturally tends to ask lots of open-ended questions and demonstrates high levels of empathy. She did not know how or why, she just was able to use these skills and talents.

As a result of this learning, she spent some time thinking about how she could use these questioning skills and empathy to greater effect. She also evaluated what else she could have done to capitalize on these skills to achieve better sales results.

Now she consciously monitors her use of questioning and empathy in the moment to maximize the application of these two skills.

EXERCISE 2.10: DISCOVERING AREAS OF UNCONSCIOUS COMPETENCE

Think about:

- Has anyone ever provided you with specific positive feedback on something you are able to do that surprised you?
- Could this be an area of Unconscious Competence for you?
- Why was this information a surprise to you?
- How did you feel?
- How did you try to build on these talents and why?

TRY IT ON!

Your Strengths...

_____
_____
_____
_____
_____
_____
_____
_____
_____
_____

As you have now had a chance to identify either an acquired strength or an innate talent, let's review the stages in the Development Process to capitalize on this ability.

COACHING POINT

There are four stages required to develop an acquired strength or an innate talent. These four stages represent an addition to the original Conscious Competence Model.

A. Begin in Unconscious Competence

B. Move to Conscious Competence

C. Move to Reflective Competence

D. Move to Emotional Competence

We will define the terms Reflective and Emotional Competence later in this chapter.

Develop Innate Talents/Acquired Strengths

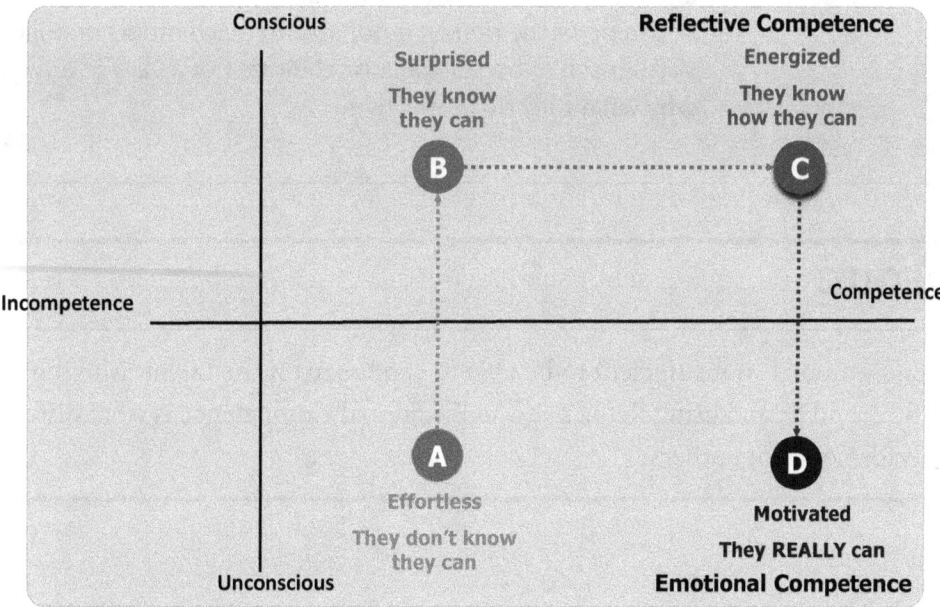

Chapter Two:
Visual Five

Let's define the Development Process in more detail.

LEVEL OF PROFICIENCY	DESCRIPTION
A. Unconscious Competence	**The mental state experienced is Effortless** • The person is not aware of the natural talent or acquired skill: **they don't know they can** – they just can! • The person is not aware that everyone is not able to perform this specific skill. In fact the person might get frustrated that others are not able to perform the task at the same level of proficiency as they can.

To move from Step A to Step B the participant has to become aware.

B. Conscious Competence	**The mental state experienced is Surprised** • The individual achieves Conscious Competence when he/she becomes aware of the existence and relevance of the skill: **they know that they can** and perhaps others can't! • A learning event may raise awareness in a participant that they had a skill that they did not know about. • The person realizes that by capitalizing on this skill or ability that effectiveness will improve measurably. • At this point the person is not able to teach others or build on the skill himself or herself because they are not aware of **how and why** what they do is effective.

TIMEOUT!

Awareness alone is not sufficient to be able to capitalize on the talent. Moving through Steps B, C, and D, and using Reflective and Emotional Competence is what differentiates star performers from others.

To move from Step B to Step C the individual needs to begin analyzing their innate talent or acquired strength. A well-designed workshop can provide relevant data in this process.

TIMEOUT! DEFINING REFLECTIVE COMPETENCE

Reflective Competence is a **new term** to differentiate this stage from Conscious Competence. This term describes the ability to mentally step back and analyze what the talent looks like and how it contributes to improved performance. If you cannot understand what you do and how this works positively for you, then you are unable to teach it to others or capitalize on it for your own performance enhancement. This internal thought process precedes taking action to enhance the talent (see the later definition of Emotional Competence). The best way to discover whether an individual has achieved Reflective Competence is to ask them to describe the What and How of their talent.

LEVEL OF PROFICIENCY	DESCRIPTION
C. Reflective Competence	**The mental state experienced is Energized** • The person achieves Reflective Competence in a skill or behavior when they can **analyze** what they do, how they do it, and why this is effective in achieving success. **They know HOW they can.** • At this point, the person is able to articulate the strength or talent to themselves and others. • The person is able to understand the dynamic of the talent and undertake a scientific exploration of the skills and abilities being used. • The person can also probably teach it to others because they are able to understand the source and structure of the talent. • The person will be reliably performing the skill, technique or behavior, and have the ability to think about it at the same time.

To move from Step C to Step D the individual needs to consciously apply the strengths and talents they have identified.

Unlike when learning a new skill or overcoming a weakness (described in the early part of this chapter), which can take three weeks to three months to develop, this Development Process is quicker. This is because strengths tend to be easier to access. In addition, we already possess capability, so we are merely adding the dimensions of awareness, analysis, and further application.

TIMEOUT! DEFINING EMOTIONAL COMPETENCE

D: Emotional Competence is a **new term** to differentiate this stage from Unconscious Competence. This term describes the ability to self-monitor performance in order to perceive, integrate, understand, and regulate additional skills and techniques to enhance the use of core talents and acquired strengths.

The term Emotional Competence is used because this process is self-regulating and is similar to Emotional Intelligence as defined by Salovey and Mayer: the ability to self-regulate emotions. In Emotional Competence, the individual is not only thinking about the skill, but also acting on the self-analysis by incorporating additional techniques, ideas and skills to further raise performance.

LEVEL OF PROFICIENCY	DESCRIPTION
D. Emotional Competence	**The mental state experienced is Motivated** • The person achieves Emotional Competence in a skill or behavior when the talent becomes so practiced that it enters the unconscious part of the mind – it becomes "mastery". **The individual REALLY can.** • At the same time, the individual is able to move from unconscious to conscious and back to self-monitor their performance and skills development. • At this point, the person is able to reassess personal competence consistently – perhaps against a new standard – and step back into Reflective Competence until new mastery is obtained. • The person will be able to teach and coach others in a coherent and streamlined way. • This requires a movement up and down from C to D to ensure complacency does not occur. There is a constant quest for improvement and enhancement of aptitude. • This process can occur when an individual participates in a series of learning events spread over 2-3 weeks.

CASE STUDY: BUILDING ON TALENTS

Effortless: Unconscious Competence.

Sarah was a Training Consultant who ran very successful programs. The number one piece of feedback from these sessions was that participants found the environment "safe." She did not know how she created that environment.

Surprised: Conscious Competence

Sarah received specific positive feedback at a Train the Trainer program about the particular skills and techniques she used to create a safe environment. Some of these included repeating the answers participants provided, saying "thank you," using names, never saying "no" if an answer was incorrect, and using positive body language to acknowledge all ideas. She also had an innate sense of the group dynamic in the room – how the group was feeling and what was the best approach to use at any specific point in time. She was unaware that she possessed this talent.

Energized: Reflective Competence

As Sarah attended a further Train the Trainer program she was able to consciously analyze what she was doing, how she was doing it and what worked. In addition, she was able to observe how other trainers created a safe training environment and recognize the specific skills they used. As she progressed, she was able to describe these skills to others. In addition, she participated in a program about personality type (as assessed by the Myers-Briggs Type Indicator®) and learned that her type (ENFJ) naturally accessed Extraverted Feeling (Fe), which helped her to read a group dynamic with ease. She gradually became more able, in the moment, to observe herself using this function and describe to others how it felt.

Motivated: Emotional Competence

Sarah now is able, when she is training, to mentally observe the skills she is using, incorporate additional skills she has seen others using, and monitor in the moment the effectiveness of these skills. She is able to train others in these skills and assess their proficiency level with ease.

Optimize the Development Process

> "The business world -- and the world at large -- is obsessed with weaknesses and finding ways to fix them. A great coach knows he or she will get the most return on investment by working on strengths."
>
> *Marcus Buckingham*

As we discussed earlier, our society tends to emphasize weaknesses and skills that need to be learned rather than helping individuals identify and build on their innate talents or acquired strengths.

However, there is an increasing body of evidence that supports the principle that working on weaknesses is like "wasting people's time on trying to excel at things in which they are inherently poor" (The Strengths Book, CAPP 2010.) Instead, a preponderance of research tends to show that humans, when utilizing strengths, tend to achieve higher quality, greater productivity, and more personal fulfillment. (See books and articles by Marcus Buckingham, Alex Linley, and Robert Biswas-Diener.)

The idea that developing strengths yields vastly superior outcomes is proven by research and application. Such research has been conducted in business (Gallup Organization), mental health (Steven and Sybil Wolin), psychology (Martin Seligman), education, athletics, optimal human performance, and nearly every other field of human endeavor.

COACHING POINT

From the substantial research noted above

- The greatest capacity for growth in human beings is not, as is commonly believed, in their weaknesses, but rather in their areas of greatest strength.
- Growing strengths requires significantly less time and fewer resources than fixing weaknesses – and yields significantly better results.
- Talents and strengths are not something "out there" that one needs to "gain," but rather something that already exists which simply needs to be identified and nurtured.
- Talents or strengths are skills, techniques, and abilities that are so automatic that they no longer require conscious thought.
- Each person has a unique and enduring constellation of talents and strengths.
- **Focusing** on strengths and talents while **Managing** weaknesses or new skills is more motivational, easier to achieve, and more effective in raising individual performance.

CASE STUDY SPORTS: FOCUSING ON INNATE TALENTS

- **Michael Jordan** is one of the world's most famous and successful basketball players. In managing his performance, he only reviewed tapes of when he played well. He wanted to focus on analyzing and understanding what exactly he had done well, in order to apply these skills in future games. He did not review tapes of when he played poorly.

CASE STUDY BUSINESS: FOCUSING ON STRENGTHS/INNATE TALENTS

- **Ben** had an innate talent for seeing future opportunites, analyzing options and recommending creative solutions. He did not enjoy the operational elements of his role. In working with an Executive Coach, he decided to focus on his strengths and hired key team members to conduct these operational aspects. By focusing on strengths and utilizing others with different strengths to conduct elements of the role that represented his weaknesses, he was able to achieve success as a Chief Operating Oficer in a retail chain of over 400 stores.

COACHING POINT

Therefore, your role as a Facilitator of learning events is to:

- Help your audience members identify and understand the skills and talents they already possess.
- Help your participants define and learn new skills in as positive a Development Process as possible

Therefore, when facilitating learning events, it is important to try to recognize where participants may lie in the Development Process. Are they on the Capability – or Incapability side? If on the Incapability side, how can you protect their self-esteem to help them move gracefully from Oblivious to Uncomfortable to Focused? If on the Capability side, how can you capitalize on this ability to move from Effortless to Surprised to Reflective to Emotional Competence? By managing the Development Process in a positive way for participants you will create more rapport and receive more positive feedback.

Chapter Summary

For a Facilitator to be Flawless, it is important for them to understand how Adults learn and to minimize negative pressure on participants. In this Chapter, we have reviewed selective key adult learning and Neuroscience theories that underlie why we use the skills that we do to facilitate learning. They answer the "So What?" question. For instance, "Why can't I just lecture?", "Why do I need to create a safe learning environment?", etc.

We first reviewed Active Learning approaches and behavioral objectives. The term Andragogy was coined by Malcolm Knowles to describe the importance of involving participants in learning, treating participants as self-directed learners, linking subject material to participants' prior experience and making learning relevant to a problem the audience need to solve.

Next we reviewed more recent research on Neuroscience and the Brain, highlighting the importance of utilizing different areas of the brain to gather data, reflect on learning, create meaning and then actively test any new concepts/skills or behavior. We briefly described how different learning approaches might stimulate different areas of the brain.

Next, we reviewed the importance of creating a Social Learning environment to help ensure participants learn from others, have the appropriate emotions for learning and maintain their attention on the learning journey.

Finally, we described the Development Process for learning a new skill and a slightly different process for building on an existing skill. Both elements can be important when running learning events both to create an environment that is psychologically safe, and to gain the performance enhancement benefits from enabling participants to focus on their strengths as well as learn new skills.

The key principles we have described are:

- The Facilitator needs to use Active Learning to achieve greater retention.
- Apply the principles of Andragogy to help make learning more relevant and participant-directed.
- Consider the stages in Zull's Learning Cycle in order to enhance how the brain learns.
- Understand the need to incorporate Gathering Data (using Sensory cortex), Reflecting (using Integrative cortex), Creating Ideas (using the front of the brain) and Active Testing (using the Motor cortex) into the learning journey.
- Evaluate which are the best activities to stimulate different areas of the brain.
- Use a Social Learning Environment.
- Create moderate arousal with minimal negative emotions.
- Maintain the attention of the audience.
- Use The T.E.A.C.H. Methodology and good design principles to accomplish these aims.
- Remember the Development Process so that you enable participants to build on existing skills as well as create new behaviors.

SCORECARD

- To what extent do you use Active Learning? How could you incorporate more Active Learning in your sessions?
- What were your key learning points about Andragogy and Pedagogy? What will you do differently as a result?
- How will you ensure you make your learning more student-centered?
- What were your key learning points from Zull's Learning Cycle?
- What will you do differently in helping your participants to gather data? How will you make sure they access as many of their senses as possible?
- What will you do differently in helping your participants to reflect? How will you create "quiet time" to facilitate this process?
- What will you do differently in helping your participants to create their own meaning? What activities might help you in this process?

- What will you do differently in helping your participants to test data? How can you make sure you allow time for this important process?
- What will you do differently to help participants learn from others?
- How will you create a safe learning environment and minimize negative emotions?
- What processes will you put in place to manage attention?
- How will you monitor the audience to evaluate which participants are developing new skills and which are refining uses of existing talents?

3

E: ENGAGE YOUR LEARNERS

Chapter Overview

As we discussed in the Introduction, the ability to engage the audience is key to being a Great Facilitator. In the previous chapter, we outlined the benefits of Active Learning. In this chapter, we will begin to document in detail the "How" – the skills and techniques that build a dynamic, social learning environment. There are two main ways to create an interactive learning context:

1. Use Facilitation Skills.
2. Practice Experiential Learning.

Active Learning

Use Facilitation Skills   Practice Experiential Learning

Chapter Three:
Visual One

In this chapter, we will focus on how to facilitate interaction with a group by understanding the skills and techniques inherent in the Communication Process. First, we will review the communication process to clarify the importance and process of two-way interaction. Then we will describe in detail Involving Facilitation skills that can be used to facilitate a group discussion between one and many. We will also review Directive Facilitation skills, when the Facilitator is presenting content and/or being more instructional in nature. We will discuss the benefits and potential challenges of each approach and explore which style is appropriate for different situations. As Visual Aids enhance the message and engage the group's visual and kinesthetic preferences, we will review how to use these tools to clarify any message. In addition, we will review typical challenging situations that might arise and share techniques to manage these effectively in order to maintain the "relaxed alertness" frame of mind conducive to effective learning. Finally, we will discuss how these skills integrate with The T.E.A.C.H. methodology.

GAME PLAN

You will learn about:

- The Communication Process: One to Many
- Involving Facilitation Skills
- Directive Facilitation Skills
- Spectrum of Collaborative Facilitation
- Visual Aids
- How to Deal with Challenging Situations
- The T.E.A.C.H. Methodology and Engage your Learners

> "The facilitator's job is to support everyone to do their best thinking. To do this the facilitator encourages full participation, promotes mutual understanding and cultivates shared responsibility."
>
> *Sam Kaner*

The Communication Process: One to Many

Engaging the audience requires an effective understanding and management of the communication process.

What is Communication?

Communication is defined as the **exchange** of information, ideas and emotions between the Sender and the Receiver.

Norbert Weiner, in *The Human Use of Human Beings – Cybernetics and Society*, writes 'Communication is a joint game between the talker and the listener against the forces of confusion.' Too often, we see communication as presenting data. However, for real communication to take place, there needs to be feedback/response from the Receiver/Listener. In order for learning to occur, the message must be clear and the Receiver must receive it, process it and act on it. Communication includes the words said, the way they are said and the body language used during the process.

Try the following activity to personally experience one-way versus two-way communication.

COACHING POINT

The purpose of this exercise is to show the complexity of the communication process.

Round One

- Divide the group into pairs and ask them to sit back to back.
- Give one person the diagram shown below and ask him/her to describe it to their partner so that he/she can draw it.
- The first time use only **one-way** communication. Only the person with the diagram can talk.
- After three minutes, ask the pairs to turn around and compare diagrams.

Round Two

- Then the pairs swap roles and each person is given a different diagram.
- The second time, use **two-way** verbal communication.
- Both partners can ask and answer questions.
- After five minutes, again ask the pairs to turn around and compare diagrams.

Learning points from the exercise are normally as follows:

- Most times the one-way communication diagram is hopelessly inaccurate, and pairs normally give up before the time for the activity is complete.
- With the two-way communication diagram, it takes more time, and tends to be more accurate. Often the drawing will be closer to a "mirror" of the diagram described.

Conclusions

- One-way communication is easier for the Sender. It takes less time, but produces less effective results. If the message is not understood, two-way communication is needed to clarify it.
- Two-way communication normally produces better results, and yet is more time consuming.

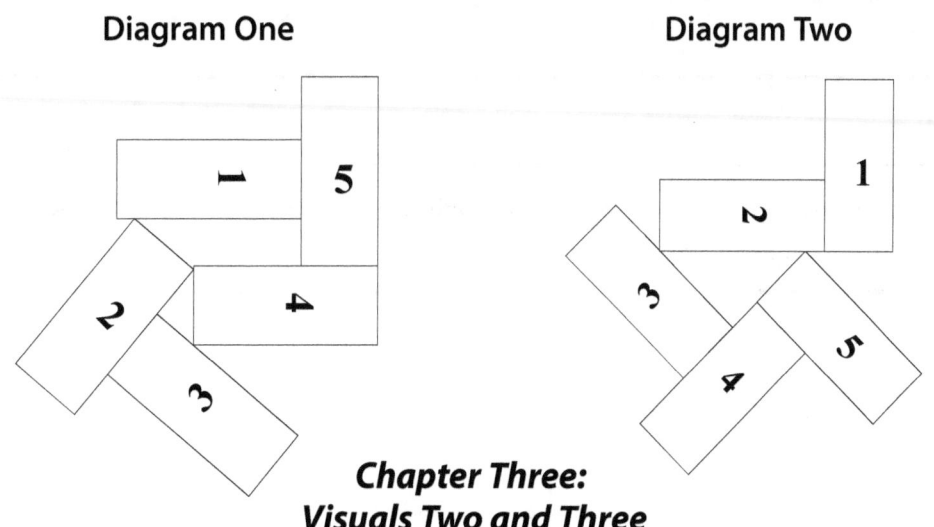

Diagram One   Diagram Two

Chapter Three:
Visuals Two and Three

The Communication Process

When you ask individuals to identify the beginning of the communication process, normally the answer is it begins with words or by getting the other person's attention.

1. In reality, the communication process begins when the Sender has an idea, thought or information that they wish to communicate.
2. The Sender then must formulate or organize the information considering, not only who will be the Receiver, but also what they wish to achieve as a result of sending the message. When the information has been mentally prepared, it is ready to be sent.
3. The Sender can then send the message using both verbal (words/word choice/vocabulary and the way the words are delivered/tone/pitch/volume, etc.) and non-verbal communication. Non-verbal communication refers to body language (expressions, gestures and posture). When we communicate with someone with whom we have an ongoing relationship, credibility also plays a role. Credibility usually comes from the amount of connection, knowledge or reliability we recognize in the communicator.
4. When we send a message, if we are lucky the other person will receive it. However, too often filters such as bias, insufficient interest, rehearsing, lack of understanding and distraction prevent the listener from receiving the message.
5. If the listener does receive the message, they then process it against their own reference bank and decode it appropriately.
6. Then, in order to "close the loop", the Receiver will either take action or provide a response.

FOUL!

The Communication Process is not complete until some type of feedback has been received from the Receiver.

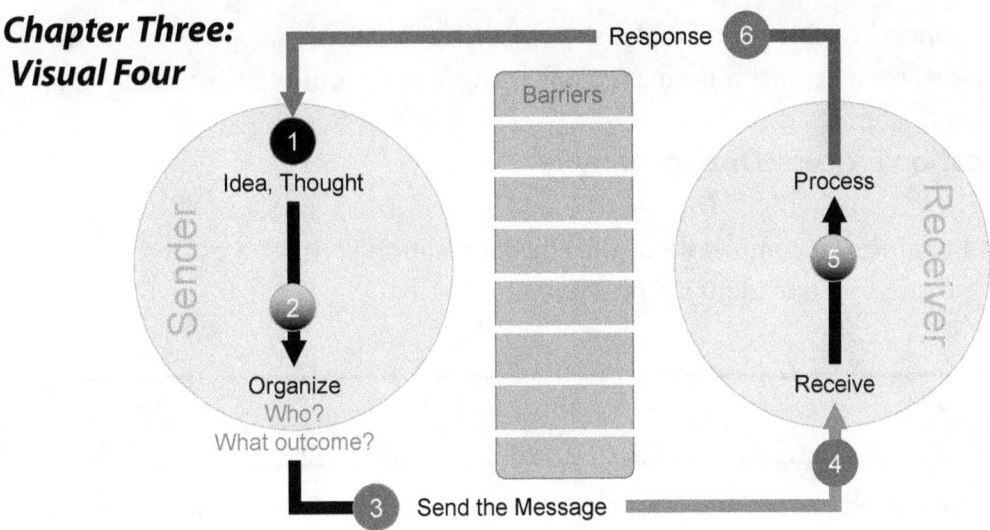

Chapter Three: Visual Four

Complexity of the Communication Process

The communication diagram represents a simplistic explanation of the communication process.

TIMEOUT!

All the steps actually happen simultaneously. As the Sender is thinking of an idea, they are formulating a sentence and possibly already sending the message. On the other end, the Receiver is sending back a complex combination of responses during the whole transmission, while at the same time processing and decoding the information.

Many things can go wrong with the communication process. The Sender may have an irrational idea, want to communicate incorrect data, or formulate the information erroneously for the Receiver. By using the wrong words (too complex, too simple, jargon, slang), the Sender could also offend, confuse, irritate or bore the receiver. In addition, he/she might not deliver the words effectively (unclear enunciation, inappropriate body language). From the other side, the Receiver might filter out the message or interpret it incorrectly because of their different frame of reference. The Receiver could also provide a completely inappropriate response. The process is so complex that it is amazing anything is communicated accurately at all!

Communication Process: One to Many

As you can imagine, the complexity of the communication process is exacerbated when facilitating learning in a one to many format.

TIMEOUT!

There are many differences in the communication process when communicating one-to-many. Each Receiver will have different experiences, education, cultural values, family background, type preferences, interests, maturity, motivation, listening barriers and communication style to name a few areas.

This diversity in terms of the Receivers' ability and willingness to accept, process and give feedback to any content presented necessitates the Sender constantly seeking two-way interaction to assess where each of the Receivers is located in the learning process. The Sender needs to use Facilitation Skills not just Presentation Skills.

Presenting Versus Facilitating

As we discussed in an earlier chapter, for learning to take place, it is important to differentiate between Presenting versus Facilitating.

TIMEOUT!

Presenting involves providing relevant information or knowledge. The focus tends to be on the Sender to deliver an effective message while using some two-way interaction. Presenting tends to sound more like "Telling".

Facilitating is far more complex. In the learning context, Facilitating involves both presenting content to the audience while at the same time, planning, managing and guiding the group process in order for active learning to occur. Facilitators tend to do more "Asking".

The Facilitator is responsible for guiding learning to achieve the course objectives from a student-centered perspective. As a result, the Facilitator uses a very different set of skills that we will review in the next sections.

EXERCISE 3-1: PRESENTING VERSUS FACILITATING

- Think about the definition of the Presenting and Facilitating
- To what extent do you "Present"?
- To what extent do you "Facilitate"?

TRY IT ON: PRESENTING VERSUS FACILITATING

Write your ideas here…

Presenting?

_____

_____

Facilitating?

_____

_____

Involving Facilitation Skills

The most important way to engage the audience, and where a Facilitator can be successful, is by continually using Involving Facilitation skills to create a two-way dialog. Involving Facilitation Skills include:

- Ask Open and Closed Questions
- Pause
- Listen Actively
- Reinforce Contribution
- Ask Follow up Questions

Ask Open and Closed Questions

TIMEOUT!

Open Questions engage the audience and stimulate thought. Open questions begin with words such as Why? How? What? Who? Where? When?

Topic-opener statements such as Tell me about, Explain and Describe also tend to begin discussions. Because these statements gain broader input from the audience, we categorize these under open questions.

Closed Questions confirm data and/or can transition from one subject to another. Closed questions begin with words such as can, could, shall, should, will, would, have, had, is, was. Closed questions tend to provide a Yes or No answer.

FOUL!

Too often, Facilitators think they are asking Open questions – and yet they are asking Closed questions. As a result, participants may not engage fully. In addition, it can be easy to close down an open question – for instance "Can you tell me about."

Both types of questions have value:

- Open questions and Topic-opener statements can build engagement.
- Closed questions can confirm learning.
- Choosing and using the appropriate type of question is a key facilitation skill.

Open Questions

Using open questions to guide learning is a proactive and complex process. Open Questions need to make participants think about the content and link their emerging understanding to their prior experience. Questions cannot appear mundane or patronizing, while at the same time, they need to focus on what you can expect the group to know. For instance, asking, 'What words begin open questions?" is a safe question to ask (if teaching communication, sales or service skills) because most people have been taught this concept in school or college. Asking the group "What is a Topic-Opener statement?" probably would not work, because this concept tends to not be commonly understood, even though most participants will know the phrase, "Tell me about". In this case, the way to facilitate this learning is to name the concept 'Topic-Opener Statements", share the acronym "TED", and then ask participants what they think the T, the E and the D stand for? In addition, a Facilitator needs to build questions to help participants move "down the funnel" of learning: from more general to more specific. For instance, move from, "What is an Open Question?" to, "Why ask Open Questions?" to, "What open questions might you ask in _____ context?"

COACHING POINTS: OPEN QUESTIONS

Below are some general guidelines for using Open questions effectively in order to create an interactive learning environment:

- **Prepare and practice** Open Questions based on the information you want to cover. As you prepare the questions, make sure they are designed to proactively guide the group through the content.

- The fundamental principle is **Trust the Group** to answer the questions. This is the attitude underpinning this key facilitation practice.
- Only ask Open Questions on information you think the **group will know**.
- Only ask **one question at a time**: discomfort with questioning skills can sometimes cause Facilitators to ask 3-4 questions without waiting for a response. This can result in participants' confusion.
- Make sure you have **suggested answers in your head**: this will enable you to prepare more questions in the moment to obtain the answer you are looking for.
- **Do not answer your own questions**: allow time for a response.
- If the group does not answer, you can **repeat your initial question at least once**, and then ensure you have other questions prepared. Half the time, the audience is not listening so they will not hear the duplication!
- If the group still does not know the answer, **prepare a leading question**. A leading question is one that gives part of the answer and thereby leads the audience to the answer.
- Worst-case scenario, if the group still cannot answer, **have an example prepared** that can help to lead them to an answer.
- If you are concerned about the audience not being able to answer questions, **create a "plant"** to give you ideal answers for critical questions.
- **Preface your questions** with phrases such as, "Let me ask you a question" to give the audience a heads-up that they need to listen.
- Ask "**Anything else**" several times when completing any large group discussion – this allows time for individuals to expand their thoughts.

When the group asks you a question…..

- If someone in the group asks you a question, consider whether to offer the question to the audience to answer – **ping-pong**. If you choose to do this, repeat the question and bounce it to the audience by asking something like, "What do the rest of you think?" This helps to reduce "The Expert Trap" that many facilitators fall into.
- Always **repeat questions** that have been asked of you so the group hears them.

Use Open Questions constantly throughout learning to stimulate thought. Each question can help individuals reflect, create their own meaning and test their understanding.

Rhetorical Questions

FOUL!

- Too often, Facilitators use Rhetorical Questions.
- While these can grab interest, they can also shut down two-way communication because the audience is not required to answer.
- They tend to make the environment feel "less safe" as there is only one "right answer" and that is the facilitator's point of view.
- They can also tend to appear a little too one-up/one-down "Parent to Child" versus "Adult to Adult" communication.

Closed Questions

Closed Questions also play a valuable role in creating a two-way learning conversation.

COACHING POINTS: CLOSED QUESTIONS

Below are some guidelines for using Closed Questions effectively in order to create an interactive learning environment.

Use Closed Questions:

- To transition from one subject to another.
- To check understanding.
- After every section: "Any questions?"
- To confirm definite information.
- To gather specific data.

EXERCISE 3-2: OPEN AND CLOSED QUESTIONS

- How effective are you at asking Open Questions when facilitating. Record a training session you facilitate and track your use of Open Questions.
- How could you improve your use of Open Questions to engage the audience?
- When do you use Closed Questions?

TRY IT ON: OPEN AND CLOSED QUESTIONS

Write your ideas here...

Open Questions?

_____

_____

_____

Closed Questions?

_____

_____

_____

COACHING POINTS: QUESTIONS

Make sure you ask some type of question minimally once every two minutes. This maintains attention and ensures the energy continues to move back and forth between the Facilitator and Learners.

Pause

It is important to pause after asking a question to allow the audience to consider their responses and to confirm that the Facilitator wants the group to answer!

TIMEOUT!

The average duration of the Pause can vary from 2 seconds (when the group is highly engaged) to 10 seconds (at the beginning of a learning event and/or when a complex question is asked.)

Remember the Pause sounds longer to the Facilitator than it does to the audience!

Some of the factors influencing the length of the pause are:

- What are the type preferences of the participants? For instance, how many prefer to talk things through (Initiating/Extraverting) or think things through (Responding/Introverting)? The pause will tend to be longer with a more reflective group. (See Appendix for more about this preference.)
- The cultural preferences of the group – what cultural values might be in play? For instance, many Asian cultures may not speak up quickly for fear of losing face.
- How safe do participants feel? If the group feels that they can respond and receive positive validation, the pause will be shorter. (See earlier notes in Chapter One on establishing a positive group process.)
- How relevant is the question? The more targeted and relevant the question, the quicker will be the response.
- How complex is the question? How much thought is required to integrate ideas and answer the question?
- What is the current group process? After a particularly thought-provoking topic, the pause may be longer as people process emotions. How long is it since you took a break? How close to lunch/end of day are you?

The Facilitator who manages the pause will also manage the group process.

COACHING POINTS: PAUSING

Below are some guidelines for managing the Pause

- Manage the silence: **4-10 seconds**. Remember, silence is golden.
- **Count to ten** to manage the silence.
- Expect the silence to be **longer at the beginning** of the session.
- Do not be afraid to **ask why** if the Pause seems longer than you expect.
- Monitoring pausing can provide the "**pulse**" of the group.
- Use silence to encourage the audience to "**think**".

Listen Actively

Listening actively is important in order for the Facilitator to create a safe learning environment and to ensure that participants perceive that their input is valued. Too often Facilitators lose the ability to listen actively because they are:

- Rehearsing what they will say next.
- Distracted by something in the environment.
- Not comfortable with the content.
- Not aware how obvious it can be to the audience when the Facilitator is not attentive to the participants.

FOUL!

Do not bluff if you did not hear what a participant said. This can be immediately obvious to the audience and can result in some closing down of the communication process.

COACHING POINTS: LISTEN ACTIVELY

Below are some guidelines to aid in Listening Actively

- Focus.
- Look at the person speaking.
- Make eye contact.
- Be prepared.
- Pay attention.
- Probe deeper for clarity – see later notes on asking follow up questions.
- Make adjustments based on the data you receive: make sure you demonstrate by behavior that you have heard what the person said.
- Always stay in the "now" moment with the group.
- Use listening cues such as "uh uh" and body language to demonstrate that you are listening.
- Be prepared to either paraphrase or repeat back the information word-for-word (see later notes).
- Use follow up questions to clarify an answer if you would like further data.
- Ask to confirm understanding if you are not sure about what the person said.
- Suspend any judgments or preconceived ideas about the person or their comment so that you hear the message in its entirety.

EXERCISE 3-3: PAUSE AND LISTEN ACTIVELY

- How effective are you at managing the Pause when facilitating? How often do you fill the space with another question?
- How effective are you at listening actively to participants' answers?
- What will you do differently to make sure you listen to audience responses?

TRY IT ON: PAUSE AND LISTEN ACTIVELY

Write your ideas here…

Pausing?

_____
_____
_____

Listening Actively?

_____
_____
_____

Reinforce Contribution

An important way to build a social learning environment with minimal stress for the audience is to validate any participant who answers a question and/or provides a point of view.

TIMEOUT!

The easiest and most effective way to reinforce participants' contribution is to **repeat each person's answer "word for word"**. The benefits for this technique are comprehensive and include:

- Ensures every participant in the room hears every answer.
- Makes you as a Facilitator listen – if you do not hear it, you cannot repeat it!
- Validates the person who speaks because you have repeated their words back to them.
- Provides an opportunity for the participant to Actively Test their understanding. Often people do not remember exactly what they said – hearing their answer repeated back reinforces and builds on learning.

- Creates the dynamic back and forth energy required for active learning.
- Means you do not need a microphone when recording – even with a large group – as all data is captured.
- Answer is neutral – no Facilitator judgment is added.
- You are giving time and space to the audience – so more Adult to Adult learning style.

COACHING POINTS: REINFORCE CONTRIBUTION

Below are some additional guidelines to aid in Reinforcing Contribution:

- Use the person's name when they say something (see the LAURA Technique for remembering names – see later notes).
- When a participant says something, say "Thank you."
- Give positive feedback when a person answers such as "Good thought", "great point, etc...
- Make sure you vary your positive feedback – "great answer" for every participant response can seem insincere.
- Refer back to examples individuals have used, using their names.
- Use positive body language.
- Never criticize a participant in front of the group.
- Watch your tone of voice and body language when you hear what you might perceive to be "stupid" questions or answers.
- If the answer is long, you can also repeat word for word key words from the answer the participant has provided.

Occasionally it is not possible to repeat word for word because either the answer is too long, or you missed part of the response. In this case, paraphrasing is a viable option.

TIMEOUT!

Paraphrasing is defined as summarizing what the other person has just said using your own words to capture the essence and the meaning in the participant's answer.

Paraphrasing is also neutral – there is no judgment from the Facilitator in the answer.

COACHING POINTS: PARAPHRASING

- Always ask for permission to paraphrase. "So if it's OK – this is what I heard".
- Check with the participant to ensure that the paraphrasing was accurate.
- Give the participant an opportunity to correct or add to your comments.
- You can also ask the individual to paraphrase if the answer was long!

FOUL!

- If the Facilitator "over-uses" paraphrasing (uses it most of the time), unconsciously the message is being transmitted that the Facilitator's words are better than the participants' contributions.
- This can create a more Parent to Child environment and may make individuals reluctant to contribute.

Another challenge in repeating word for word can be if someone provides a "wrong" answer or one that is drastically different from the answer you were expecting. In a positive learning context, it is important to answer "No" as little as possible – so what do you do?

COACHING POINTS: WRONG ANSWER

- Repeat the answer word for word.
- Use Ping Pong and give the answer back to the audience, "What do the rest of you think?"
- 90% of the time, the audience then regulates and manages the answer ensuring that the communication climate remains Adult to Adult.
- If the group cannot correct, then you know that something has been misunderstood and it enables you to revisit your content.

Below is a simple technique to help you remember names. As names can act like music to our ears, using a person's name consistently and authentically can contribute to a productive learning environment.

TIMEOUT! LAURA

Learn names as quickly as possible using LAURA:

L: **L**ook at the Person to get a visual image – try not to get the name until you have the picture otherwise you will forget the name immediately!

A: **A**sk for the person's name

U: **U**nderstand the name – how is it constructed? Whom else do you know with that name? What are the origins of the name?

R: **R**epeat the name – not obsessively, but enough to cement this knowledge in your brain.

A: **A**ssociate – where is the person sitting? What is their job role? Whom might they look like? Etc.

Asking Follow Up Questions

Asking follow up questions is another way to demonstrate interest in your participants, stimulate more in-depth learning and validate involvement.

TIMEOUT!

Asking follow up questions is the process of probing for more information on the answer provided.

It involves taking the basic information received, repeating it, and asking further open questions to gather more specific data within the subject area.

The reasons for asking follow up questions are many and include:

- There is a need for greater clarity from the participant about meaning.
- You want the participant to expand the answer they gave as this will add value to the group.
- You believe that a further example will clarify the meaning for the audience.
- You want to utilize "experts" in the room to validate their insights.

FOUL!

- There can be a temptation, if there is time pressure, not to ask relevant follow up questions.
- This can be a mistake because this might mean that the pressure for quantity has negatively affected the quality of the overall learning. (See Chapter Two for Must, Should and Could Model).

EXERCISE 3-4: REINFORCE CONTRIBUTION, PARAPHRASE AND ASK FOLLOW UP QUESTIONS

- How often do you repeat word for word what participants have shared with you?
- What other skills do you use to reinforce contribution e.g. use of names, positive feedback, etc.
- How often do you use paraphrasing? Could you use paraphrasing less and repeating more?
- How often do you ask follow up questions to deepen participants' knowledge and engagement?

TRY IT ON: REINFORCE CONTRIBUTION, PARAPHRASE AND ASK FOLLOW UP QUESTIONS

Write your ideas here...

Repeating word for word?

_____

_____

Other reinforcement techniques

_____

_____

Paraphrasing?

_____

_____

Asking Follow up Questions?

_____

_____

CASE STUDY: TRAIN-THE-TRAINER

The best way I have found to gain an understanding of an individual's Involving Facilitation skills is to record each Facilitator and provide specific feedback on the extent to which these skills are used. Individuals then have an opportunity to watch their practice and listen to the feedback. In addition, using a "buddy" as a coach can develop observation and feedback skills.

Directive Facilitation

Directive Facilitation encompasses the following:

- The Facilitator uses effective presentation skills when teaching content. We will review specific guidelines for words, the way we say the words and body language. This can be when the Facilitator moves into "Lecture-only" mode.
- When the Facilitator shares examples or stories that are relevant to the context and/ or skill being presented.
- The Facilitator provides clear instructions for activities – we will review these in more detail in Chapter Four.
- When the Facilitator needs to correct a misconception or set clearer boundaries.
- When the Facilitator faces a challenging situation – see the guidelines later in this chapter.

FOUL!

If you only use Directive Facilitation, you will not be able to capture the benefits of Active Learning and you may appear more Parent to Child or Pedagogic.

Sending an Effective Message

TIMEOUT!

We communicate our message using Words, the Way we Say the Words and Body Language.

Words are defined as **Word Choice, Vocabulary or Word Selection** (They represent part of verbal communication.)

The Way we Say the Words is the second part of verbal delivery and includes elements such as **Tone, Pace, Volume, Accent, Enunciation, Emphasis,** etc.

Body Language represents the non-verbal element sending the message and includes elements such as **Eye Contact and Movements, Gestures, Facial Expressions, Posture and Stance, Movement,** etc.

FOUL!

- Credibility can also play an important role in whether participants receive and understand our message or whether they discount and/or misunderstand it.
- We will review credibility in Chapter Five when we discuss Temperament as there are general and specific ways to build credibility based on participants' preferences.

Words

According to Mehrabian's research, the actual words we use represent a small percentage of the communication message. Yet, often this is the area in which Facilitators spend the most time preparing and rehearsing.

Below are some simple guidelines for optimizing your word choice when using Directive Facilitation.

COACHING POINTS: WORD CHOICE

- Avoid saying "no" as far as possible (see earlier notes).
- Use positive and encouraging words.
- Prepare in advance so as to manage filler words such as "um", "ah", "like" etc.
- Be careful about humor.
- Self-disclose to connect.
- Use examples and stories, but practice them first.
- Use transition phrases to "bridge" from one topic to the next.
- Don't use too many words.
- Don't use jargon or slang.
- Select "easy" words (depending on the audience).

Way We Say the Words

The Way we Say the Words can change the meaning of the message received, so make sure you provide the most effective Verbal Delivery. Try the activity below to experience the influence on meaning of verbal delivery.

EXERCISE 3-5: THE WAY WE SAY THE WORDS

Repeat the following sentence placing an emphasis on a different word each time.

- **_I_** did not say you stole the watch.
- I **_did not_** say you stole the watch.
- I did not **_say_** you stole the watch.
- I did not say **_you_** stole the watch.
- I did not say you **_stole_** the watch.

- I did not say you stole *the* watch.
- I did not say you stole the *watch.*

TRY IT ON: WAY WE SAY THE WORDS

Write your ideas here for the different meanings:

I did not say you stole the watch – meaning?

_____

I *did not* say you stole the watch – meaning?

_____

I did not *say* you stole the watch – meaning?

_____

I did not say *you* stole the watch – meaning?

_____

I did not say you *stole* the watch – meaning?

_____

I did not say you stole *the* watch – meaning?

_____

I did not say you stole the *watch* – meaning?

_____

Below are some simple guidelines to optimize the way you say the words when using Directive Facilitation.

COACHING POINTS: WAY WE SAY THE WORDS

- Use a variation of tone to add interest.
- Demonstrate enthusiasm and interest in your topic (where appropriate).
- Use a variation of volume.
- Manage your pace so that you do not rush when nervous.
- Slow down if you are giving instructions or making key learning points.
- Emphasize key words: new terms, etc.
- Use pauses to manage the group dynamic and maintain audience interest.
- Manage your emotions so you do not use sarcasm or sound patronizing.
- Make sure you know how to pronounce difficult terms.
- Enunciate clearly.
- Make sure the delivery matches the content of the message.

Body Language

Body Language has a high influence on the understanding of the message that we send. If participants have to select between the message communicated by body language and the message communicated by words, they will tend to believe the body language message.

Below are some simple guidelines to optimize how you use body language when using Directive Facilitation.

COACHING POINTS: BODY LANGUAGE

- Become aware of your body language – ask for feedback and/or record yourself.
- Learn about cultural differences to meet all participants' needs.
- Be careful about power roles when training, don't get too close to participants.
- Use body language mirroring to help listening and in reinforcing participants' contributions.
- Shake hands with delegates: this creates a human connection and can contribute to building rapport.
- Remember body language will show how you are feeling: make sure you "go on stage" when training.

Here are some guidelines about specific aspects of body language

EYE CONTACT	• Make 2-4 seconds of eye contact with everyone in the room. • Remember you will have a favorite side – be aware of it and modify it. • Everyone should receive eye contact several times during the training. • The eyes are the windows to the soul, so everything will be reflected in your eyes.
EYE MOVEMENTS	• Watch rolling your eyes. When you are thinking, your eyes may roll upwards – preparing and practicing will help reduce this.
FACIAL EXPRESSION	• Smiles generate more smiles. Watch the positions of the eyebrows, tension in the mouth and forehead.
MOVEMENT	• Adds energy to an interaction. • Move in a controlled way – don't pace. • Make the movement in alignment with your natural pace (see later Chapter on Interaction Styles for more information). • Watch "fiddling with gadgets" or moving around a lot, as this could be perceived as a lack of interest or nerves.

POSTURE STANCE	• Stand firm and upright – this tends to be interpreted as confidence. • A change in posture indicates that a change in communication mode is required. • Stand upright with your feet 6-9" apart and the weight on the balls of your feet. • Don't wriggle or twitch. • Don't cross your legs one in front of the other. • Don't lean unnecessarily. • Watch barriers and move around them when it is realistic to do so.
BREATHING	• When we are stressed, we tend to stop breathing. • Use stress reduction techniques to manage your breathing patterns. • Do not sigh when someone asks you what you might perceive to be an irrelevant question.
SPACE	• We each carry around our unique bubble of space. • If we go into someone's space, they will pull back and feel pressured. We have three space bubbles: intimate, personal, and professional. • Respect your participants' space bubbles.
GESTURES	• There are over 30 gestures in all. • Use gestures that are comfortable. • We can make all gestures larger than normal in front of a group. • Unacceptable gestures are pointing and beckoning. • Remember to use open hand movements to replace these gestures.
DRESS	• This makes an impact on the group until credibility has been established. • The guideline initially is to dress "one level up" from the audience. • When you are working with a regular group, the guideline is to dress "on the same level" as the audience.
NATURAL SELF	• We each possess a unique identity when communicating. If we try to modify our style based on other people's styles, we will come across as insincere. • So by all means, watch other techniques, but adapt them to your own natural style.

EXERCISE 3-6: YOUR DIRECTIVE FACILITATION SKILLS

- What do you think works well for you in terms of Word Choice? How can you improve your Word Selection?
- What do you think are your strengths in the Way you Say the Words? How can you improve your verbal delivery?
- What are your Body Language strengths? What might you need to improve?

TRY IT ON: YOUR DIRECTIVE FACILITATION SKILLS

Write your ideas here…

Words?

_____

_____

Way you Say the Words?

_____

_____

Body Language?

_____

_____

Provide Facilitator Examples

Facilitators also use Directive Facilitation when they provide examples to bring content to life.

FOUL!

Most of the literature about how to share examples is grouped under the subject area of Stories, a subject we explored briefly in Chapter One. Stories are fundamentally different from examples:

- The purpose of a Story is often to entertain, educate or inform.
- The purpose of a Facilitator example is to connect with the audience and increase learning and retention.
- Examples tend to put the Facilitator and Group on an equal footing and demonstrate how the Facilitator has personally applied the skills/techniques or knowledge in a similar context.

Below are a few principles for introducing effective examples.

COACHING POINT – FACILITATOR EXAMPLES

- Make them relevant and relatable – do not give examples from very different contexts or where skills are not directly applicable.
- Ensure they are concise and specific with a clear application focus.
- Consider how they might connect with the Audience's emotions.
- Get examples from the audience first and supplement with yours – if needed.
- Be prepared not to use your examples.

While it is important to prepare and rehearse your examples, you may only have a chance to use a small percentage of those in your "tool bag".

Spectrum of Collaborative Facilitation

When using the facilitation skills outlined in the previous sections, there exists a Spectrum between Involving and Directive Facilitation. To summarize:

TIMEOUT!

Involving Facilitation engages the audience in the Learning Journey. The Facilitator may have designed the content and the flow, and yet the Facilitator trusts the Learners with this methodology to create their own insights.

Directive Facilitation involves the Facilitator being more proactive in guiding the Learning Journey. This may occur if the flow needs to be changed, if the group process needs some support or if the learning is going off track.

Spectrum clarifies that, at any time, a Facilitator may be anywhere on an axis from very Directive to very Involving. This location is dependent on each individual, group and context so is impossible to predict.

Collaborative Facilitation means that the ownership of a successful learning outcome is shared between the Facilitator and the Participants.

The table below outlines the key elements of Involving and Directive Facilitation.

INVOLVING FACILITATION	DIRECTIVE FACILITATION
Mental Approach	

INVOLVING FACILITATION	DIRECTIVE FACILITATION
Focus on group learning the content	Focus on covering the key content
Trust the group to support the process	Trust yourself to guide the process
Approach tends to empower student to be a self-directed learner	Approach tends to make student more dependent on expert teacher
Aim is to begin with, and build on, participants' knowledge	Aim is to begin with teacher knowledge to expand participants' knowledge
Higher level of participant choice	Lower level of participant choice
Skills	
Ask primarily open questions	Ask primarily closed questions
More active listening with follow-up questions in the moment	More script-based with limited response to questions
Tend to ask more leading questions	Tend to ask more rhetorical questions
More listening than talking	More talking than listening
More intentional use of body language to engage the audience	More intentional use of body language to illustrate a point
Tends to encourage pausing for audience reflection and engagement	Tends to fill silence with knowledge and content
Responding to the Group	
Tends to repeat word for word or paraphrase to confirm listening	Tends to acknowledge audience contribution
Refers back primarily to participants' input	Refers back primarily to Facilitators' prior experience
Examples primarily from the group	Examples primarily from the Facilitator
Deals with "wrong" answers by repeating and reframing	Deals with "wrong" answers by correcting
Tends to use ping-pong to encourage the group to answer questions	Tends to fall into the "expert" trap – answering all audience questions
Uses Facilitator knowledge and/or examples to supplement group input	Uses Facilitator knowledge and/or examples before group input
Admits lack of knowledge – and offers to explore solutions	Closes the subject and moves on
Environment	

INVOLVING FACILITATION	DIRECTIVE FACILITATION
Group is given space to manage and explore feelings	Group is not given space for sharing and exploring feelings
Participants tend to be active and contributing	Participants tend to be passive for more than five minutes
Can appear more Adult to Adult	Can appear more Parent to Child
Participants feel valued and "safe"	Participants may feel inhibited in providing responses
Energy is primarily multi-directional	Energy is primarily one-way
Power mostly with students	Power mostly with Facilitator
Participants create their own understanding	Participants are provided with learning points

COACHING POINTS: INVOLVING VERSUS DIRECTIVE FACILITATION

- Neither style is right or wrong – they are just different.
- The balance ideally will be 80% Involving and 20% Directive.
- If the Facilitator uses too much Directive Facilitation, the group may shut down.
- At any time, the Facilitator's role is to balance whether to use Directive or Involving Facilitation to optimize learning effectiveness.
- Subject material can also influence the extent to which Directive facilitation is used e.g. technical training.

FOUL!

- Technical training can still be taught using Involving Facilitation Techniques.
- Many experiential learning activities can be used in technical training thereby incorporating Involving Facilitation Practices (see Chapter Four).

CASE STUDY: TEACHING TEMPERAMENT AND INTERACTION STYLE

Much of my work involves teaching the knowledge of psychological type.

Originally, when I taught Temperament (see Chapter Five), because this was heavily theoretical I would "lecture" for about 15 minutes about each type. As a result, the group dynamic would become static and one-way.

Having worked with developing trainers at PUMA University, I realized that by using well-designed activities in a structured learning process (incorporating large group discussion, team exercises, open space activities, case studies and card sorts), I could minimize my "lecture" time and capitalize on the group "learning by doing". As a result, the group dynamic improved, content became more immediately relevant and retention increased.

COACHING POINT: INVOLVING FACILITATION AND MILLENNIALS

Teaching technical content in an experiential way is even more important for Millennials who tend to want to be constantly engaged in the learning process.

EXERCISE 3-7: INVOLVING AND DIRECTIVE FACILITATION

- To what extent do you use Involving Facilitation?
- To what extent do you use Directive Facilitation?
- How can you ensure you balance the two styles effectively?

TRY IT ON: INVOLVING AND DIRECTIVE FACILITATION

Write your ideas here...

Involving Facilitation?

_____

_____

_____

Directive Facilitation?

_____

_____

_____

Balance?

_____

_____

_____

Use Visual Aids

Visual Aids make the learning process more effective (most people are visual learners) and also provide kinesthetic stimulation (movement/touch). Visual Aids can also serve as a support to the Facilitator.

TIMEOUT!

The most common Visual Aids are:

- Presentation Slides combined with Projector/Beamer or TV
- Flip Charts
- Handouts
- Videos
- Samples or Photos

FOUL!

Used incorrectly, Visual Aids can detract from the learning and confuse or distract the audience.

Visual Aids do not replace a Facilitator's role – they supplement it!

Presentation Slides

TIMEOUT!

- Presentation Slides are designed to provide the structure for any learning event – the "Red Line".
- They contain the overview for the key content and flow.
- Slides describe key knowledge, skills, techniques, or behaviors that are being taught so that participants can see and hear this important data.
- Slides should also contain the instructions for any activities to supplement the Facilitator's guidelines.

COACHING POINT: USING SLIDES EFFECTIVELY

Below are some guidelines for making effective use of slides and the technology that supports them.

Dos	Don'ts
• Use simple bullets: no more than nine.	• Read from the slide.
• Use animation to avoid cognitive dissonance – you are talking about one bullet yet participants are reading other bullets.	• Use unnecessary visuals.
• Ask one open question per bullet to make the slides interactive.	• Have too much information on them: key words only.
• Check the animation works.	• Use a small font – should be 24 ideally.
• Practice so you are familiar with the animation.	• Have distracting animations.
• Have a paper copy of slides available 6 to a page for reference.	• Rely always on slides: use other tools.
• Ensure spelling is correct.	• "Show up and throw up!" limit the number of slides in a specific period. Use no more than 12 per hour.
• Use prepared slides as a visual memory to cover key learning points.	• Use copyright images – it can be easy in today's world to assume all images on search engines are common domain but this might not be the case.
• Organize/sequence slides effectively – follow the flow of the day.	
• Use divider slides to separate sections.	
• Think of quantity versus time.	
• Provide a summary at the end.	
• Have consistent layout: headers/footers/numbers/slide master.	
• Use company-specific font and colors.	
• Use relevant visuals.	

Flip Charts

Flip Charts provide another tool to engage participants in the learning journey.

TIMEOUT!

- Flip Charts can capture the learning from the group.
- They can also capture insights from a large group discussion or from some type of team activity.
- They can document key models that need to remain visual throughout a learning event. (For instance, The Communication Model in a presentation skills workshop.)
- Used effectively, they can act as a visual memory of key learning points.

COACHING POINT: USING FLIP CHARTS EFFECTIVELY

Below are some guidelines for making effective use of flip charts when facilitating learning.

Dos	Don'ts
• Use simple bullets: no more than nine.	• Read from flip chart: ask questions to gather information.
• Use color, pictures and key words.	• Stand in front of the flip chart.
• Ensure spelling is correct.	• Write too small for people to read.
• Use prepared flip charts as a visual memory.	• Use colors that cannot be seen easily such as yellow.
• Write in pencil before the session as a guideline if flip charts are being used for models.	• Use confrontational colors such as red.
• Use to energize the group.	• Run out of paper/pens/tape.
• Work with a scribe if you are worried about spelling: repeat the words from the audience to go onto the flip chart to ensure the scribe knows what to write.	• Write long sentences.
• Use upper case for easier reading.	• Put too much content on them.
• Use a consistent size of words and keep writing straight.	
• Love your flip chart!	
• Position it in the room for ease of use. Make sure it is stable	

Handouts

Handouts are slightly controversial in today's "conserving paper" society. There can be a tendency to provide soft copy of slides and/or rely on individuals to make their own notes.

TIMEOUT!

- Handouts can supplement the information from the slides.
- They can contain detailed content information together with workshop agenda and objectives.
- Handouts can also contain the instructions for any activities to supplement the Facilitator's guidelines with space for writing notes. This can help to ensure that notes are gathered in the relevant content area.
- Writing notes on a handout activates our neocortex more than if we simply observe the content and flow.

FOUL!

Merely providing copies of the slides does not support learning.

Individuals can be tempted to read ahead and so may become bored quickly.

COACHING POINT: USING HANDOUTS EFFECTIVELY

Below are some guidelines for making effective use of handouts.

Dos	Don'ts
• Allow time for reading.	• Overload with details.
• Constantly reference page numbers to keep participants on the same page.	• Use information that you are not explaining in the training session unless this is in the Appendix section.
• Distribute before the session – but use Prisoner/Page Turner to keep on same page (see Chapter One).	• Have different terms in the handouts and the slides.
• Alternatively, distribute after the presentation to encourage people to write and minimize distractions.	• Use the presentation slides as a handout because this encourages reading ahead.
• Hold up the handout and show the page when you are using it.	• Use too many abbreviations.
• Keep content simple.	• Make them a book!
• Check spelling, grammar and punctuation.	
• Use bullet points.	
• Include references for further reading if required.	
• Use a clear visual layout.	
• Make sure they are relevant.	
• Establish use of handout in ground rules (stay on same page; watch your partners, etc.).	
• Make sure handouts and slides "match".	
• Love your Participant Handout!	
• Tell them what to write, where and when.	
• Make sure everyone can read them.	
• Make sure there are enough plus at least 3-5 extra.	
• Use the corporate font, look and feel.	

Video Clips

Videos, when used correctly can build energy, raise emotions and convey important learning points.

TIMEOUT!

- Video clips can consist of clips available on the internet.
- It can also be beneficial to create customized videos for certain skills being taught.

COACHING POINT: USING VIDEOS EFFECTIVELY

Below are some guidelines for making effective use of Video clips.

Dos	Don'ts
• Introduce the video clip.	• Use to replace a live person.
• Set the scene on why the clip is being used.	• Make it too long.
• Know the technology and make sure it works.	• Use clips if they are not relevant.
• Build some involvement strategies: tests, worksheet.	• Be inappropriate (remember cultural differences).
• Start at the right point.	
• Make clips short, simple and relevant.	
• Make sure everyone can see and hear the video.	
• Try to ensure there is a WOW factor with the clip.	

CASE STUDY: VIDEO

In an interviewing workshop, two videos were customized for an Interviewing Skills workshop:

- An Interviewer making common interviewing mistakes.
- An Interviewer demonstrating the skills taught.
- The benefit of this approach was that the content was highly customized to the participants' context, which helps increase learning and retention.

Photos and Products

For specific learning e.g. product knowledge, use of photos and/or products can increase interest and retention as participants physically engage with these materials. As we discussed in Chapter Two, the more we can engage all the senses when Gathering Data the better.

COACHING POINT: USING PHOTOS/PRODUCTS EFFECTIVELY

Below are some guidelines for making effective use of photos or products.

Dos	Don'ts
• Make sure the products/photos are relevant and high quality. • Organize how you will present them: you hand them out or walk around with them. • Have enough for the group. • Explain what they reference. • Categorize and highlight key points. • Allow time for exploration – touching any products will stall the group process.	• Rely solely on products or photos – remember content. • Keep talking as you pass them around – the group will get distracted. • Have too many products. • Rush the distribution of products.

We use Visual Aids to maintain audience involvement and ensure multiple senses are engaged in the learning journey.

EXERCISE 3-8: USE VISUAL AIDS

How will you use Visual Aids differently as a result of this section?

TRY IT ON: USE VISUAL AIDS

Write your ideas here…

Use Visual Aids Differently?

_____

_____

_____

Dealing With Challenging Situations

When the facilitation skills we have just described are used well, they are often "transparent" to the learners. All that participants might note is that they thought the facilitator was excellent, or environment felt comfortable and they felt willing to share their point of view. If these skills are not used effectively, or other factors are in play, then you may need to address certain challenging situations in order to restore the positive learning environment. Let us look at some of these situations now. Some of these challenges may require you to use more Directive Facilitation techniques to re-establish or cement a positive group process.

TIMEOUT!

There can be three types of challenging situations:

- One to one: between you as the Facilitator and one member of the audience (One Person).
- One to many: between you as the Facilitator and multiple members of the audience (Group).
- From you – as the Facilitator.

Below are a few examples of each type of challenging situation:

ONE PERSON	GROUP	FACILITATOR – YOU
• Talks all the time • Challenges every data point • Does not participate • Derails the content with non-related issues	• Has side conversations • Is non-responsive • Is chatty and/or multi-tasking	• Forget your content • Have too much/too little content • Struggle with technical issues • Don't know the answer

COACHING POINT: CHALLENGING SITUATIONS

Managing challenging situations is situational – success can vary for the same situation at different times, to different situations for similar audiences. It is important to remember, "You cannot win them all!" They are a natural outcome of the complexity of managing task and group process for a diverse group of Learners.

Managing One to One Challenges – Use Assertive Communication

When under pressure in a one-on-one challenging situation, it can be easy for our emotions to take over and innately respond using either Aggressive or Submissive Communication.

If we wish to achieve a win-win outcome from the discussion, it is better to use Assertive Communication. Assertive Communication is a Directive Facilitation Technique.

TIMEOUT!

Aggressive Communication can be defined as standing up for our rights in such a way that we violate the other person's rights. It originates in our **fight** response, can sound louder and have body language that includes leaning forward. It can result in a win-lose outcome because both parties' needs are not given mutual respect.

Submissive Communication can be defined as failing to stand up for our rights and allowing the other person's needs to dominate. It originates in our **flight** response, can sound quieter and have body language that appears hesitant. It can result in a lose-win outcome because we can lose credibility when we do not clearly communicate our position.

Assertive communication is the most misunderstood style of communication. Assertive communication can be defined as standing up for our rights at the same time respecting the other person's rights. It is a **learned behavior** and can sound calm, with balanced body language. It can result in a win-win outcome because it focuses on shared interests (rather than differing positions) and both parties' needs are given mutual respect.

Using aggressive communication with participants can result in not only closing down an individual but also in negatively affecting the group dynamic. Using submissive communication can result in losing control of the group dynamic. Using assertive communication with participants can positively influence the group dynamic as well as help to resolve challenging situations.

Here is an example of how each style could appear if someone asks to be able to leave the one-day training to attend three meetings,

- **Aggressive** "How on earth do you expect to learn anything if you are not in the room half the time?"

- **Submissive** "Well I don't suppose it really matters…. If these meetings are really important……"
- **Assertive** "I understand how difficult it is to clear meetings for an entire day in order to attend training and it sounds like these meetings are important. From my perspective, my role is to maximize group and individual learning. I have two concerns – when people come and go it can disrupt the group dynamic and influence learning, plus it may be difficult for you to get what you need from the session if you have to leave and come back. Are there some different options? Could you get someone else to attend one/both of those meetings? Could you attend just your part of a meeting so that you can do it in a break? Would it be better to reschedule?"

The technique that is used to facilitate effective Assertive Communication (and which we used in the example above) is called "The Four P's"

COACHING POINT: THE FOUR P'S

<u>P</u>: **Paraphrase the Other Person's Position.** This can help to ensure the other person's position is understood, validates the person and can provide time for the Facilitator to calm emotions and reframe the position. You may also need to ask questions to gain more understanding about the other person's point of view.

<u>P</u>: **Pause.** This unconsciously signals that you are changing communication mode. You can also use a bridging word such as "and".

<u>P</u>: **State your <u>Position</u>** in a calm steady tone of voice. This is important so that both sides of a point of view are articulated.

<u>P</u>: **Explore <u>Possibilities</u>.** Move into generating Possibilities (ideally 2-3) using questioning or by suggesting options.

FOUL!

DO NOT use "however" or "but". Both of these are blocking words and tend to negate any words spoken before them.

In addition, Paraphrase FIRST before stating your position because stating your position first sounds more confrontational and the other person will not feel heard.

P: Paraphrase
I understand how difficult it is to clear meetings for an entire day in order to attend training and it sounds like these meetings are important.

P: Pause

P: Position
From my perspective, my role is to maximize group and individual learning. I have two concerns – when people come and go it can disrupt the group dynamic and influence learning, plus it may be difficult for you to get what you need from the session if you have to leave and come back.

P: Possibilities
Are there some different options? Could you get someone else to attend one/both of those meetings? Could you attend just your part of a meeting so that you can do it in a break? Would it be better to reschedule?"

EXERCISE 3-9: USE ASSERTIVE COMMUNICATION

- Think of one challenging situation you have faced where you think you could have used Assertive Communication.
- Map out the four P's below.

TRY IT ON: USE ASSERTIVE COMMUNICATION

Write your ideas here…

Challenging Situation?

_____
_____
_____

P: Paraphrase

_____
_____
_____

P: Pause

_____
_____
_____

P: Position

_____
_____
_____

P: Possibilities

_____
_____
_____

Assertive Communication can show how you might address an issue – let's also review a few possible alternative solutions.

PERSON WHO TALKS ALL THE TIME	• Acknowledge the value of the person's input. • Ask the rest of the group to help. • Shift eye contact. • Manage whom you call on. • Move body language to "close them down" • Paraphrase their point of view. • Remain positive. • Divide the group into teams/pairs to do an exercise. • Give them a "role" where they are monitoring an activity rather than talking. • Discuss with the person offline/on a break and explain the importance of the group participating (using the four Ps).
PERSON WHO CHALLENGES EVERY DATA POINT	• Stay factual. • Acknowledge their input. • Make sure you have all relevant sources and data prepared. • Reframe how you perceive the challenge: remember it could be an indicator of interest. • Facilitate the group managing the situation, "What do the rest of you think?" • Give relevant examples. • Suggest putting the points on hold to discuss when all content has been introduced. • Have an off-line discussion about key issues (using the four Ps).

PERSON WHO IS NOT PARTICIPATING	• Make stronger eye contact: pull them in non-verbally. • Ask, "What do you think?" • Use interactive techniques. • Find out why. • Remember that some people learn by listening and reflecting. • Make sure you recognize their contribution when they say something. • Refer back to their input. • Involve them when you know they have specialized knowledge on the subject you are discussing. • Do not obsess about this – if the majority of the group is engaged, focus on those participants. • Use breaks to find out about their interests. • Have a one-on-one discussion (using the four Ps).
PERSON WHO DERAILS CONTENT WITH NON-RELATED ISSUES	• Use the "parking lot". • Set up ground rules to keep content focused. • Give positive feedback and put off until later. • Point to other resources to get answer. • Explain that it is out of the field of discussion. • Suggest having a discussion off-line in a break.

Managing One to Many Challenges

As we have discussed, facilitating learning with a group can be difficult because you have to try to balance individual learning needs with the overall group dynamic. Below are a few tips to help manage challenges in this arena.

GROUP HAS SIDE CONVERSATIONS	• Set up ground rules. • Arrange seating beforehand. • Move the group around for an activity. • Ask the group to share their point of view. • Use humor – as appropriate. • Use silence – do not say anything until they have finished.

GROUP IS QUIET/ NON-RESPONSIVE	• Repeat the question. • Use "repeat after me" (see Chapter Four). • Ask questions. • Use a flip chart in a group discussion. • Use an activity. • Use ground rules to encourage participation. • Use Ice Breakers at the beginning to set an interactive tone. • Use quizzes. • Do some type of "pair and share" activity. • Take a break. • Get people to stand up and/or move seats. • Use some sort of short physical energizer. • Change order of program (only if you are comfortable with the sequence). • Ask them why? This can build credibility as it shows you are tuned into the group.
GROUP IS CHATTY AND/OR MULTI-TASKING	• Incorporate a team exercise. • Split up the group: rearrange seating. • Establish the ground rule of raising hands to participate (depending on learning culture). • Stand behind/close to the "chatterers". • Positively call out and ask the group to share their comments. • Ask for their participation. • Use humor to acknowledge and move on. • Ask why? • Hold a one-on-one discussion with individuals/group (using the four Ps).

FOUL!

Many of these ideas may look like common sense. In the moment, when emotions are raised, common sense may not necessarily be common practice!

Facilitator Challenges

The role of the Facilitator is complex and it can be easy to "lose the way". Below are several ideas to aid in some of those situations.

YOU FORGET YOUR CONTENT	• Prepare, prepare, prepare. • Have copies of PowerPoint slides or notes on hand. • Pause. • Give the group a break to regroup. • Do not say or show you have lost track: you are the only one who knows. • Move on: circle back later to include this information if it is important. • Remember retention levels can be low so they would not have remembered it anyway!
YOU HAVE TOO MUCH CONTENT	• Pick out key points. • Schedule a second presentation. • Reduce presentation material and create supplementary handouts. • Acknowledge time limit (+ and -). • Work through the break: but ask permission. • Don't try to speak more quickly to cover the content: you will lose the group. • Ask specific questions to focus on key learning points.
YOU HAVE TOO LITTLE CONTENT	• Add extra exercises/group work into existing materials. • Try it out first: run through the presentation and time yourself. • Finish early and give the group recognition. • Bring extra exercises and group activities. • Engage the audience to the maximum extent. • Develop the topic further. • Ask yourself if they have achieved the key learning objectives: remember it is about quality not always quantity. • Remember it's OK to finish early!

YOU STRUG-GLE WITH TECHNICAL ISSUES	• Prepare, prepare. • Practice, practice. • Allow enough time for set up for things to go wrong. • Find/organize an internal expert to help. • Make sure you are using the right medium for the message. • Is there a plan B? For instance if the projector does not work – have copies of slides.
YOU DON'T KNOW THE ANSWER	• Use an expert in the group. • Defer until later. • Refer to other materials. • Don't pretend!! • Say you don't know and will find out – and make sure you do. • Capture the question on a flip chart/parking lot. • Use Ping-Pong – is there someone in the audience who could help you.

Challenging situations, when handled well, can build individual and group commitment.

EXERCISE 3-10: YOUR FACILITATION CHALLENGES

- Think of one challenging situation you have faced.
- What would you do differently to manage this challenge

TRY IT ON: CHALLENGING SITUATION

Write your ideas here…

Challenging Situation?

_____

_____

_____

Do Differently?

_____

_____

_____

TEACH and Engage your Learners

Engaging your Learners using Involving and Directive Facilitation, incorporating Visual Aids effectively and managing challenging situations to a positive outcome all help to support the TEACH methodology with its inherent back and forth energy flow.

TOPIC AND HOOK	• Use an involving question to act as a Hook to engage the audience. • Apply effective Directive Facilitation skills to ensure the topic content and outcome is clear.
ENGAGE THE AUDIENCE	• Use Involving Facilitation skills to engage the audience and ensure a productive and ongoing two-way dialog.
ABSTRACT INFORMATION:	• Implement both Involving and Directive Facilitation skills to teach key concepts, models and skills. • Use Visual Aids to engage multiple senses in the learning journey.
CONCRETE APPLICATION:	• Set up activities effectively with Directive Facilitation skills. • Stimulate learner's reflection in debriefing and surfacing learning points from the application of skills, knowledge and techniques with Involving Facilitation skills • Use Directive Facilitation skills to reinforce key learning points from activities.
HOW TO APPLY	• Set action ideas with a Learning Log (Directive Facilitation) • Share action ideas with Involving Facilitation Skills.

Chapter Summary

A key element in being perceived as a great facilitator is to engage the audience and create an adult-to-adult learning culture. In this Chapter, we have reviewed the communication process that underlies our one to many learning context. We have described the role of the Facilitator and clearly shared best practices in using Involving Facilitation skills to create a real-time two-way dialog. We have discussed how to present your message effectively when using Directive Facilitation Skills. In addition, we defined and explored how and when to balance the use of Involving versus Directive facilitation skills along a Collaborative Spectrum. We reviewed how to use Visual Aids to appeal to multiple senses. Finally, we reviewed skills and techniques to use if and when challenging situations arise to maintain the positive engagement of the participants.

Key Principles Reviewed

- Understand The Six Steps in the Communication Process and recognize how this process varies when communication is one-to many.
- Use Involving Facilitation skills to manage group conversations; these skills include ask open and closed questions, listen actively, reinforce contribution and ask follow up questions.
- On occasions, use more Directive Facilitation Skills and consider the words selected, the way the words are expressed, body language and examples to share.
- Consistently balance Directive and Involving Facilitation to optimize Task and Group Process.
- Use Visual Aids to engage participants' visual, auditory and kinesthetic preferences.
- There are a variety of challenging situations that can be faced when engaging the audience. Use Assertive Communication to help to negotiate win-win solutions with participants one-on-one. Take different actions to manage a challenging group processes. Finally, prepare and plan to overcome potential personal challenges.
- Engage the audience in every stage of TEACH for learning to occur.

SCORECARD

- What were your key learning points about the one-to many Communication Process? What will you differently as a result?
- How effective are your Involving facilitation skills? What can you do to improve your facilitation effectiveness?
- What were your key learning points about Directive and Involving Facilitation? Which style do you think you use most?
- What will you do differently in your use of Visual Aids to appeal to different learning styles?
- How do you think you will use Assertive Communication in managing challenging participant interactions?
- What will you do differently to help manage a group process that is not working?
- What challenges might you face and how do you plan to proactively avoid these situations?
- How can you make sure you engage the audience at every stage in TEACH?

4

A: APPLY EXPERIENTIAL LEARNING

In this chapter, we will review the second key element in Active Learning – how to use activities to help ensure maximum engagement, retention and application.

Active Learning

Use Facilitation Skills

Practice Experiential Learning

Chapter Three:
Visual One

TIMEOUT!

Experiential learning is constructivist learning. Adults are active learners, constructing their own knowledge rather than solely observing the demonstrative behavior of a facilitator. It engages the learner at a more personal level by addressing the needs and wants of the individual. Adults remember relevant activities and appreciate Facilitators who design and run memorable exercises.

We will define and explain the different types of learning activities and define key principles about the use of any experiential technique. We will explore how to use each of these activities successfully and evaluate which activities might be most effective in the four stages of the Learning Cycle. Then, we will share tips and techniques to design customized learning activities. Finally, we will evaluate how The T.E.A.C.H. Methodology integrates with experiential learning. Applying these techniques will build your Flawless Facilitation "tool kit".

GAME PLAN

You will learn about:

- Experiential Learning Activities
- General Principles for Activities
- Specific Guidelines for Each Activity
- Learning Cycle: Which Activities to Use When
- Guidelines for Designing Effective Activities
- T.E.A.C.H. and Experiential Learning

Experiential Learning Activities

> "You can discover more about people in an hour of play than a year of conversation."
>
> *Plato*

There is a wide range of experiential learning activities. In this book, we will focus primarily on "indoor" activities designed to teach and/or reinforce key skills, knowledge or techniques (the task element of any development event) within a learning environment. In addition, Facilitators can use a wide range of outdoor learning events to create individual insight and growth, as well as enhance team effectiveness. Many of these outdoor activities do not contain a teaching or "content" component. We will not cover these activities in this book as our focus is on enhancing learning where there is both a Task and Group Process component.

FOUL!

In this chapter, we will NOT be providing a resource of activities. There are lots of these available on the web and in various publications. What we WILL be doing is describing in detail HOW to use activities so that they are effective for the audience and build the Facilitator's presence and credibility.

Below is a sample list of activities that you can incorporate into the T.E.A.C.H. framework to help create an active and impressive learning environment.

TIMEOUT!

Some activities to use are:

- Open Space Activities
- Brainstorming
- Jigsaw Learning
- Games
- Quizzes
- Read and Teach
- Role-plays
- Simulations
- Case Studies
- Card Activities
- Team/Pairs Exercises

- Individual Reflection or Learning Journal Compilation
- Debate
- Observations
- Fieldwork
- Problem solving activities
- Project-based learning
- Repeat After Me
- Group Reading
- Show of Hands

Below is a definition of all the activities listed above with an example for each in a workshop environment:

TYPE OF ACTIVITY	DESCRIPTION
Open Space Activities	• Flip charts are posted around the room with one question/comment relevant to a specific topic per flip chart. • Individuals are instructed to visit each flip chart IN NO SPECIFIC SEQUENCE and add one comment to each flip chart. • The exercise is debriefed by reading each individual flip chart back to the group. • By inviting people to take responsibility for what they care about, Open Space establishes a marketplace of inquiry, reflection and learning, bringing out the best in both the individuals involved and the group.
Case Study	In a coaching module, four flip charts were created to set the scene on coaching. The questions one on each flip chart were: • How would you define coaching? • What are the benefits of one-on-one coaching? • How can a coach motivate an individual to perform? • What constitutes positive feedback? • This content was then linked to the content of the program.
Brainstorming	• Brainstorming is a group process that collects as many ideas as possible in a short time, without concern for quality. Ideas do not have to be practical or original. • An entire group can answer a question to explore ideas around a subject. • Brainstorming can also be included as part of pairs or team exercises. • The goal is to get as much group input into a specific subject as possible.

TYPE OF ACTIVITY	DESCRIPTION
Case Study	In a communication module, the group brainstormed ideas for improving listening skills. Ideas were written on a flip chart by the Facilitator and included: • Focus • Pay attention • Paraphrase to check understanding • Stay in the now • Eliminate distractions, etc.
Jigsaw Learning	• Jigsaw Learning is a cooperative learning technique where students have to rely on each other. • The group is divided into teams or "jigsaw" groups. • Assignments are divided into pieces – one piece for each "jigsaw" group. • Each "jigsaw" group completes a different assignment and every individual in the group writes down the output from their team. • The students are then reorganized into "expert" groups containing one member from each "jigsaw" group. • Each team member in the new "group" presents part of the solution. • The summary requires the pieces to be put together. • This is a highly structured learning activity with an element of "required" interdependence. • It encourages the students to take an active part in their learning. • In becoming a teacher of sorts, each student becomes a valuable resource for the others. • The set up for this activity is complex and really important. From this point, it requires the least input from the Facilitator during the exercise and in the debrief. It can appear "Facilitator independent".

TYPE OF ACTIVITY	DESCRIPTION
Case Study	In a facilitation skills workshop for experienced Facilitators, each team or "jigsaw" group was provided with one type of Visual Aid out of Five e.g. Slides, Flip Chart, Handout, Video and Products. • Groups were created by counting 1-5 and one Visual Aid allocated to each group. Therefore, in a group of 20, there were five "jigsaw" groups with four members each. • Each jigsaw group was asked to list five Dos and Don'ts for making effective use of this specific Visual Aid. • The groups were then divided into new "Expert groups" by counting A, B, C, D for each person in the Slides "jigsaw" group, A, B, C, D, for each member of the Flip Chart "jigsaw" group, etc. Thus, there will be one member from each of the five teams in each of the A, B, C or D groups to share the knowledge of all the Visual Aids. • The "jigsaw" will have been reassembled and the knowledge of how to use the five Visual Aids shared with the entire group.
Games	• Games can help participants to learn about certain subjects, expand concepts, reinforce development, understand an historical event or culture, or assist them in learning a skill as they play. • They can involve physical activity, board, card or video games. • Games are designed to reinforce learning, teach content and make knowledge relevant. • They also can provide an energizing, fun way to raise retention rate.
Case Study	In a team building session, the group was divided into four teams and each team was provided with building equipment with instructions to build the tallest possible tower. Each team assumed competition, but the best solution was when all teams collaborated to build one structure. This was used to introduce how innately many people go first to competition. It also helped to preview the important of positive mental attitude, good allocation of roles and effective communication – all of which are essential for effective teamwork.

FOUL!

Make sure the game is relevant to the learning objectives. Using games that are not linked to the course purpose actually minimizes learning and simply creates unnecessary distractions. Participants remember the game but not the subject!

TYPE OF ACTIVITY	DESCRIPTION
Quizzes	• These can include Informal quizzes at the end of each subject, "What have we reviewed in this section?" • Quizzes can also be more formal, for example Knowledge Checks on the important content, which can be scored and returned. • Quizzes can also be used to raise awareness of a specific subject. • Quizzes can allow individual participation and can act as non-threatening interest raisers.
Case Study	In a customer service workshop, six multiple-choice questions about general customer service knowledge were researched and used to raise awareness and to assess participants' existing knowledge. The questions were used in an "Open Space" format where each participant marked what they thought was the correct of four answers for each question with a sticky arrow. This meant that no individual was embarrassed at getting any answers wrong and yet the group could observe the overall group knowledge and accuracy of the answers. It set the scene for the methodology to be introduced later in the workshop.
Read and Teach	• Read and Teach is a learning technique where students have to read some specific information, data or theory and then present the key learning points to other students. • The content to be shared is divided into sections and each section allocated to a person or team. • Each section is then presented back to the rest of the audience/other team members. • When participants have to digest information and teach this to another person it helps them move through the stages of data gathering, reflection, creation and active testing in the Learning Cycle.

TYPE OF ACTIVITY	DESCRIPTION
Case Study	In a product-training workshop, each participant was allocated a new product and provided with a product information sheet. They then had to pair up and teach another person about the product they had been allocated.
Role-plays	• Role-play refers to activities where students simulate a scenario by assuming specific roles. In the classroom, students can work through a situation and practice behavior for the real world. • Alternatively, the role-playing activities may be used to shed light on any complicated topic. • They provide an opportunity to experience in real time specific ideas techniques and skills, practice skills in a non-threatening environment, and obtain feedback.
Case Study	In a negotiation skills workshop, individuals played the role of the sales person and the customer to negotiate with some pre-set criteria, receive feedback and to gain a better understanding of the customer's perspective.
Simulations	• These activities replicate and amplify real experiences. • They are immersive in that participants engage in them in a fully interactive dynamic way. • They tend to be extensive and complex, with multiple "stages" and decision points. • They tend to last considerably longer than Role-plays and Case Studies, and may include a complex collection of analysis, scenario planning, reflection and demonstrations. • It enables participants to practice skills and techniques while avoiding unnecessary risks.
Case Study	In a sales training program introducing selling skills involved in a complex sale, teams ran a complex sale from beginning to end with regular check ins. The Simulation was divided into multiple progressive build stages. At regular decision points, teams presented data and approaches and were ranked in terms of effectiveness. The simulation lasted two days.

TYPE OF ACTIVITY	DESCRIPTION
Case Studies	• Case studies are defined as student centered activities based on topics that demonstrate theoretical concepts in an applied setting. • They tend to be customized, practical examples from the past of either a specific skill or technique. • They provide an opportunity to raise awareness, analyze data or discuss a specific subject. • They differ from role-plays because they require individuals to talk about what they would/might do –the approach is more cognitive versus behavioral. Participants do not necessarily have to demonstrate the skills.
Case Study	In a managing priorities program, individuals were provided with Case Studies to analyze what prioritization errors the individuals in each Case Study made, to suggest (based on the day's content) techniques that they might recommend to help with each area.

Card Activities	• Cards can be used to divide the group or as part of an exercise (see later notes).
	• Because people have to "touch" the cards, they make any session more hands-on and experiential. They also access our background experience as children/adults with card games and can make any subject feel more active.
	• Content on cards is pre-prepared and can be used to check knowledge (which category does _____ fit into), raise awareness (sort cards in a specific way) and teach content (match the following statements).
	• The advantages of using Cards are substantial and include:
	  · Participants engage multiple senses in learning: talking, listening, movement, observation and this process maximizes the Data Gathering stage in learning.
	  · In sorting cards, participants have the opportunity to Reflect and Create their own understanding by discussing answers and moving the cards around.
	  · In checking whether the cards are laid out accurately, participants have the opportunity to Actively Test their knowledge.
	  · In addition, cards stimulate a social yet psychologically safe learning environment that is proved to aid retention.
	  · For many, this means they enjoy the process, learn faster, retain the information with ease and are more easily convinced that this content is valid.

TYPE OF ACTIVITY	DESCRIPTION
Case Study	In a coaching workshop, a set of 20 cards was created; 10 documenting "Ask" Coaching techniques and 10 documenting "Educate" Coaching phrases. The cards have been used two ways: 1. Each person is allocated a card and asked whether they think their statement reflects "Ask" or "Educate Coaching". They then move to one side of the room or the other and explain why they think their card belonged in that category. This enables the entire group to move. 2. The group is divided into teams and each team is allocated a set of 20 cards. They decide where each card fits in terms of "Ask" and "Educate Coaching". This allows for more discussion and learning from other team members.
Team/ Pairs Exercises	• This involves dividing the group into smaller teams of pairs, threes or more to complete specific tasks (see later notes for more ways to divide the group). • They provide an energizing and safe way to learn, and enable all to participate. • They tend to take more time than a large group discussion. • Often other types of experiential learning takes place in teams or pairs e.g. Case Studies, role-plays, etc.
Case Study	As an ice-breaker, people were asked, in their table groups, to identify their expectations for the learning session.
Individual Reflection or Writing in Learning Journal	• Time is provided for individuals to reflect and identify individual learning or action ideas. • Normally worksheets are provided to facilitate this learning and reflection time. • This activity can be helpful for those with an Introverting preference (those who like to reflect before speaking) and for helping groups to make meaning after a data gathering experience.
Case Study	In any workshop, provide a "Learning Application Log" and allocate five minutes for individuals to capture their key learning points and action ideas at the end of each section. (This can also represent the H in T.E.A.C.H.).

TYPE OF ACTIVITY	DESCRIPTION
Group Discussion	• Group discussion is an interactive oral process where the group members need to listen to each other and communicate their point of view effectively using gestures, clear language and persuasive style. • A Group Discussion is a structured exchange of ideas led by a Facilitator in a systematic and structured way. Each of the participants gets an opportunity to refine and/or express his/her views and comments on the views expressed by other members of the group. • The skills used here have been described in detail in Chapter Three: Engage your Audience.
Debate	• A formal debate can be used as a framework for learning. A debate has been described as a form of argument that "has strict rules of conduct and quite sophisticated arguing techniques". • Participants conduct comprehensive research into the topic, gather supporting evidence, and present on one of two sides of a topic. • A more Informal debate can be used by setting thought-provoking questions and/or asking teams to explore both sides of a point of view.
Case Study	In a Conflict Management workshop, the group was divided into two groups. One group had to argue for Conflict being positive. The other group had to argue for Conflict being negative. Both perspectives have some validity so this approach enabled the group to explore and understand both sides of this issue.
Observations	• Observational learning can be described as the process of learning through watching others, retaining the information, assessing the effectiveness of the skills and then later replicating the behaviors that were observed. • It can also encompass situations when participants are assigned a task and provided with specific elements to observe. Participants then observe and provide feedback on these key elements.
Case Study	In a Presentation Skills workshop, participants are allocated a partner ("Buddy") and a detailed behavioral checklist for skills the Presenter should use when presenting data to a group. After the presenter has completed their five-minute session, the Buddy is responsible for providing feedback on skills used and areas that could be improved. If an individual can observe the skills, it is more likely that he/she will be able to apply the skills in their presentations.

TYPE OF ACTIVITY	DESCRIPTION
Fieldwork	• Fieldwork represents a consciously planned set of experiences occurring in a practice setting designed to move students from their initial level of understanding, skills and attitudes to more advanced levels of comprehension. • Participants are assigned specific tasks relating to the subject matter that has been shared.
Case Study	In a Talent Development program spread over six months, participants were allocated a project on which they had to work with other team members, apply the skills they had learned in the associated workshops (four two-day sessions), and present their result to the Executive Committee. This cemented their learning and produced a tangible result for the organization.
Problem Solving Activities	• Problem-based learning encourages students to learn about a subject through the experience of solving an open-ended problem. Students learn both thinking strategies and domain knowledge. • The goals of this approach are to help students develop flexible knowledge, effective problem solving skills, apply self-directed learning and use effective collaboration skills.

TYPE OF ACTIVITY	DESCRIPTION
Case Study	**The Tennis Ball Exercise** in a Problem Solving session. The goal was to move the ball so that all participants interacted with it in a specific sequence in the shortest possible time frame. A team of 18 people was asked to stand in two parallel lines, nine people in each, facing each other. The Facilitator stood at one end of the two rows of participants. The sequence was as follows – The Facilitator gives the ball to the person on their right. Each person then was told to throw it to a person on the other side – not directly opposite but one person to their right. They continued in this way until the ball was given back to the original person. The main instruction was, "The sequence of touch has to stay the same". The "perfect" sequence was then timed. The challenge was set to minimize the time for this sequence while keeping the same team members all of whom had to touch the tennis ball in the predetermined sequence. The group is given 2-4 opportunities to reduce their time. The normal time initially is about 18 seconds and this can be reduced, with effective team problem solving, to 2-3 seconds. The group had to challenge two assumptions: 1. They had to **stand** in the sequence they had been allocated. 2. They had to **throw the ball** – versus pass it from one person to another. The problem solving activity highlighted the importance of listening to all ideas while not being restricted by perceived rules: core principles inherent in the rest of the program.

TYPE OF ACTIVITY	DESCRIPTION
Demonstrations	• Demonstration means 'to clearly show'. • Through demonstrations, the Facilitator can demonstrate (with or without help) concrete examples of the skills, technique or approach that has been taught. • Demonstrations often occur when students have a hard time connecting theories to actual practice or when students are unable to understand application of theories.
Case Study	In an interviewing workshop, the Facilitator demonstrated how to ask effective behavioral interviewing questions, how to pick out the Moments of Truth (those areas when further information is required) and ask follow up questions to gain more in-depth knowledge. (You could also ask someone who is an expert in a specific technique or skills to conduct the demonstration.)
Project-based Learning	• This instructional approach utilizes multifaceted projects as a central organizing strategy for educating students. • When engaged in project-based learning, students will typically be assigned a project or series of projects that require them to use diverse skills—such as researching, writing, interviewing, collaborating, or public speaking—to produce various work products. • Project-based learning gives students a more "integrated" understanding of the concepts and knowledge they learn, while also equipping them with practical skills they can apply throughout their work. • This approach is probably more common in academic study. Fieldwork, the similar alternative strategy tends to be more common in an organizational context.
Case Study	In an employee engagement program, "work stations" were established to describe the different elements of the company's business (an airline – so departments included sales and reservations, cabin crew, pilots, baggage handling, etc.). Individuals were divided into teams and then each team moved from one workstation to another for 45 minutes running the airline for a day. At the end of the day, the team who had achieved the greatest success was awarded a prize.

TYPE OF ACTIVITY	DESCRIPTION
Repeat after me	• This is an instructional approach where the Facilitator asks the group to repeat key concepts to cement learning. • While this may appear to be more "parent" to "child", when used very selectively with humor, the process can help to improve memory and long-term retention.
Case Study	In a sales training program, to help differentiate between product/service Features and Benefits, the group was asked to say, "Who Cares?", "So What" after each Feature was listed. If a statement answered those two questions, the content was more likely to be a Benefit. Then they were asked to repeat, "which means that" to bridge from Features to Benefits. So for instance, "A table has four legs." Repeat, **"Who Cares?" "So What" "Which means that"**, "It is stable." (See later notes for guidelines on using this technique to reduce the perception of being too Parent to Child.)
Group Reading	• This is an instructional approach where the Facilitator asks individuals from the group to read aloud certain information from a participant guide/reference manual.
Case Study	In an assertiveness workshop, participants were asked to read the detailed definition of aggressive, submissive and assertive communication.
Show of Hands	• This is an instructional approach where the Facilitator asks the group to raise hands to answer a question. • It can be an either/or question to gain knowledge of the group, question about experience, etc. • This is one of the safest and simplest types of activities. It uses a physical movement and yet remains relatively emotionally safe.
Case Study	In a leadership program participants were asked, "How many of you left a job because you did not respect/get on with your manager even though you liked the work?" and then "How many of you stayed in a specific role because you respected and got on well with your manager even though the work was not all you wanted it to be?" This immediately highlighted the importance of the leadership role in employee retention.

As you can see, there is a wide variety of experiential learning activities. Many of us have our "preferred" activities that might work for us, and yet might not suit all participants.

COACHING POINT: ACTIVITIES

The more variety of activities we use, the more likely it is that we will meet the learning needs of different participants.

EXERCISE 4-1: EXPERIENTIAL LEARNING ACTIVITIES

- Look at the previous list of activities.
- Which of these activities do you use frequently?
- Which activities are you not familiar with?
- Which new activities do you think you will try?

TRY IT ON: EXPERIENTIAL LEARNING ACTIVITIES

Write your ideas here…

Activities you use?

_____
_____
_____

Activities not familiar with?

_____
_____
_____

New activities you might choose to use?

_____

_____

_____

General Principles for Activities

Think about you as a participant in an activity – how did you feel when it was set up poorly? Normally the response is frustration, annoyance and negative emotions towards the Facilitator. In this way, activities can **make or break** the learning experience. If used well, participants appreciate the Facilitator's expertise and the exercise can stimulate retention and contribute to a safe, interactive learning environment. If facilitated poorly, they can disrupt learning, cause stress for the participants and resentment towards the Facilitator.

TIMEOUT! MAKE OR BREAK

Make – Make a Training Experience More Positive

- Raises energy.
- Increases focus and reduces Partial Attention Syndrome because it is active.
- Involves people.
- Increases learning.
- Brings new ideas.
- Allows the group to share experiences.
- Can be fun.
- Can provide clarification.
- Builds a social learning environment.
- Activates the brain's Learning Cycle.
- Helps to cement the Development Process. (as described in Chapter Two)

Break – Make a Training Experience Less Effective

- You can lose the attention of the audience when the point of an activity is not clear.
- If the instructions are confusing, activities can cause frustration to participants who may get upset with the Facilitator.
- Some participants might be offended by certain types of activities.
- Activities can cause conflicts.
- Activities can be complex to manage – you never quite know what will happen.
- People may not want to "play".
- There might not be enough room/resources for an activity.
- If the activity appears irrelevant and/or superficial, some participants may switch off.
- Individual types may prefer different types of learning techniques and switch off from those they do not like.
- Language and cultural barriers might make an activity ineffective.

FOUL!

New Facilitators can make the mistake of not preparing activities thoroughly and/or treating them as time to prepare their next piece of content. Both mistakes can reflect negatively on the Facilitator.

Consider the following tips when using any activity:

COACHING POINT: GENERAL PRINCIPLES

Set Up:

- Explain the purpose of any activity – why are we doing this activity?
- Prepare the instructions in detail: script on separate cards if necessary.

- Take instructions step-by-step. Individuals need time to digest each instruction before acting.
- Speak slowly and calmly.
- Have the instructions in multiple places: on a slide, in a handout, and verbally. This maximizes sensory input.
- Always "Prime the Pump". Get one correct example for each part of the exercise from the group. This can help you to ensure the instructions have been understood.
- Anticipate any potential objections to the activity.

During the Activity

- Be prepared to clarify instructions/approach as required.
- Monitor progress – are all the groups/teams completing the activity?
- Watch group dynamics – are there any issues that need to be addressed?
- Listen in to be able to describe important learning points in the debrief.
- Give regular time checks.
- DO NOT join in with the activity in a group or a team – your role is to be a neutral third-party observer.

Debrief is Key:

- Remember the Purpose and Outcome.
- Create open-ended "learning" questions.
- Ask "What?" (have you learned), "So What?" (Why is this important or relevant), and "Now What?" (What do you plan to do differently?)
- Debrief through Task (What?) and Group Process (How?). The purpose and/or the flow of the activity influences which element you debrief first. Which you choose is completely situational.
- Balance learning from the group (what did you learn) with Facilitator "wisdom" (examples, stories, key messages).
- Share relevant observations from your perspective only after the group has shared their insights. This encourages participants to make sense of the activity and

progress through the Learning Cycle: data gathering, reflection, creating meaning and active testing.

- Be prepared to confirm verbally the link between the learning and the "real world."
- Always ask, "Anything else?" This allows individuals who need more time to reflect to make sense of the learning experience.

FOUL!

Do not provide the learning point from an activity before you ask the group for their thoughts. If you do this, you put yourself in the Teacher mode versus the Adult-to-Adult mode

EXERCISE 4-2: GENERAL PRINCIPLES

- Look at the guidelines above.
- What do you think you will do differently in the set-up of activities?
- What will you do differently during an activity?
- What will you do differently when you debrief an activity?

TRY IT ON: GENERAL PRINCIPLES

Write your ideas here...

Set up?

_____

_____

_____

During?

_____

_____

_____

Debrief?

_____

_____

_____

Dividing the Group

The way the Facilitator divides the group can also enhance learning and add energy to any activity.

COACHING POINT: DIVIDING THE GROUP INTO PAIRS

- Turn to the person next to them – make sure you move around the room and confirm, using body language, who is with whom.
- Count the number of people in the room. Divide by 2. Count off that number and the individuals with the same number get together. For instance, 24 people, 12 are half the group. Count to 12. 1's together, 2's together, 3's together, etc. This facilitates movement and can add energy to the room.
- Create a series of matching cards with one word on each card showing opposites such as:

Good	Bad
High	Low
Competent	Incompetent
Conscious	Unconscious

Hot	Cold
Big	Small
Early	Late
Short	Long
On Time	Late
Bad	Good

- Shuffle the cards: give each team member one card and then get them to find their matching other half. (Just make sure you confirm that the cards were only for dividing the group – not for use in the activity…)
- Create a mixture of different shaped/colored cards with two of each shape/color such as those listed below. Shuffle the cards and ask people to find their matching shape/color.

White square	Blue square
White circle	Blue circle
White triangle	Blue triangle
Red square	Yellow square
Red circle	Yellow circle
Red triangle	

When dividing the group into teams, many similar approaches can be used:

- Grouping people with those close to them.
- Counting for the number of teams: so four teams, 1,2,3,4, and then 1's together, 2's together, etc.
- Using cards that match (for instance playing cards – four teams – four suits)
- Individuals with the same color work together.
- Allocating team names.

CASE STUDY

PUMA used names of football teams sponsored by the company to divide the group.

COACHING POINT: DIVIDING THE GROUP INTO TEAMS

When dividing the group into teams, it is important to consider factors such as:

- Experience – Is it necessary or appropriate that individuals with more experience help those who have less experience?
- Knowledge – Is this a subject for which you have content knowledge experts? In addition, if so, how could you distribute these participants into different teams?
- Optimal mix – Do you want different departments working together or people working within departments (depending on the purpose of the activity and learning focus)?
- Cultural mix – What cultural sensitivities if any are there?
- Language – Will it be helpful (for instance if subject matter involves complex terms) to group individuals in language proficiency groups to help understanding?

As you can see, activities can require detailed knowledge of the audience and learning objectives to ensure teams are set up in the most effective way to achieve the maximum learning.

FOUL!

Do not talk about "little activities" – this can devalue the importance of the experience. It can communicate a subconscious message that the Facilitator's lecture is more important than group contribution. Use the word "short" instead!

Specific Guidelines for Each Activity

For each activity, we will suggest a few examples of when to use each activity together with specific guidelines for what would help to ensure that this activity runs smoothly to achieve the team's learning outcomes. While many of the ideas below might seem like common sense, as we know, common sense is not always common practice!

TYPE OF ACTIVITY	WHEN?	HOW?
Open Space	• When people are getting tired and you want to change the energy. • As a way of getting to know the group in the introduction. • When a subject is not too complex e. g. for answering a quiz. • When you want to gain the entire audience's involvement. • When you want to gather lots of data in a short time	• Make sure there are enough flip chart pens. • Be clear about making writing legible. • Set ground rules about acceptable content. • Monitor the group process because individuals can quickly get bored with this exercise and divide into small sub-groups to "chat". • Use flip chart pens or get individuals to add Post-Its to a flip chart. • With large groups, create multiple versions of each flip chart. • Debrief by asking different individuals to read out each flip chart to the rest of the group (a more thorough debrief) and discuss insights/themes, learning points, etc. • You can also ask the group to walk about and read each chart individually (this can be quicker although you cannot be as sure that each chart has been reviewed thoroughly)

TYPE OF ACTIVITY	WHEN?	HOW?
Brainstorming	• Make sure the subject is understood by the audience. • You want to expand knowledge or go more in depth on a specific subject. • You wish to check understanding from the group. • You wish to stimulate participants to create individual learning.	• In a large group, make sure the question is asked multiple times, and all answers repeated so that the group gains the full knowledge from the brainstorming. • In teams, make sure the subject to be explored is clear and teams have materials or a process with which to capture their results to share with the group (flip chart, work sheet, etc.). • If the purpose is to explore options, clarify the importance of not "shooting down" what might appear to be impractical ideas.
Jigsaw Learning	• The group has some knowledge of the subject and you want to facilitate sharing best practices. • You want the team to collaborate and break down divisions between groups. • To help ensure all participants contribute to an outcome. • You want multiple pieces of data in the debrief to be connected.	• Prepare in detail the different sections to be separated out. • Make sure you have prepared how to divide the group in order to make sure the pieces come back together smoothly. • Make sure all group members have the knowledge of the first subject discussed and/ or a reference source. • Ensure all participants are writing down the group's answers. If they do not, this can cause embarrassment and frustration during the second part of the activity. • Create a worksheet to help capture all the pieces of the "puzzle". • The Facilitator can choose whether or not to do a large group debrief – it is often worth adding one "general" question to use in the debrief afterwards. For instance, for the Visual Aids activity described earlier, the Facilitator could ask, "What general principles work for all Visual Aids?"

TYPE OF ACTIVITY	WHEN?	HOW?
Games	• As an Icebreaker. • Before the topic is presented as an engagement activity. • In the middle of two big "chunks" of content. • At the end of the session – provides time to relax and finish with entertainment and laughter.	• Ensure the game is closely linked with the purpose of the training. • Make sure the game is simple to organize and easy to understand. • Check that the time required for the game will produce the required return in terms of learning. • Ensure you highlight the reason you have used the game and link the learning back to the real-life skills, knowledge or techniques that you are teaching. • Make sure the game is well-prepared with correct materials, rules and logistics.
Quizzes	• As an icebreaker. • As a summary after a session. • As a motivator with a prize.	• Make sure the quiz is relevant and interesting. • Have the reference resources available for the answers in case of challenges. • Make sure the questions are clear with accurate instructions. • Watch double negatives. • Make sure the quiz has a clear learning point. • Make sure the audience can answer the questions. • If the answers have an element of "surprise", such as communication statistics make sure you can quote the source of the data. • Do not make the quiz too long. • Have answers available. • Anticipate the barrier to quizzes that they might be too reminiscent of school. • Ensure that they remain "safe" so that you do not disrupt learning.

TYPE OF ACTIVITY	WHEN?	HOW?
Read and Teach	• To help the team be more engaged with technical content. • To teach technical content. • To help ensure all participants internalize the content. • You want multiple pieces of data to be shared. • To minimize "lecture" time	• Prepare in detail the different sections. • Make sure you are clear on the mode and process for reporting out. • Have key learning points from each section prepared so that you can supplement and/or correct as necessary.

TYPE OF ACTIVITY	WHEN?	HOW?
Role-plays	• You need individuals to practice the skills so that you can assess skills proficiency and learning effectiveness. • You want to raise awareness that the individuals might not be using the skills already (even though they might think that they are – to help them move from Oblivious to Uncomfortable in the Development Process). • When you want to bring certain skills and activities to life.	• Anticipate that individuals may not enjoy role-plays: they may say they are unrealistic, they don't like to "act", or it is hard for them to pretend without their equipment around them. • Be prepared to emphasize the importance of being able to practice new skills and receive feedback in a safe environment. • Customize any role-play to make it relevant to participants' current work responsibilities and/or the problem they are trying to solve. • Pilot or practice any role-play before you use it in a learning context. • Put participants into groups of two or three, either with an observer or without. • Demo the format for the role-play before you begin to ensure they are clear on the instructions. • Encourage them to "play" around the structure they are given, by practicing the skills they have been taught. • Be prepared to have additional space (two rooms for more than ten). • Consider an additional Facilitator so that you can monitor the skill level and ensure people are completing the exercise as instructed. • You may also choose to conduct the role- plays as a "fish bowl" in front of the entire group. The advantage is group learning. The disadvantage can be that individuals may be really scared by this idea. • Define and monitor the time; for preparation and conducting the role- play. • You can also build in time to script complex role-plays. • Clarify the outcome that you expect from the role-plays.

TYPE OF ACTIVITY	WHEN?	HOW?
Simulations	• Learning needs to be progressive and skills/Knowledge and techniques need to be shown to build from simple to complex or from one period to another. • To provide extensive opportunities for practice. • For complex skills, knowledge and techniques.	• Make sure the outcomes of the simulation are clear and reinforce the learning point that you are trying to make. • Ensure all relevant support materials, worksheets, and support tools are available in the correct sequence when required. • Pilot the simulation before rolling it out. These are the most complex of activities to make a success. • Expect emotions to vary between storming, norming and performing during the length of the simulation.
Case Studies	• You want to "connect the dots". • To demonstrate how skills, techniques or behaviors have been used in the past. • To stimulate analysis of a specific subject in terms of skills, knowledge or techniques.	• Customize the case study to the specific group or context to ensure validity. • Make sure the outcomes of the case study are clear and reinforce the learning point that you are trying to make. • If the case study is complex, you may choose to demo an ideal answer in front of the group. • Consider the breakdown of the teams in terms of knowledge and experience to complete the case study in the most effective way. • Have "ideal" answers prepared with the supporting rationale in case groups have different perspectives.

TYPE OF ACTIVITY	WHEN?	HOW?
Card Activities	• Questions can be put onto cards to stimulate discussion at the beginning of a section or program, or at the end of a section or program. • Matched sets of cards can be used to highlight contrasting behaviors. • Cards can be used to check understanding of a topic.	• Identify key attributes for each model or concept you are trying to Teach. For instance for Temperament, you might select Needs, Values, Talents, Time Orientation, etc. • Make sure there are always equal numbers of each attribute for each model for balanced understanding. • Create one header card per model (so for Temperament – Improviser, Stabilizer, Theorist and Catalyst.) • List one attribute for each model/concept/framework on each card. • Number the cards in such a way that when they are in numerical order they are mixed up and ready to use. • Prepare a Facilitator "master set" in the correct sequence for debriefing. • Check the logistics: numbers of cards/number of people/etc. • Demo the use of the cards to clarify. • If teaching a concept, make sure the number of cards match to apply the theory of parallel construction. • Encourage individuals to write down the correct answers learned from the cards to ensure active learning. • Have the summary of the data on the card available either on a slide, in the Participant Guide or as a handout to help ensure accuracy.
Team/Pairs Exercises	• When the energy of the group is low. • When you want individuals to internalize the content. • To allow individuals who prefer one-on-one or smaller interaction to engage with the process.	• Provide a means to report out. • Twenty minutes is enough; keep a check to ensure the group does not stray off topic. • Watch that the discussions remain focused on the subject. • When summarizing, ensure you receive balanced feedback from all pairs/teams. • Make sure dynamics of teams/pairs are well balanced.

TYPE OF ACTIVITY	WHEN?	HOW?
Individual Reflection or Learning Journal Writing	• Recap at the end of a section. • When there is an important learning point. • To raise awareness of a skill. • When you want to change the pace and provide more mental space around a content area.	• Provide time to write in materials. • If you are not providing a handout, make sure there is paper to write on and additional pens available. • Make sure you ask for examples of what is written. • You can also "pair and share": ask individuals to discuss their ideas with a Buddy. This can take longer but tends to cement learning.
Debate	• When there are valid perspectives on both sides of a potential issue. • When you want participants to explore specific concepts in more detail. • When subjects are controversial. • To foster critical thinking skills.	• Decide how formal or informal you wish the debate to be. • Educate the participants about the process you will be using for the debate. • Be clear about roles: For, Against, Time Keeper, Chairperson. • Be clear about the two positions. • Allow time for preparation. • Facilitate the debate and key learning points.
Observations	• You have introduced a specific range of skills and you wish to assess comprehension.	• Provide a checklist to help reinforce the skills/techniques to be observed. • Video what is being observed in order to assess accuracy of observations. • Be prepared to use Ask and Educate Coaching to expand participant observations.
Fieldwork	• Learning is separated by time and you wish to maintain continuity of development. • You want participants to apply the knowledge they have gained from formalized training/learning events in the actual work context.	• Make sure fieldwork is relevant to real-time work opportunities, • Evaluate the extent to which teams can complete an actual work assignment. • Include a formal review process, ideally to actual stakeholders.

TYPE OF ACTIVITY	WHEN?	HOW?

Problem solving activities	• To encourage students to take on responsibility for their own learning
	• To stimulate discussion of alternatives and personal action planning.
	• To develop higher thinking skills.
		• Provide some sort of problem solving methodology: For instance
		  • Present position
		  • Problem
		  • Possibilities
		  • Plan
		• Ensure trial and error is supported by creating a safe learning environment.
		• Make sure the Facilitator's role is to give hints and stimulate thought – not provide answers.

Project-based learning	• To encourage critical thinking, collaboration and communication skills.	• See ideas around Fieldwork and Problem Solving activities.
Repeat after me	• There is an important learning point that you don't want the group to forget.	• Highlight that this is a fun way to reinforce learning (to overcome the possible barrier that some people may find this childish). • Expect the first reaction to be hesitant so do not be afraid to try it again, and use body language to "play it up". • Be aware of the learning culture – could this be perceived as one-up, one-down? • Use sparingly – for only one or two key points.
Group Reading	• For key points and/or important definitions. • For quotations. • If the energy is low.	• Consider the culture of the participants – is this acceptable or not? • Ask for volunteers. • Be clear about content.

TYPE OF ACTIVITY	WHEN?	HOW?
Show of Hands	• Ideal at the beginning of a session. • Also works when people are appearing disinterested or disengaged. • Can be useful to ascertain a knowledge level in a specific subject.	• Raise your hand to show you want their hands raised. • Make eye contact with those who do not raise hands. • Pause to allow time for everyone to raise his or her hands. • Review the results in terms of learning points- how many raised their hands for each question? • If individuals do not raise their hands, make a joke such as "Does that mean you are always or never…..?" • Use as a tool to ask further follow up questions e.g. "How many of you are familiar with ……?" Then ask follow up questions to those who have raised their hands. • Try to remember who answered key questions a specific way, then you can refer back to these individuals by name later.

As you can observe, each activity can be appropriate for different subjects, contexts and learning outcomes. Varying activities and selecting the most effective exercise can increase retention and ensure different learning styles are stimulated.

EXERCISE 4-3: PRINCIPLES FOR SPECIFIC ACTIVITIES

- Look at the guidelines above.
- What do you think you will do differently in choosing different activities – When?
- What will you do differently to make sure the activity runs successfully – How?

TRY IT ON: GENERAL PRINCIPLES

Write your ideas here…

When?

_____

_____

_____

How?

_____

_____

_____

Learning Cycle: Which Activities to Use When

To review from Chapter Two, there are four main stages in the Learning Cycle:

- Gathering Data – using as much sensory input as possible.
- Reflection – where individuals are able to step back and assimilate data.
- Creation – where learners begin to develop their own understanding from learning.
- Active Testing – where learners test out their newly developed skills, knowledge or techniques.

Earlier, we suggested certain activities that would help address different stages of the Learning Cycle. Below is a more comprehensive reference guide.

COACHING POINT: ACTIVITIES AND LEARNING CYCLE

The overall principle is that many activities can stimulate multiple stages of the learning cycle. By carefully considering each module, the learning context and objective, you will be able to choose the most relevant and effective activity.

WHAT APPROACH	GATHERING DATA	REFLECTION (PERSONAL)	CREATION	ACTIVE TESTING
Open Space Activities	Students are up and moving. They gather input from others.	Less likely, as there may not be enough space to step back and think.	May happen as participants absorb others input and add their ideas.	May work here, depending on the content on the flip charts, as there is action and movement.
Brainstorming	If in teams, people are moving. Input is gathered from self and others.	May not allow mental "breathing time."	Can be applicable when taking existing knowledge and using discussion to enhance an individual's perspective	May depend on the subject being explored.
Jigsaw Learning	Within jigsaw group, individuals may gather new information.	Reflection will probably take place as the individual writes down ideas and begins to process what to share back with the new group.	Will probably happen in deciding what information to share from the "expert" when jigsaw is assembled and as information is discussed.	Will emerge as jigsaw is reassembled and discussion is stimulated.
Games	The combination of physical and mental activity will stimulate multiple senses.	May not allow time for individual reflection.	Depending on relevance of the game, individual meaning and learning points could emerge during the game and in the debrief.	May provide an opportunity for applying learning if the game is designed to apply skills/techniques learned.

WHAT APPROACH	GATHERING DATA	REFLECTION (PERSONAL)	CREATION	ACTIVE TESTING
Quizzes	May work as an awareness activity.	May stimulate internal reflection if it pulls on knowledge that has been taught. It can also identify knowledge gaps.	May happen in the debrief as ideas are explored using learning questions.	This is a great way of testing knowledge.
Read and Teach	Can be used to begin data gathering process.	This will stimulate a degree of analysis as individuals decide what they wish to teach others.	As individuals present their point of view about their reading, they will have created individual understanding.	As individuals question the information being presented, this can provide the "presenter" with an opportunity to assess the resilience of their knowledge.
Role-plays	Can be used for awareness: for instance good and bad examples of specific skills.	The Observer role can provide an opportunity for reflection on the feedback they plan to provide.	If time is allowed for preparing or scripting role-plays, this could allow time for meaning to be created.	Role-plays are extremely effective in trying out new skills because they are both behavioral and mental.
Simulations	Data gathering will tend to occur during the simulation.	Depending on the duration and timing for the simulation, there may be opportunity for reflection.	Learning within the simulation can help participants create their own knowledge, based on the real-life element of the activity.	Simulations provide an exceptional opportunity to test out skills, knowledge and techniques as the simulation progresses from one stage to another.
Case Studies	Case studies can provide historic and practical examples for data gathering.	If Case Studies are analyzed individually, they can provide scope for individual reflection.	During the analysis, individuals can make their own judgments.	Case studies can confirm understanding.

WHAT APPROACH	GATHERING DATA	REFLECTION (PERSONAL)	CREATION	ACTIVE TESTING
Card Activities	Cards provide a mental, physical and kinesthetic experience that can stimulate all the senses.	There may not be enough time with all the activity involved in sorting cards for individuals to have quiet thinking time.	Discussion around the cards can stimulate integration of knowledge.	Cards being laid out or organized accurately can confirm comprehension.
Team/Pairs Exercises	Discussion and movement can stimulate ideas.	May not be time to reflect.	Discussion can stimulate insights.	May provide an opportunity to practice a skill thereby assessing learning.
Individual reflection or writing	If individuals complete pre-work or preparation for a workshop, this can begin the data gathering process ahead of time.	This is an ideal activity to ensure learning is internalized.	In surfacing learning, this provides an opportunity to link learning to prior experience.	Sharing insights with a partner or the group can test decisions and thoughts.
Debate	Debates tend to necessitate participants researching and collecting information around a specific point of view.	Dissecting the research to formulate an argument forces a degree of reflection.	Debates tend to require formulating a specific point of view and getting feedback on this approach.	Debate provides a fantastic way of gaining real-time feedback.
Observations	Watching others can provide mental and physical input.	Providing time to summarize notes and/or watching a recording can provide time for further reflection.	The process of watching others and providing feedback stimulates individual interpretation.	As feedback is provided, there is an opportunity to assess the effectiveness of the observation and learning.
Fieldwork/ Project Based Learning	Some new data will be collected in any project.	If each individual has a clear role, then participants will have an opportunity to reflect between meetings.	These two approaches provide an excellent way of stimulating self-directed learning.	The result of the project can act as a real-life test.

WHAT APPROACH	GATHERING DATA	REFLECTION (PERSONAL)	CREATION	ACTIVE TESTING
Problem solving activities	Problem solving normally includes a degree of data gathering.	Problem solving may provide some time for individual analysis	The problem solving process involves creating opportunities to solve a problem.	Whether the problem is solved or not will provide insight.
Repeat after me	Effective at reinforcing a specific point by repetition.			
Group Reading	Can provide a different energy in repeating data.	May provide an opportunity for reflection for those listening.		
Show of Hands	Quick and easy way to gather data.		Individuals might create meaning from observing different responses within the room.	Quick way of assessing knowledge.

EXERCISE 4-4: LEARNING CYCLE

- Look at the table above.
- What was your learning from this information?
- What actions might you take as a result?

TRY IT ON: LEARNING CYCLE

Write your ideas here…

Learning?

_____

_____

_____

Actions?

_____

_____

_____

Guidelines for Developing Activities

There is a wide range of activities that are available on the web – some of which are free, some have an annual subscription and some can be bought individually. While these resources can provide some excellent learning, customizing activities to your workshop can be more beneficial in terms of replicating the "real world", and helping to make more explicit and tangible the link between participants' experience, problem to solve and desired behavior change. Developing relevant and realistic activities reflects positively on the Facilitator – ideally, you want to hear participants say, "I really felt this activity was like doing my real job." Below is a simple process to help you to design an effective activity.

TIMEOUT!

STAGE	QUESTIONS	ADDITIONAL INFORMATION
Big Picture	**Who** is the audience?	Who will be attending? What is their existing level of knowledge on the subject? What are their job roles and responsibilities? What cultural influences might there be, if any? What types of activities might they gravitate towards and why? What types of activities might they not like and why?
	What are you trying to achieve?	What does the group want to learn? Why? How is this relevant in their current context? What challenges are there in their current context for which this content might be relevant? What skills, knowledge or techniques might be helpful in addressing these challenges?
Preparation	What are the **logistical constraints**?	How much time do you have? Where will the session be held – both the room, locale and country? What physical space is required? Will you need observers?
Decide the type of activity you will use based on this data.		
Which Activity?	What **activities** might work for this audience and outcome?	List two-to-three activities. Look at the pros and cons of each activity. Consider other activities you have used. Think about which activity is most likely to achieve the outcome you are aiming for. Consider the extent to which this activity addresses different steps in the Learning Cycle.
Select One Activity	Think about the **stages and steps** in this activity?	How will you customize the activity to the audience? Words? Terms? Examples? Stories? What steps are involved? Will you need to do some type of demonstration? How will you divide the group into teams/pairs and why? What materials might you need? What might need to be handed out when? What might be the barriers to this activity and why? How could you overcome these barriers?
Test the Activity	How can I **test** the activity?	How could you test the activity? Whom could you use as an advisor?

COACHING POINT: DESIGNING AN ACTIVITY

When using any activity, it is normally a good idea to do some sort of pilot. Testing the activity can help to ensure the instructions are clear, no offense is provided and potential barriers can be identified and overcome.

T.E.A.C.H. and Experiential Learning

Using Experiential Learning is an essential component of the T.E.A.C.H. Methodology: it does not work without it! While experiential learning is obvious for at least two stages in The T.E.A.C.H. Methodology, (The E and The C), there is an opportunity to use this type of development process at every stage in TEACH as shown below.

Topic and Hook	Many types of activities can be used as Hooks. In addition, you might use an activity, such as a test, to define the Topic.
Engage the Audience	Any type of activity will engage the audience.
Abstract Information	While it might appear that experiential learning cannot be used when teaching or sharing the main content, in fact, many activities such as Read and Teach, Cards, Project-based Learning, etc. can be utilized to involve the audience in active learning.
Concrete Application	This is the main area in which experiential learning is used – a wide variety of activities can help to cement learning for participants.
How to Apply	Personal reflection, learning journals, Pair and Share are typical examples of how experiential learning is applied in deciding future action plans.

Chapter Summary

An effective Facilitator is able to design, develop, set up, run and debrief relevant exercises. In this Chapter, we have reviewed a diverse range of activities, some of which are used frequently and others that tend to be more innovative and/or comprehensive. We covered general principles to apply to ensure an activity is set up successfully, runs smoothly and is debriefed to capture relevant learning points. We explored different ways to divide the group to ensure maximum energy and learning. We examined in more detail when each type of activity might prove to be effective and how to run each activity. We evaluated at a high level how each activity might meet the needs for the differing steps in the Learning Cycle of data gathering, internal reflection, creation of meaning and active testing and introduced some steps for developing a customized learning activity. Finally, we summarized how Experiential Learning can be used in all stages of The T.E.A.C.H. Methodology.

Key Principles Reviewed

- A Flawless Facilitator uses a range of diverse activities to provide an opportunity for active adult learning.
- Select the correct activity and vary the types of activities used.
- Set up any activity carefully and thoroughly. Failure to do so can impact the learning experience and cause negative judgments on the Facilitator.
- Think about how different activities influence the four stages in the Learning Cycle.
- Design customized activities for the context to accelerate learning and retention.
- Explore how to incorporate activities into The T.E.A.C.H. Methodology.

SCORECARD

- What were your key learning points about the different types of activities? What will you do differently as a result?
- How effective are you at facilitating learning activities? What can you do to improve your effectiveness in setting up, monitoring and debriefing activities?
- How will you divide the group into teams/pairs differently?
- What is one activity that you had not heard of before? How will you test this activity in a workshop that you design and run?
- How will you approach designing a customized activity? How will you test this out with the potential audience before using?

5

R: RECOGNIZE DIFFERENT LEARNING STYLES

So far, we have introduced a range of general learning principles and practices to add to your Flawless Facilitator tool kit to stimulate Active Learning. In the next two chapters, we will introduce three different personality frameworks that can help you become a more versatile Facilitator by building greater self-understanding in addition to recognizing different types of participants.

TIMEOUT!

There are many differing personality frameworks. In this book, we will focus on the concepts of Temperament (as originally articulated in modern day reading by David Keirsey and Linda Berens), Interaction Style (as described by Linda Berens) and Cognitive Processes (as originally articulated by Carl Jung and the theoretical framework underlying the Myers-Briggs Type Indicator tool (MBTI®).

In this chapter, we will define Temperament, which can help to explain **Why we do what we do.** This can help us understand more about our personal needs, strengths and challenges as a Facilitator. It can also help to explain different participants' learning needs and provide insight into how to motivate different types to learn. We will provide background information on the Temperament patterns, demonstrate how to use this knowledge to build self-awareness, and finally explore how to use this framework to position knowledge/learning to appeal to all Temperaments. We will also briefly explore how we might unintentionally cause stress to each of the four Temperaments when learning and identify simple techniques to restore a safe learning environment.

We will also explore Interaction Style, which can help to describe **How we engage with others** to get our Temperament's core needs met. It can help to explain our innate energy patterns as we relate to others. This information can be useful to understand our core drive, strengths and challenges as a Facilitator. In addition, we can use this information to build rapport and engage more effectively one-on-one with students. This can also help us adapt our style so our delivery is most effective for the learning context.

For both theories, we will revisit the T.E.A.C.H. methodology to show how this approach complements different learning styles for each type.

GAME PLAN

You will learn about:

Four Temperament Patterns

- Understanding Facilitator Strengths and Challenges
- Speaking Four Languages
- Four Temperaments as Children
- Temperament and TEACH
- Temperament and Stress

Four Interaction Style Patterns

- Understanding Facilitator Strengths and Challenges
- Flexing Interaction Style
- Four Interaction Styles and Learning
- Four Interaction Styles and TEACH

Combining Temperament and Interaction Style: 16 Types

Four Temperament Patterns

> *"The two most important days in your life are the day you are born and the day you find out why."*
>
> *Mark Twain*

Four Temperament patterns have been recognized and described for over 25 centuries. David Keirsey popularized this concept alongside psychological type in his original book, (written with Marilyn Bates), *"Please Understand Me"*. Linda Berens has further expanded and enhanced these concepts for the 21st century in various publications.

TIMEOUT!

Temperament is defined as a pattern of needs, values, talents and behaviors that underlies our way of acting and being in the world. Temperament helps us to understand WHY we do what we do. Each of us views the world through our own set of lenses, distorting reality to match our own mental picture. We are all unique individuals with our own complexities and idiosyncrasies, and yet four basic patterns have been consistently and cross-culturally recognized in the human personality for over 25 centuries.

Temperament theory is based on four sets of themes. People with the same Temperament share the **same core needs and values.** This similarity does not mean that these people are all the same! There are wide varieties, but with strong shared needs. For example, string instruments are part of a family of musical instruments, but there are huge differences between a guitar and a double bass.

The four Temperaments are listed below with their equivalents through history.

Improviser (Berens)	**Stabilizer (Berens)**
• Sanguine (Hippocrates)	• Melancholic(Hippocrates)
• Hedonic (Aristotle)	• Proprietary (Aristotle)
• Innovative (Adickes)	• Traditional (Adickes)
• Changeable/Salamander/Fire (Parcelsus)	• Industrious/Gnome/Earth (Parcelsus)
• Aesthetic (Spranger)	• Economic (Spranger)
• Eagle (North American Indians)	• Mouse (North American Indians)
• Mistaken goals: Revenge (Adler)	• Mistaken goals: Service (Adler)
• Dionysian (Keirsey/Bates)	• Epimethean (Keirsey/Bates)
• Sensing/Perceiving: SP (Myers)	• Sensing/Judging: SJ (Myers)
• Artisan (Keirsey)	• Guardian (Keirsey)
Theorist (Berens)	**Catalyst (Berens)**
• Phlegmatic(Hippocrates)	• Choleric (Hippocrates)
• Dialectical (Aristotle)	• Ethical (Aristotle)
• Skeptical (Adickes)	• Doctrinaire (Adickes)
• Curious/Sylph/Air (Parcelsus)	• Inspired/Nymph/Water (Parcelsus)
• Theoretic (Spranger)	• Religious (Spranger)]
• Buffalo (North American Indians)	• Bear (North American Indians)
• Mistaken goals: Power (Adler)	• Mistaken goals: Recognition (Adler)
• Promethean (Keirsey/Bates)	• Apollonian (Keirsey/Bates)
• Intuiting/Thinking: NT (Myers)	• Intuiting/Feeling: NF (Myers)
• Rational (Keirsey)	• Idealist (Keirsey)

* **Adapted from information from Linda V. Berens Ph.D. and David Keirsey Ph.D.**

In this book, we will use the Berens' Temperament names of Improviser, Stabilizer, Theorist and Catalyst.

Temperament is reviewed thoroughly in an organizational context in ***Turning Team Performance Inside Out*** and the ***Teamwork from the Inside Out Field Book,*** within the context of relationships in ***Dating Mating and Relating,*** in the process of verifying best-fit type in ***Let's Split the Difference*** and in coaching in ***The Type Trilogy Card Set and Guidebook.*** In this book, we will focus on the importance of Temperament theory in ensuring targeted effective learning.

Understand Facilitator Strengths and Challenges

As we continue to expand the descriptions of Temperament, consider which Temperament sounds most like you. Try to avoid thinking of only your current role. Think instead of which description seems to best capture your natural behaviors, values and talents. You may choose to read each description and rank them into "Most Like You" (1) and "Least Like You" (4)

Self-Assessment

In describing the four Temperaments, David Keirsey identified specific animals, which he believed demonstrated specific behaviors that could be used as a metaphor to help understand each Temperament. The animals and their high-level descriptions are listed on the next page.

Catalyst **Diplomatic Skill Set** **Animal mascot – Dolphin**  **Driving force/core needs – be unique, develop self and others' potential, have greater meaning and purpose for actions** The Catalyst's core needs are for the meaning and significance that come from having a sense of purpose and working toward some greater good. They need to have a sense of unique identity. They value unity, self-actualization, and authenticity. Catalysts prefer cooperative interactions with a focus on ethics and morality. They tend to be gifted at unifying diverse people and helping individuals realize their potential. They build bridges between people through empathy and clarification of deeper issues.	**Improviser** **Tactical Skill Set** **Animal mascot – Fox**  **Driving force/core needs – be noticed or make an impact, get a result, act swiftly and practically, in the moment** The Improviser's core needs are to have the freedom to act without hindrance and to see a marked result from action. Improvisers highly value aesthetics, whether in nature or art. Their energies are focused on skillful performance, variety, and stimulation. They tend to be gifted at employing the available means to accomplish an end. Their creativity is revealed by the variety of solutions they create. They are talented at using tools, whether the tools are language, theories, a paintbrush, or a computer. They want to be impressive.

Stabilizer Logistical Skill Set Animal mascot – Beaver	Theorist Strategic Skill Set Animal mascot – Owl

Driving force/core needs – be part of a group or team, act responsibly, contribute to concrete accomplishment or goal The Stabilizer's core needs are for group membership and responsibility. Stabilizers need to know they are doing the responsible thing. They value stability, security and a sense of community. They trust hierarchy and authority, and may be surprised when others go against these social structures. Stabilizers know how things have always been done, and so they anticipate where things can go wrong. They have a knack for attending to rules, procedures, and protocol. They want to belong.	**Driving force/core needs – be an expert, demonstrate competence and mastery, retain autonomy and control in activities** The Theorist's core needs are for mastery of concepts, knowledge, and competence. Theorists want to understand the operating principles of the universe and to learn or even develop theories for everything. They value expertise, logical consistency, concepts and ideas, and seek progress. They abstractly analyze a situation and consider previously un-thought-of possibilities. Research, analysis, searching for patterns, and developing hypotheses are quite likely to be their natural modus operandi.

Chapter Five: Visuals One through Four

Further detail on each of the Temperaments is on the table below.

CHARACTERISTICS	IMPROVISER	STABILIZER	THEORIST	CATALYST
Driving Forces/ Core Needs	• Be noticed or Make an impact • Get a result • Act swiftly and practically in the moment	• Be part of a group or team • Contribute to a concrete goal or accomplishment • Act responsibly and dutifully	• Be an expert • Retain autonomy and control in activities	• Be special • Have a greater purpose and meaning for actions • Develop their own and others potential
Work Approach	• Seek to make an impact with their style and skills • Able to do tactical troubleshooting and fire fighting	• Get the right thing, to the right place, in the right quantity at the right price at the right time • Put in repeatable processes	• Seek to improve systems and redesign processes • Able to think logically and see strategic connections	• Build bridges between groups • Provide connection and enthusiasm
Time Preference/ Focus	The present: here and now	The past: what was done before	Infinite time orientation: scanning past, present and future	The future: life's a journey forward
Thinking Style	**Contextual Thinking:** reference data to present context	**Sequential Thinking:** reference data step-by-step from start to finish	**Differential Thinking:** where distinctions in points of view are seen first.	**Integrative Thinking:** where similarities behind different data or points of view are naturally connected.
Communication Style	Net it out/get to the point Concise communication – less is more	Linear and sequential: 1,1a, 1b, 2, 2a, 2b. 3 etc. Structured: beginning, middle end	Abstract around models Critical questioning to examine a point of view	Empathetic Flowing and effusive

CHARACTERISTICS	IMPROVISER	STABILIZER	THEORIST	CATALYST
Language	• Informal/casual with occasional slang • Creatively and humorously economical	• Respectful and appropriate to the group • Conventional	• Precise and articulate • Avoids redundancy	• Generalizations and impressionistic • Employ hyperbole
Relationships	**Fraternal:** associated with buddies all on the same level	**Group Bonding:** associated with the family, team or interest	**Expert:** associated with any type of specialized knowledge or expertise	**Empathic:** associated with genuine, authentic connections

FOUL!

Remember, individuals can demonstrate behaviors from all four Temperaments at different times. The key difference between each Temperament is reflected in the core needs and values.

EXERCISE 5-1: YOUR BEST-FIT TEMPERAMENT

- From the previous descriptions, which do you think might be your best-fit Temperament and why?
- Review the grid below. Circle the answer you feel is your best fit for each category and then total the numbers for each column.

COLUMN	1	2	3	4
Value...	Authenticity	Expertise and Competence	Honor and Duty	Excitement and Adventure
Need...	To make a difference	To be logical	To be responsible	Freedom to make things happen
Want more...	Romance	Precision	Ownership	Stimulation
Enjoy...	Growth and Development	Theory and Debate	Nurturing and Contributing	Making an impression
Descriptive Verb ...	Becoming	Knowing	Protecting	Doing
In Setting a direction, need a...	Meaningful Purpose	Strategy	Step-by-Step Approach	Action Plan/Goal
Give Feedback on...	Individual Strengths	Accuracy and Competence	Areas for Improvement	What was done with skill and style
Like Feedback that is...	Genuine and specific	Recognizes Intelligence and Ideas	Constructive and Specific	Frequent and Direct
Words tend to be...	Dramatic and Flowing	Precise	Specific and Clear	Colloquial and to the Point

COLUMN	1	2	3	4
Admire...	Realized Potential	Knowledge and Design	Achievement	Skill and Beauty
Seek in Life...	Meaning	Mastery	Membership	Opportunity
Would hate to be...	Average	Incompetent	Not needed	Confined
Ideal Work Environment...	Expressive and Personal	Innovative and Intellectual	Organized and Secure	Stimulating and Varied
Learning is Easier when...	Relationship-Centered, Growth-Oriented	Knowledge-Centered, Competence-Oriented	Authority-Centered, Practical in Application	Experiential-Based, Practical/Tool-Oriented
Core Abilities...	Diplomacy/ Building Relationships	Developing Strategies and Analyzing Frameworks	Logistics/ Operations	Tactics/ Performance with Skill
Motto	"Be all that you can be."	"Knowledge is power."	"To Protect and Serve."	"Carpe Diem."
Total				

TRY IT ON: YOUR BEST-FIT TEMPERAMENT

Which Temperament did you rank (1) in the first two descriptions?

Total each column in the table in the boxes provided.

If your lowest total was in Column One, this could be an indicator for the Catalyst Temperament.

If your lowest total was in Column Two, this could be an indicator for the Theorist Temperament.

If your lowest total was in Column Three, this could be an indicator for the Stabilizer Temperament.

If your lowest total was in Column Four, this could be indicator for the Improviser Temperament.

Write your ideas here…

Which do you identify as your best-fit Temperament?

_____

_____

_____

What are your quick insights from this knowledge?

_____

_____

_____

If you are struggling with identifying your best-fit Temperament, there are several options:

- Continue reading the additional data in this chapter.
- Review some of the resources in the Appendix.
- Check out web sites such as type-academy.com, lindaberens.com, and keirsey.com

COACHING POINT: TEMPERAMENT

Understanding Temperament has many benefits in teaching and learning.

- As a Facilitator to understand your strengths and challenges.
- To apply different learning approaches for different Temperaments.
- To motivate students to learn.
- To avoid causing stress to students by inadvertently challenging core needs.

Strengths and Challenges

> "We do not see things as they are. We see things as we are. We do not hear things and they are, we hear things as we are."
>
> *The Talmund*

As you can see from this quotation, we tend to view the world through our distinct type profile, and can distort reality in order to meet these perceptions. As a Facilitator, it is important to be aware of our Temperament. This can enable us to understand our strengths and potential blind spots. In addition, it provides a framework to use to flex our approach in order to meet the needs of different students. Here are a few sample ideas for the strengths and potential challenges of each Temperament as a Facilitator.

IMPROVISER STRENGTHS	IMPROVISER POTENTIAL BLIND SPOTS
Ability to make learning hands-on and relevant to the current context	May not reference concepts or articulate theoretical frameworks
Now-focused – so ability to respond in the moment	May be reluctant to follow a teaching agenda
Tactical – so able to focus on short-term action steps	May miss the big picture – and might not see implications from actions
Aware of classroom dynamics – able to read body language and current sensory data	May get distracted by current events and resist instituting structure into workshops
STABILIZER STRENGTHS	**STABILIZER POTENTIAL BLIND SPOTS**
Understand process – how to create a structured learning experience	May be reluctant to deviate from the lesson plan
Past-focused – so ability to remember previous examples and ideas to make learning tangible	May be reluctant to try something new without prior experience in the approach or content
Realistic – so able to focus on what is practical, useful and achievable in learning	May dismiss abstract ideas as unrealistic
Ability to set concrete goals	May become stressed with children and/or participants not following the "rules"
THEORIST STRENGTHS	**THEORIST POTENTIAL BLIND SPOTS**
Focus on the what and why of any learning content	May be reluctant to follow and/or use tried and true approaches or data
Aim is to present the most relevant and accurate information through applying research and independent thought	May appear overly theoretical or analytical
Strategic approach can encourage intellectual independence	May neglect to provide positive feedback and instead use primarily developmental feedback to increase quality
Ability to view information from a logical perspective	May miss the emotional connection and/or group dynamics

CATALYST STRENGTHS	CATALYST POTENTIAL BLIND SPOTS
Create a safe, inclusive learning environment	May be too "soft" on participants focusing on potential versus actual performance
Future-focused – so ability to see potential in individuals and groups	May be reluctant to consider realistic, more practical, options
Empathic with different learning styles	May not provide sufficient logical data
Ability to self-disclose to connect and provide genuine positive feedback	May struggle with providing "tough" messages

EXERCISE 5.2: YOUR STRENGTHS AND POTENTIAL CHALLENGES

- Based on your Temperament assessment, what do you identify as your 2-3 strengths as a Facilitator?
- What could be your potential challenges?

TRY IT ON: YOUR STRENGTHS AND CHALLENGES

Write your ideas here…

Strengths as a Facilitator?

_____

_____

_____

Potential Challenges?

_____

_____

_____

Speaking Four Languages

Once we have gained an insight into our personal needs, values, talents and behaviors, this framework is also important to understand and appreciate different communication styles of participants.

Communication Style

Each Temperament tends to have an innate communication style as described in more detail below. Understanding these facets can enable Facilitators to "speak four languages" i.e. adapt their content and approach to different Temperaments to increase acceptance and retention.

Improviser Communication Style

Ideas and Information

- Tend to like practical tangible data and information that is exciting and current that they can use immediately.
- Talk about actions and will get frustrated if forced to talk for too long about something with no action associated with it.
- Tend to focus on, "What's in it for themselves or others".

Organization of Data

- Method of data organization may not be immediately obvious because they often either go straight to the point, or weave a story around a theme.
- Will often organize their message around a concrete object, such as a demo of software operation, and use this current reality to "facilitate thinking."
- Tend to start with concrete sensory details and build (maybe) to big picture.

Types of Words

- Tend to use jargon or colloquial language to make their point. Words such as "cool", "stuff," "trash and trinkets" (for course giveaways) are examples.
- Tend to use concise, to the point language and choose to "net it out" in the communication process. Communication style can appear terse, direct and abbreviated: get to the point – less is more, "Keep It Short and Simple" (KISS), 1, 2, 3, that's it. Just give them the facts and the bottom line. They can't stand long-winded speeches!
- Use colorful words that paint a picture with lots of action verbs. Key words you will hear from Improvisers are fun, risk, excitement, luck, deals and adventure. They will talk about what is happening now.

Delivery/Body Language

- Tend to enjoy using tools and gimmicks to support their point and will sometimes fiddle with objects when talking to others.
- When bored, body language can become fidgety and there might be constant movement, often getting up in the middle of a conversation and walking around.
- They tend to tune into sensory stimuli, so may create a unique, stylish look for themselves, or may dress more casually for comfort.

Building Involvement

- Improvisers build involvement through stimulating others to experience physically as much learning content as possible. They can make others feel that they are part of the interaction through descriptive stories and anecdotes. They bring the situation to the active, three-dimensional here and now versus the conceptual level of theory land.
- Improvisers tend to observe and mirror language, which allows them to connect with others. They love to see a person's eyes light up as they pick up a topic of the person's interest. This ability to connect and consider the desires of all involved is also at the core of their persuasive skills.

- Improvisers can read others motives easily, and yet they may have to be careful about pressing others "hot buttons" in interaction. What they mean in fun, can alienate other Temperaments.

Stabilizer Communication Style

Ideas and Information

- Like practical, tangible ideas and information that can produce results and that are related to concrete discernible outcomes.
- Want to talk about what is tried and true and has proved effective. Tend to talk about the process for getting things done: "How did we do this last time", "How can we ensure consistency in outcome?"
- Tend to talk about saving and wasting money/resources, as this is linked to their economic values.

Organization of Data

- Organize data sequentially when they are communicating. They start at the beginning and tend to move through the information in a step-by-step manner: "First I did this, then I did that, next I did this, etc."
- Like data grouped into sections and subsections. In notes and reports, they often use numbers and bulleting. For example, 1, 1.a, b, c., etc. When presenting, naturally follow the process, "Tell then what you are going to tell them, Tell them, and then Tell them you told them!"
- Like to present examples from the past and practical information.

Types of Words

- Relate data to past experience. They tend to say things such as, 'In my experience", "Last time I…" "What's this person's experience?" "In the past…." They like to talk about what is "tried and true" and what has been proven.

- Stabilizers tend to use traditional language in regards to protocol and politeness and/ or use language appropriate to the group.
- Stabilizers tend to compare and contrast one thing to others regularly using such words as "better than, worse than" to show where components are located on their internal ratings scale.

Delivery/Body Language

- Tend to use a methodical mode of delivery.
- May sometimes go into lecture mode, especially when conveying information to a group. Their desire to express the seriousness of the material and establish their role as the instructor in the hierarchy can be the main motivation behind this behavior.
- They can come across as responsible and sensible. Sometimes they may seem burdened by the all responsibilities they take on.

Building Involvement

- Like to build involvement by creating a group culture and observing team traditions.
- May be reluctant to build two-way communication when in the role of expert and may appear authoritative and directing.
- Listen carefully to historical data when others share it, but may discount what appears to them as overly abstract or unrealistic.

Theorist Communication Style

Ideas and Information

- Tend to gravitate to concepts and abstract data, in their search for the operating principles of the universe without necessarily articulating practical application. Subjects of interest tend to be strategy, trends, long-range goals, future possibilities, new modes of operating and different mental models.
- Enjoy debating issues and pride themselves on their intellectual rigor.

- Talk about logic, systems and principles and will tend to ask 'What and Why?" In their examination of possibilities, they may often be unaware of physical time/ resource constraints.

Organization of Data

- Categorize data in order to communicate, although the extent to which this is obvious varies between Directing and Informing Styles (see later notes on Interaction Styles).
- Tend to be reluctant to state what they see as obvious because they don't want to be perceived as redundant.
- Organize information based on their reasoning and use patterns of statements and conclusions to explain their point.

Types of Words

- Use words as tools and normally have extensive vocabularies. They tend to be extremely selective in their word choice, often correcting others' and their own words, and deliberating over the most accurate word to use. They tend to react negatively to words and information that they feel are illogical. They want to select the right word, to convey the exact nuance of meaning desired, even if the word they choose may be too esoteric for others to understand. They can also become frustrated when they cannot think of the precise word they want.
- Use analogies and metaphors to make their points (as do Catalysts). Theorists prefer to take all the facts of the situation and drop them into another scenario in order to point out the flaws of the argument, identify hidden inconsistencies or errors, and prove a theory.
- Like to use their critical questioning skills to highlight what might be missed. Have this innate ability to see what's present and what's not, and in this process may forget to give positive feedback.

Delivery/Body Language

- May appear confident in demeanor (sometimes to the point of arrogance), as they speak from their areas of competence.
- May also appear self-doubting because of their use of qualified language.
- May appear disassociated, with their innate ability to step back and analyze data from a variety of perspectives.

Building Involvement

- Their knowledge and confidence can inspire trust and following from others.
- Tend to show genuine interest and connect easily with those who they consider are experts. They are eager to gather as much data as they can in order to build their own store of knowledge.
- Can appear competitive, as they argue principles or try to establish their competence.

Catalyst Communication Style

Ideas and Information

- Naturally tend to gravitate to conceptual data that allows individuals to fulfill their potential such as psychology, self-help, etc. They tend to be attracted to information that builds individual identity.
- Talk a lot about relationships. Empathy and intimate communication are important to them. They will tend to reject instinctively conversations that are non-authentic, and will try to establish genuine meaningful interaction. They tend to recognize others' unique qualities and provide genuine, often spontaneous, positive feedback on these attributes.
- Often discuss what is meant or intended. They have a particular interest in understanding interactions and appreciate symbolic significance.

Organization of Data

- Integrate information from various sources around a unified theme by seeing the connections between what might seem like disparate categories.
- Tend to focus on the big picture and then consider the details. They are often concerned with the natural flow of information.
- They may appear to jump from one point to another and some of their comments may seem to come out at random with no logical connection. However, the theme on which they are focusing is often just not apparent to others.

Types of Words

- Often use flowing dramatic language, full of "larger than life" words such as, "epiphany," "fabulous" and "everyone." They can speak in global language— the feeling or the big picture without concrete details. They also tend to talk about their impressions of a specific situation, and may have difficulty when trying to articulate the specific data behind an impression.
- Use metaphors as a teaching tool and to bridge communication barriers between individuals. These can bring groups to a common understanding.
- Tend to have a verbal fluency, particularly around subjects core to their passion. Use phrases such as, "connect with…", What's the purpose?", "What's the meaning of …"

Delivery/Body Language

- Tend to use flowing gestures and expressive body language when they talk about something meaningful or personal to them.
- As they tend to be absorbed in the world of people and ideas, they may appear clumsy and struggle with using tools and equipment.
- They can be quite intense when talking from the heart.

Building Involvement

- Tend to ask open-ended questions to identify what is important to other people.

- Coupled with their ability to listen empathetically and put themselves in the other person's shoes, this tendency often results in finding out lots personal information about the other person, while not necessarily self-disclosing important information about himself or herself.
- Instinctively recognize and value the uniqueness in others and try to encourage individuals to actualize their potential.

TIMEOUT!

In order to meet the needs of all four Temperaments in a one-to-many interaction (workshop, classroom, etc.), a Facilitator can vary the types of ideas introduced; the organization used, and type of content shared.

This approach is called "Speaking Four Languages. Below are two examples of this technique in action.

The first demonstrates how to sell a cooking school to each of the four Temperaments. The second indicates how to change language, to position the benefits of attending a specific sales training workshop. Each bullet includes why this statement/approach might appeal to each Temperament's core needs and talents.

CASE STUDY: SPEAKING FOUR LANGUAGES

TEMPERAMENT	COOKING SCHOOL	ATTENDING A SALES WORKSHOP
Improviser	You can look good when you throw great dinner parties for family and friends. (*Be impressive*) You can change the recipes and create your own version. (*Freedom and flexibility*) The classes are fun and hands-on! (*Tactical talent*)	You will pick up tips and tricks to raise sales. (*Meet a challenge*) You'll be one of the first to use this approach – you'll make an impression. (*Be noticed*) The program is experiential so you get to learn by doing. (*Tactical talent*)
Stabilizer	The Cooking School has been in existence for 25 years. (*Experience*) You will receive structured step-by-step recipes that are guaranteed to produce excellent, consistent results. (*Sequential thinking*) There are many courses: the introductory (Essentials Series) starts you at the basics and then you can move onto more advanced courses. (*Structure and consistency*)	The sales process defines key roles and accountabilities. (*Responsibility and team*) You will receive a Certificate showing achievement of sales standards. (*Concrete achievement*) The course content includes best practices with practical skills and techniques to meet customer needs more effectively. (*Logistical talent*)
Theorist	You will learn the chemistry of cooking and become an expert in the kitchen. (*Mastery, concepts and logic*) You will know the "what and why" of ingredients, cooking equipment and presentation. (*Strategic talent*) You will understand the universal principles of categorizing a menu and creating a meal. (*Autonomy and control*)	Leading edge methodology providing a new way of directing a complex sale. (*Strategic talent*) You will have an innovative way of collecting, analyzing and presenting client data. (*Concepts and logic*) Provides a strategic approach to addressing clients' multifaceted problems with a state-of-the-art solutions approach. (*Strategic talent*)

TEMPERAMENT	COOKING SCHOOL	ATTENDING A SALES WORKSHOP
Catalyst	Learning to cook fresh and healthy foods will improve the quality of life for your family. (*Self-actualization and empathy*) Quality relationships tend to develop over a good meal. (*Relationships*) You will be able to create special meals for the important people in your life. (*Unique identity*)	Focuses on building authentic relationships during the sales process. (*Relationships*) The course introduces a collaborative, partnership approach to meeting client needs. (*Diplomatic talent*) Provides an ethical approach – not "hard sell". (Auth*entic and genuine*)

EXERCISE 5.3: SPEAKING FOUR LANGUAGES

- Think about a subject that you want to teach. How would you describe this course to each of the four Temperaments?
- Focus specifically on core needs, talents and values.

TRY IT ON: SPEAKING FOUR LANGUAGES

Write your ideas here…

The Course/Subject you plan to teach

_____

_____

Improviser

_____

_____

Stabilizer

_____

_____

Theorist

_____

_____

Catalyst

_____

_____

Four Temperaments as Children

Temperament is also valuable to understand our audience so that we can recognize needs and flex our approach accordingly. In this section, we will describe briefly how each Temperament might look as a Child. In the following section, we will share some general principles about how to incorporate Active Learning to appeal to all four Temperaments.

The Improviser Child

The Improviser Child tends to be drawn to **explore the physical universe in the now moment** in an adventurous way. This can look like constant movement. You might observe the Improviser Child being drawn to discover the **concrete environment** by touching switches and equipment (normally those that are not toys!), picking up bright things, spotting unusual items and climbing and jumping with gay abandon. This absorption in the sensory environment serves to help them keep things interesting and varied. A mother commented that her daughter was like an explosion when she got home from school and needed to run out some energy. The school environment seemed to be too physically confining and she was like a spring that had been held down and suddenly let go, bouncing even higher than normal.

Chapter Five: Visual Five

For an Improviser child, restriction of **physical or emotional free-dom** tends to be very difficult and you may see a reaction and/or the child may become disruptive. For instance, a parent tried to put a backpack with a guiding harness onto a two-year old Improviser child's back and she became hysterical because this appeared to restrict her freedom of movement. Rules introduced for safety seem to have less significance for an Improviser Child because they trust in their innate physical dexterity to deal with any challenge.

In their **enjoyment of the current context,** they tend to jump in first and then think later. As a result, they can appear adaptable, positive and eager to try new things. Every moment can give them joyful sensory stimuli, for instance playing in the dirt, running into and out of waves next to the ocean, coloring, doing finger painting, climbing, running, etc. In fact, the more able we are to provide immediate excitement and stimulation, the happier and more joyful our Improviser Child will be. Our Improviser children tend to enjoy wheeled toys, games, contests and sports where they are able to test the limits of the activity and demonstrate their physical acuity.

In the search for stimulation, it is important for our Improviser Child **to be impressive**, to stand out and demonstrate their tactile ability and be noticed. They want to see a reaction from those who look after them. It is best if this is positive, however a negative reaction is better than no reaction at all. Prompting a negative reaction when they are bored is what can get them into trouble. They might also do even more adventurous or risky activities to keep that adrenaline going and to get that attention.

While all children might tend to be somewhat impulsive, our Improviser Child can appear to **respond more consistently to what is happening in the immediate context** and this could be viewed as disruptive in a school setting. We might observe our Improviser Child being restless, constantly testing other people's limits, appearing reckless as they continue their bold and daring exploration of the environment. A parent talked about arriving at a park and within two minutes the three-year old Improviser child is at the top of a 12-foot slide peering over the top at you (While her four-year old Stabilizer sister turns to her parent and says "this it too high".)

Improvisers often **learn best when they are moving** and prefer discovering by doing. The more they can move around the classroom the better. They enjoy **daily variety** and quick incremental rewards to get work done. They respond well to contests, challenges and recognition of desired (good) behaviors. This is important because it can be easy to be caught up in negative behaviors and forget the positive. They tend to enjoy reading action-oriented books. Reward them with activity.

Improvisers tend to be **independent and resourceful** both physically and mentally. The experience of learning is important versus the completion. Once they feel they have mastered something, they want to move on very quickly. They can be quick to find excuses or reasons to do things their way. They tend to enjoy solving problems and yet can get bored if the solution isn't quick or they perceive a task to be unproductive, repetitive or dull. One primary school teacher talks about encouraging students to run to the football posts and back when they get fidgety to provide that sensory activity.

Improvisers can be great at motivating others to join in with their activities. Their best friends will be those who agree with their choice of game and join in most often. They also tend to have **high contextual awareness**, which gives them insight into other's motives. When an adult or child says one thing and yet their body language says something different, they will read the motive accurately.

Improvisers tend to want an **immediate answer** when they ask a question. Recent feedback from kids who have struggled in a school environment says that one of the main issues they had was not getting an answer to their questions quickly enough and then they tuned out. Improvisers can find practical jokes very entertaining. They can frequently be the class clown.

When our Improviser child is bored, is unable to move and/or feels like his/her freedom is being restricted, we might observe extreme restlessness, playing up and **testing all the boundaries**. As teachers, it can be tempting to reiterate the rules, lecture and impose more structure and punish what might be perceived to be disruptive behavior. This tends to exacerbate the situation as it further impacts the core needs for freedom to act in the moment, ability to be noticed, and be impressive. Rather teachers could instead try to provide freedom of choice with a more fluid structure, provide opportunities for the children to demonstrate their tactical expertise (and be impressive) and provide logical consequences with neutral emotion.

The Stabilizer Child

The Stabilizer Child tends to like to be in an environment, which is **safe and secure**, with structure, consistency and stability. Security is important to them on all levels: physical security, emotional security and, later in life, financial security. If anything enters their life to disrupt this security, they can become stressed.

The Stabilizer Child enjoys **knowing what will happen** and can find a chaotic environment unacceptable even at a young age. If they are going to a new school or any other new situation, if possible go there in advance. Show them round every part of their new environment so that they know it well. This will help them settle much more quickly. Again, time taken at the beginning will mean less stress for the child. A Stabilizer four-year old child was taken to Legoland for a treat by her grandparents. The first time she was visibly stressed because she had not stayed away from home in a hotel before without her mum and dad. The second time, she was obviously more relaxed as she remembered the previous outing – even the location of the Whoopee cushion!

The Stabilizer Child can appear serious and cautious, and, of all the Temperaments as children, are the most likely to **worry** about what will happen. They naturally tend to "Look before they leap". I heard a six-year-old Stabilizer worry about bears and as a result did not want to go camping.

They tend to be **careful and orderly with possessions**, looking after what is theirs, knowing what belongs to whom and getting stressed if their toys, clothes, etc. are not respected by others. They enjoy sorting and organizing toys – a two-year old Stabilizer lined her Easter Eggs up in size sequence after an Easter Egg hunt. They naturally tend to be conscientious, enjoy tidying up their environment and do things like help around the house and support the teacher at school. They often act as positive role models for desired behavior when learning.

They have an **innate sense of responsibility** and respect the hierarchy. Give them any task where they can prove their organizational abilities and complete the task on time, and they will thrive. They tend to find saying no to a request for help is almost impossible. Group work can be very annoying when other students don't pull their weight. They will often end up doing all the work and may become overloaded.

They tend to look for **guidelines about what is right and wrong**, what is OK or not OK from authority figures such as teachers and parents. They tend to respect rules and get concerned when other children disrespect processes. Sitting on the top of the bus at the zoo, the driver says, "No standing up on the top of the bus" – the three year old Stabilizer would not stand up because she had been told not to and she respected the instruction.

They tend to be **dutiful dependable and reliable** – "good little boys and girls" and may act as the natural "police" of the classroom or house, sometimes telling tales of others. This can cause them some tension between their need to be part of a group and their respect for the rules. Bad behavior of other kids (as they perceive it) can cause great upset.

They naturally tend to **look after** younger siblings and enjoy learning about family events and history. They can demonstrate their concern for people in a concrete way by doing kind things for adults and siblings. They tend to remember past experiences and use them as examples in conversation, "Last time we did…". Traditions such as Christmas are very important.

Chapter Five: Visual Six

The Stabilizer child values **linear, sequential and methodical learning,** building on one idea to the next. They may have difficulty with, or a lack of interest in, what they perceive to be abstract ideas and concepts without specific application. Invite these children to observe first, then help them do the task, then watch as they do the task and then let them be independent. This can appear to be a slow process but learning will stick this way. Making a mistake in public can be a big source of stress.
Stabilizer children tend to **learn best by repetition** in pursuit of perfection. Moving on before they are ready will make them feel stupid. They can be quick at copying or imitating

others' actions and often have a high ability to memorize word-for-word. In fact, they may convince you that they can read way before they can, simply because they have memorized whole pages of text.

They **value reality** and respond well to recognition such as certificates, gold stars, and other physical expressions of success. Providing specific, concrete positive feedback on good behavior can build strong self-esteem in Stabilizers and is fundamental to strong self-confidence. They are happy to play once the work is done, but would rather play a game they know well.

The **need for belonging**, whether it is to a family, class at school, guide group, etc. can be seen in their membership and recognition of social status in these groups. They enjoy being part of a community of learners as long as it's all going well.

When our Stabilizer child is faced with constant change, loss of membership in a group (family break up, new school) or a feeling of not belonging, we might observe an increase in anxiety and a pulling back from demonstrating their normal sense of responsibility. As teachers, it can be tempting to say there is nothing to worry about, and criticize them for not contributing in their normal way. The better approach would probably be to help the Stabilizer child identify areas of continuity and consistency as well as clarifying roles in, and membership of, key groups to reestablish their sense of belonging. Providing specific timely positive feedback can also help rebuild self-esteem.

The Theorist Child

The Theorist child tends to demonstrate **autonomy** and **independence of thought** at a young age. They tend to be individualistic and prefer not to be dictated to – being told what to do, think or feel.

A need for **mastery** and competence is a very important drive for Theorist children. If they find themselves lacking in skills in a given task or sport, and they cannot see that they will improve, they will probably drop it quickly. They gravitate towards knowledge in **the areas that are of interest to them** and also to people who are knowledgeable in those subjects in which they want to gain expertise. They like to be informed and will respond well to any source of relevant knowledge.

Chapter Five: Visual Seven

They tend to be **verbally fluent** and may develop language at a young age or – as per Einstein – refuse to talk until they can speak in sentences. Early in their lives, you may hear them correct others word choice and engage in debate. In fact, often the first words from a Theorist child may be, **"Why?"** as they seek to understand what is going on and why any behavior is expected of them. This tendency may also show up in the questioning of authority and sharing their viewpoint in how something should be accomplished, using the  words, "I think…" or, "I know". The Theorist child often enjoys developing their **reasoning skills** and there can be a danger in giving them your reasons – if the Theorist child perceives your reasoning as flawed, they may dismiss you as incompetent. They can use advanced language to debate well. As they question everything, they are quite happy for a question to be responded to with another question; this will just continue a favorite pastime of asking more questions.

Theorist children tend to be **logical** and want to learn how and why things work. They tend not to take things personally – unless the feedback hits their internal drive for mastery. They enjoy games of the imagination and expressing their ingenuity as they play with building blocks, collections (rocks, coins), electronic sets, video games etc. They set themselves high personal standards and when something is completed successfully once, then this becomes "the norm" and they set the bar even higher the next time. They also expect a logical rationale from those with whom they interact and may make a judgment if a teacher appears illogical or overly emotional or affectionate.

They tend to be **more cerebral** – their minds are like Rubik's cubes that constantly turn and re-shape ideas and patterns. As a result, they may struggle with the day-to-day realities such as tidying up, getting dressed, being organized, etc. They also might appear self-contained or distant and detached as they internally analyze and wonder, "what would happen if…?".

They tend to **appear confident** with an innate belief that they are right – and may think that they are ready to be independent before they are. One ENTJ said, "I thought I was ready to leave home at age five and could not understand why I kept being brought back." They may also pretend to know more than they do.

Theorist children may appear **oblivious with social skills and interpersonal dynamics**. They might be naïve about people's motives or appropriate behavior and may not try to fit in. They may have an unusual sense of humor, which can both be successful and make everyone laugh, or be seen as offensive. There are times when no offense was meant but they may lack the judgment and personal insights to know what might be appropriate.

Theorists tend to want to be **equal partners in any learning experience**. They need to feel listened to, as this is a sign of respect. They enjoy working on projects, particularly creative or scientific projects, rather than homework. This can show in making model airplanes, growing plants, etc. They tend to engage well when something is intellectually challenging or entertaining. If neither of these facets is present, they can appear disinterested, become bored and tune out. You can help Theorist children by providing general principles and strategies to help in areas of challenge and to understand potential risks versus benefits. If the Theorist child is not accepting your reason, then provide them with some autonomy to experiment on their own so that the results of the experiment can convince them. They like **the freedom to follow their own train of thought**, which might mean they go off task for a while. Not permitting these distractions in thought is very limiting and can lead to rebellious behavior. They can have a dedication to topics of interest that can be all consuming. As far as possible, build this desire to learn by taking them anywhere you can to show them the best possible example of whatever they are interested in. If Theorist children are being taught by someone who understands them, things can go well. If not, they might alienate a teacher who could consider them to be a smart Alec, or have an attitude problem that needs fixing.

Theorist children often enjoy a **range of reading materials**, which require thinking, such as mysteries, science fiction, etc. When asked what present a Theorist child would like for his birthday, he said, "A book to learn about….". They tend to respond well to encouragement (not praise) specifically around aspects such as originality, because this reinforces their drive for competence.

When our Theorist child perceives that he/she has failed (by his/her own standards not necessarily that of others) and/or loses autonomy and control, we might observe him/her stepping back and becoming more obviously solitary, disengaging from reality and dropping schoolwork. As teachers, it can be tempting to say that they need to be more participative and this can increase the stress, as they might perceive themselves to be "failures" in social interaction. The better approach would probably be to help the Theorist child identify areas of competence and concentrate on activities in which they can be self-sufficient and demonstrate their ability for independent thought.

The Catalyst Child

The Catalyst Child needs and **values key relationships**, whether with parents, siblings, friends or teachers. Having a strong web of positive interactions helps to build resilient self-esteem and provide a sense of self. Catalyst children may also demonstrate altruism at a young age as they build special relationships with those who appear less well, either physically or emotionally, than themselves. Personalized attention is meaningful to them as this demonstrates to them both valuing of the relationship by the communicator as well as an appreciation of the special characteristics of the child.

We might observe our Catalyst child search for **unique identity** at a young age, maybe looking for a doctrine to believe in to help build their sense of individuality. You might observe the tendency to name animals and pets, as this gives these toys a distinctiveness. For this reason, many Catalysts enjoy playing with soft toys. The Catalyst child also often prefers collaborative versus competitive games, reading stories about people and relationships with happy endings such as fairy tales, and helping others (although in a more emotional versus practical way compared to our Stabilizer child). They may also explore a vivid imaginary world sometimes with fantasy friends.

The Catalyst child prefers face-to-face communication, and eye contact is important when interacting with them. They often exude personal warmth as they use **empathic communication** and may feel guilty if others are punished. They may begin speaking early as they reach out to interact with others, although the content of the message may relate more to the person than to the logic of the Theorist child. The language they use in written work may initially be less precise than other types. Recounts of events or retelling a plot from a book can be frustrating as this has already past. The possibilities for the future are far more compelling. Reflecting on poetry or lyrics can be a source of great pleasure.

Catalyst students may get themselves into a bind, as they want to do well and want to please others simultaneously. This can lead to them being unsure whether to display their competence or withhold it so that they are well liked. They have a tendency to think the best of people and have a charming naivety and **trust in others**. They will often give people who upset them a second chance, but when deeply hurt, they can be influenced by this for a long time and hold a grudge.

Chapter Five: Visual Eight

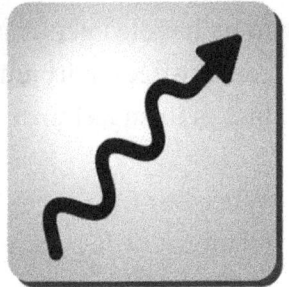

Catalyst children tend to seek a harmonious environment. In addition, they tend to enjoy some of the ceremonies and traditions in schools and families because they can give the environment a sense of **purpose and meaning**. Conflict can be stressful for the Catalyst child because of their ability to put themselves in the other person's shoes. In addition, like our Theorist children, they may get a feeling of being out of step with the environment as they represent a smaller percentage of the population.

Catalyst children tend to like being given **time to dream and imagine**. They often enjoy drama classes and writing, even if it is short such as journal entries, short stories, poetry, etc. The stories may have a dream-like quality to them and do not need to be based in the known. Happy endings tend to be important to show that evil does not win! Literature often offers a means to escape reality and enter a new world. They may grow into adult books as children and adult novels as teens as they tend to appreciate the depth of interactions sooner than the other children. They tend to have an ability to read between the lines, are keenly attentive of psychology both in peers and adults, and can often understand a story from a variety of perspectives. Their questions can be very insightful and often reflect a quest to know what the characters are feeling. With their innate preference for concepts and ideas, they trust their intuition and may struggle initially with the early practical focus of the school curriculum.

Catalyst children learn best with **teachers they like** and sympathize with, and with teachers who demonstrate that they like them. In fact, they may get distracted from the subject as they try to focus more on what the teacher wants versus the content of the lesson. Many Catalyst children prefer small group discussions as this can feel more inclusive and personal. Metaphors and analogies can help them to understand ideas so be sure the dramatic explanations are accurate! Learning about facts and dates can be boring but learning about beliefs, motivations and people of influence can be inspiring. Multiple choice or forced choice questions can be very challenging as they can often see possibilities behind every answer.

Catalyst children respond well to **genuine positive feedback** and often seek validation for who they are. This can come across as attention seeking – it is rarely intended that way. They just want to know they are OK and are following a natural desire to feel valued. With no feedback there might be a tendency to negative fantasize. Developmental feedback has to be handled gently as any critiques may be taken personally. Because Catalysts prefer a conflict-free environment, if they sense hostility or if they believe they are in a situation that makes them feel unsettled, they may close down.

When our Catalyst child faces excessive emotional turmoil or conflict, or loses a significant relationship, (e.g. family break up, betrayal) we might observe him/her emotionally disengaging and becoming lethargic. As teachers, it can be tempting to tell them to cheer up and this might be viewed as asking them to be inauthentic. The better approach would probably be to provide genuine positive feedback about the Catalyst child's strengths to reinforce their sense of self, as well as to ask and listen to their viewpoint about what has changed. Genuine empathy will also build the relationship and demonstrate that you care for the child.

FOUL!

Understanding a child's Temperament is not limiting. Children can develop ability in areas where they have a passion and may demonstrate behaviors from any of the four Temperaments based on context. The benefit of understanding Temperament is to give insight into the child's core needs, values and talents in order to support and validate these attributes.

EXERCISE 5.4: FOUR TEMPERAMENTS AS CHILDREN

- What have been your key learning points from understanding how Temperament might look in children?
- What will you do differently when facilitating learning as a result?

TRY IT ON: FOUR TEMPERAMENTS AS CHILDREN

Write your ideas here…

Learning Points?

_____

_____

_____

Do differently?

_____

_____

_____

TEACH and Temperament

As we have already reviewed, each Temperament tends to have different innate communication styles. In the same way, each Temperament tends to gravitate towards different Active Learning approaches. To maximize facilitation effectiveness, we can use this knowledge to adapt our course design to motivate all four Temperaments to learn.

FOUL!

These are high-level, flexible suggestions to consider in designing content. Other factors can also influence learning preferences such as intelligence, culture, interests, etc.

Below is a simple table describing some of these differences.

Facilitating for Improvisers	Facilitating for Stabilizers
• Learn best by doing.	• Learn best by linking learning to past experience.
• Communicate using concrete informal language with similes.	• Communicate using sequential language with specific examples.
• Be flexible in your approach.	• Be structured in your approach.
• Provide hands-on experience.	• Provide opportunities to practice skills.
• Build your credibility by being impressive.	• Build your credibility by talking about past experience.
• Use activities that are challenging and fun.	• Use activities that are practical and realistic.
• Make sure the goal includes "What's in it for me?"	• Make sure the goal includes concrete, tangible outcomes.
Facilitating for Theorists	**Facilitating for Catalysts**
• Learn best by independent study.	• Learn best with social engagement.
• Communicate using precise language with metaphors and analogies.	• Communicate using global language with analogies and metaphors.
• Be logical in your approach.	• Be genuine in your approach.
• Provide relevant facts and research.	• Provide opportunities to interact and share.
• Build your credibility by being knowledgeable.	• Build your credibility by being authentic.
• Use activities that are intellectually stimulating.	• Use activities that are meaningful.
• Make sure the goal includes the What and the Why?	• Make sure the goal includes how the content can foster personal growth.

Let's also review how each Temperament might respond when following the TEACH Methodology.

Topic and Hook	Improvisers tend to gravitate towards subjects that are relevant, challenging and provide scope for being impressive. Any Hook that is active and hands-on will tend to draw them in. Stabilizers tend to gravitate towards subjects that are realistic, related to their past experience and provide scope for development. Any Hook that is practical and linked to the subject will tend to draw them in. Theorists tend to gravitate towards subjects that are intellectually interesting, appear to be leading edge and provide scope for independent thought. Any Hook that is relevant and thought provoking will tend to draw them in. Catalysts tend to gravitate towards subjects that relate to personal development, incorporate a focus on individual differences and provide scope for interacting with others. Any Hook that stimulates genuine interaction will tend to draw them in.
Engage the Audience	Improvisers and Stabilizers will tend to gravitate towards engagement activities that are hands-on and practical – the more senses engaged the better. Theorists and Catalysts will tend to gravitate towards engagement activities that are more conceptual and abstract – for Theorists, the more abstract, the better!
Abstract Information:	Improvisers and Stabilizers will tend to want to make sure that any abstract concepts, theories and models relate to current role/work/context and will want time spent in this area to be balanced with as much concrete practice as possible so that the link between the theory and the content is explicit. Theorists and Catalysts will tend to enjoy abstract content without necessarily wanting to focus on practical application. They tend naturally to imply the action from the theory.

Concrete Application:	While Active Testing is a key part of the neuroscience of learning, each Temperament tends to vary in the extent to which time and energy is invested in this stage.
	Improvisers will tend to want to focus in this area until they have developed tactical competence and/or become bored.
	Stabilizers will tend to want to focus in this area if this involves repetition to develop skill and if the activity directly relates to their current role.
	Theorists will tend to enjoy limited practical workshop application followed by time spent independently developing mastery.
	Catalysts will tend to enjoy application if they see growth, individual differences are validated and explored, and they have the opportunity to work collaboratively with others.
How to Apply	All Temperaments can benefit from personal reflection, which enables them to create their own meaning.

As you can see, understanding each Temperament's innate strengths and potential challenges can be very helpful for the Facilitator, both in terms of self-understanding and in developing and delivering lesson plans that appeal to all types.

Temperament and Stress

If Facilitators do not understand Temperament, they may un-intentially stress audience members by appearing to not honor individual participant's core needs. As a result, participants may react unconsciously to try to protect their core needs, and in this process display negative behaviors.

TIMEOUT!

If the Facilitator tries to address the negative behavior, rather than help the participant meet his/her core needs, this might escalate the situation, result in negative perception of the Facilitator and cause ripples in the group process.

This methodology and approach was originally described by Dr. Eve Delunas in her book *Survival Games Personalities Play.* In this book, we will briefly review some of the typical learning stressors, behaviors you might observe and present simple techniques for helping each Temperament regain balance. A more in-depth understanding of these Survival Strategies can be gained by reading Eve's book and/or referring to resources on the Type Academy web site.

Learning Stressors for Each Temperament

Below is a high-level list of the types of things that might stress each Temperament in the learning journey.

Improviser Stressors	Stabilizer Stressors
• Boredom, waiting, monotony. • No freedom to choose. • Appearing unimpressive to others. • Unnecessary structure, rules and restrictions. • Not able to demonstrate tactical competence, be noticed or make an impact. • Losing.	• Perceived lack of structure: no agenda, time lines for modules etc. • Unclear instructions and expectations from activities. • Not belonging or being needed in the team. • Facilitators they perceive to be unprepared or unprofessional. • Others who seem to be "getting away with something." • Lack of clear responsibilities.
Theorist Stressors	**Catalyst Stressors**
• Facilitators who appear incompetent or emotional. • Poorly constructed illogical arguments or points of view. • No ability to refine thought or ideas. • Lack of autonomy. • No opportunity to debate or question models. • Bureaucratic roadblocks or no big picture.	• Not being true to themselves. • Ethical violations. • Pressure from others to violate their own sense of integrity. • Witnessing mistreatment of others. • Betrayal, in-authenticity on the part of others. • No purpose or meaning.

Possible Stress Indicators

Below is a high-level list of the types of behaviors you might observe when each Temperament is experiencing stress when learning.

Improviser Possible Stress Indicators	Stabilizer Possible Stress Indicators
• Testing the boundaries; not doing tasks as assigned or disregarding policies and rules. • Appearing distracted – side conversations, doodling, etc. • Diverting the group into areas not associated with content. • Displaying angry outbursts or using humor to disrupt learning. • Taking advantage of the system. • Giving excuses for poor performance.	• Complaining about how others are allowed to "get away with things." • "Critical parenting" of other participants. • Rigidly adhering to policies and rules – getting frustrated with perceived disorganization. • Disengaging if not following a structure. • Worrying if agenda seems to be going off track. • Resenting others who seem to dominate.
Theorist Possible Stress Indicators	**Catalyst Possible Stress Indicators**
• Projecting an arrogant, superior, know-it-all attitude. • Offering frequent criticism and no positive feedback. • Constant critical questioning. • Being oblivious to the feelings and concerns of others. • Excessive debate over concepts, models or theories. • Developing extreme performance anxiety.	• Being overly accommodating and then becoming resentful. • Avoiding direct conflict. • Taking things too personally. • Using inaccurate mind reading; negatively interpreting the motives of others. • Being extra sensitive to criticism. • Finding themselves in the middle of others' conflicts.

Implementing Stress Solutions

The most effective solutions focus on enabling each Temperament to get core needs met and/or demonstrate their individual talent. Below are a few simple ideas for preventing escalation and restoring balance to the learning journey.

Improviser Stress Solutions	Stabilizer Stress Solutions
• Provide exciting, new challenges in terms of activities. • Give freedom to make choices. • Provide opportunities to be impressive. • Use movement and hands-on tasks to physically engage. • Avoid "critical parenting" messages: use choices with consequences. • Demonstrate appreciation with surprises. • Focus on learning outcomes not just process.	• Outline intended structure, objectives and time line. • Explain when and why changes need to be made to the flow of the session. • Be clear and calm about responsibilities, time expectations and outcomes when setting up activities. • Assign them roles and projects that are integral to the functioning of the group. • Demonstrate respect and use rewards to acknowledge their contributions. • Take responsibility for the workshop: admit errors/mistakes. • Hold people to performance standards and conduct regular temperature checks.
Theorist Stress Solutions	**Catalyst Stress Solutions**
• Offer maximum autonomy and intellectual independence. • Provide complicated problems to solve. • Specify outcomes--not procedures. • Use cause and effect logic. • Ask them to do research and to teach others what they know. • If you don't know – don't bluff – find relevant data.	• Highlight how content can foster personal growth in self and others. • Demonstrate that people matter. • Integrate creative activities that have a positive impact on group process. • Encourage them to identify, acknowledge, and express their needs and wants. • Emphasize the positive. • Appreciate them with a genuine acknowledgment of their meaningful contributions.

By refocusing on helping individuals meet their core needs, the group process can be restored and individuals will feel once more motivated to learn.

Four Interaction Style Patterns

In this section, we will introduce you to the Berens' Four Interaction Styles' Model. This is a separate theory from Temperament, and for each Temperament, there is one of each of the four Interaction Styles.

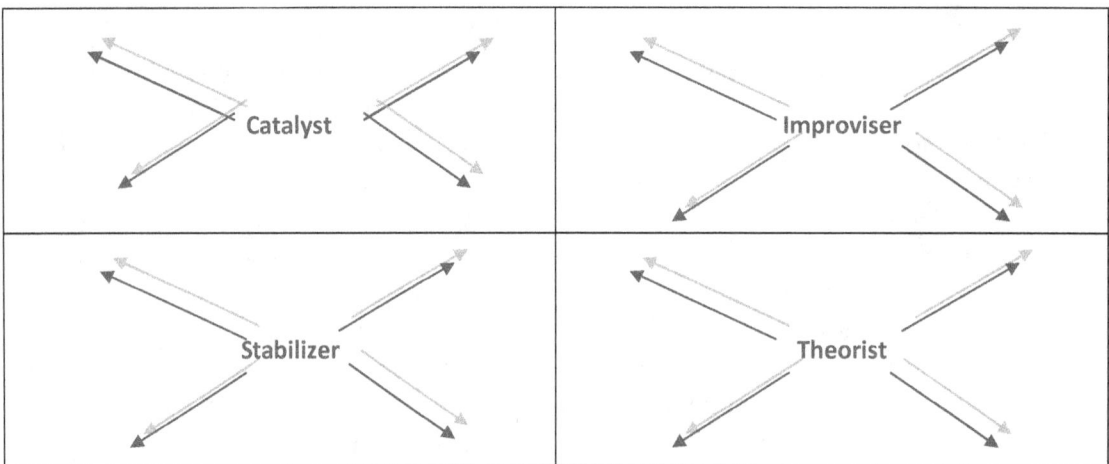

Chapter Five Visual Nine

This theory can help explain **"How"** we engage with others to get Temperament needs met. First, we will explore the Strengths and Challenges of each style as a Facilitator. From there we will learn how to flex your Style and approach to build rapport with students, as well as tips for how to adjust your delivery approach to the type of content you are covering in your workshop.

In the late 1990s, after working with psychological type for over 20 years, Linda Berens identified four holistic patterns of behavior and energy. As these patterns became more and more apparent, she found they were very similar to the Social Styles described by Bolton and Bolton as well as the basic patterns of DiSC based on the work of William Marston in **The Emotions of Normal People.**

Interaction Style can be defined as kinds of motoric predispositions (physical patterns of movement) to react to stimuli in certain ways. These patterns are characterized by a drive towards an aim, with an underlying core belief. The styles show up as observable energy flows and movements as we interact with others.

COACHING POINT

Interaction Style can be defined as a pattern of physical energy, pace, movement and outward behaviors correlated with mental aims, beliefs and innate talents that underlie the ways in which we engage with others to achieve our goals.

Interaction Style represents our mental-physical drive in relating to others.

Each of us has an innate preference for one of the four styles: one that we are naturally inclined to use. However, our style can also be influenced by the context in which we are operating. As a Facilitator, it can be helpful to understand our innate style in engaging with others so that we can choose the best Interaction Style for a specific context. The four Interaction Styles are:

- In-Charge
- Chart-the-Course
- Get-Things-Going
- Behind-the-Scenes

Understanding Facilitator Strengths and Challenges

> *"Only when there is difference between two persons in contact is it possible for those persons to achieve a new understanding."*
>
> *Gregory Bateson*

Self-Assessment

In the next few pages, we will introduce the four Interaction Styles using descriptions and a simple sorting activity. The purpose of this section is for you to self-identify your best-fit Interaction Style. As you review each description, try to identify which Interaction Style best describes your natural drive, energy and style as you engage with others. Rank "Most Like Me" with (1) and "Least Like Me" with (4).

COACHING POINT

By "Best-Fit" Interaction Style, we mean the style that you are most naturally inclined to use—the description of that style fits your normal behavior best.

Most of us have learned to demonstrate behaviors from all four Interaction Styles in different roles and contexts.

Our goal for this process is to help you differentiate between your innate versus learned behaviors.

Below are four statements. Review the statements and identify which decision making style best expresses your natural preference when engaging with others. Think particularly about the "Drive" statement. Which statement best reflects How you engage with others?

Statement One	Statement Two
My drive is to ensure that some action is being taken by me or others towards the attainable goal. I like to make quick decisions to get an achievable result.	My drive is to anticipate obstacles and have a process to achieve the expected goal. I like to make deliberate decisions to get a desired result.
Statement Three	**Statement Four**
My drive is to involve others in order to obtain buy-in to the agreed goal. I like to make collaborative decisions to get an embraced result.	My drive is to get as much input as I can from relevant sources to achieve a goal with quality. I like to make consultative decisions to get the best result possible.

Each statement is written to appeal to one of the four Interaction Styles for the reasons listed below.

Statement One: In-Charge

Those with an In-Charge Style share a drive to take action towards an achievable result. As a result, they tend to be comfortable taking risks, make quick decisions and experience a degree of stress when nothing is happening when it needs to.

Statement Two: Chart-the-Course

Those with a Chart-the-Course Style share a drive to think through a process to the desired result. As a result, they tend to naturally see potential obstacles and plan out a course to mitigate risk and achieve reward. They can experience a degree of stress when they unable to anticipate what might happen.

Statement Three: Get-Things-Going

Those with a Get-Things-Going Style share a drive to involve others and get them to buy into a process/action. As a result, they tend to be comfortable reaching out to others for input and gaining consensus to any decision. They may experience a degree of stress when people appear to demonstrate a lack of interest.

Statement Four: Behind-the-Scenes

Those with a Behind-the-Scenes Style share a drive to gain as much relevant input as possible so they can achieve the best result. As a result, they tend to be comfortable stepping back, integrating information and reconciling ideas. They may experience a degree of stress when others take credit for their ideas or when there is not enough time or input to make a quality decision.

Chapter Five: Visuals Ten – Thirteen

Get-Things-Going: Let's Think Together Representing the ability to reach out and engage people as part of the process. 	**Behind-the-Scenes: Let's Think About It** Representing the ability to gather all relevant data in an unobtrusive way and respond as required. 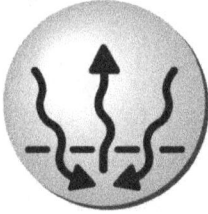
In-Charge: Let's Action our Thinking Representing the ability to move quickly and directly from one point to another. 	**Chart-the-Course: Let's Think Ahead** Representing the ability to establish the milestones and correct mid-course if necessary. 

Credit to "Type Trilogy Card Set and Guidebook" – see Appendix for more information

Below are some high-level descriptions for each Interaction Style pattern.

IN-CHARGE
• Like to move quickly toward a goal.
• Believe that it is worth taking a risk to decide now; corrections can be made later.
• Tend to appear quick moving, confident, and determined.
• Have a fast-paced tone of voice and energy.
• Tend to have a straightforward communication style.
• Tend to naturally take action and lead a group to an objective.
• Innately focus on executing tasks and removing obstacles.
• Help to get things accomplished (often through people).
• Possess an urgent need to complete tasks.
• Are stressed by the appearance of nothing happening at the time that it needs to.
• People will see you: taking the reins, setting the goals, showing energy and resilience, and controlling the environment.

CHART-THE-COURSE
• Like to think ahead and identify the goal.
• Believe that it is worth taking the time to look forward to envision what might happen.
• Tend to appear calm, intense, and self-contained.
• Have a measured tone of voice and energy.
• Tend to have a formal communication style.
• Tend to naturally define the goal, foresee potential obstacles and then map the key milestones required to reach the goal.
• Innately focus on defining a sensible course of action.
• Help to keep projects and teams on track by comparing ideal status with current position.
• Experience a pressing need to anticipate.
• Are stressed by not knowing what will happen.
• People will see you: preparing thoroughly, creating and monitoring a time line, expecting problems, and defining the process.

GET-THINGS-GOING
• Like to facilitate involvement from the group.
• Believe that it is worth the time spent to engage others.
• Tend to appear expressive, upbeat, and casual.
• Have an enthusiastic tone of voice and energy.
• Tend to have a persuasive communication style.
• Tend to involve others naturally in decisions to achieve buy-in.
• Innately focus on motivating others and raising energy levels.
• Help to raise commitment by focusing on exploring options.
• Possess an urgent need to draw in others.
• Are stressed by being left out or by others not appearing eager.
• People will see you: encouraging participation, bringing everyone together, motivating people to act, and using fun to engage others.

BEHIND-THE-SCENES
• Like to invest in the inclusion of many inputs.
• Believe that multiple points of view can be reconciled.
• Tend to appear approachable, friendly, and patient.
• Have a gentle tone of voice and energy.
• Tend to have an unassuming communication style.
• Tend to naturally gather input from various sources and then repackage that data in an original way.
• Innately focus on listening to others.
• Help to avoid mistakes by gathering as much relevant information and data on a subject as possible.
• Experience a pressing need to integrate.
• Are stressed by not having enough time/input or not being given credit.
• People will see you: supporting performers, "stage managing the production," listening to and accommodating many needs, and employing a consultative approach.

Credit to "Understanding Yourself and Others: An Introduction to Interaction Styles 2.0" – see **Appendix for more information**

Let us compare and contrast now some of the key characteristics of each style.

Chapter Five: Visual Fourteen

In-Charge

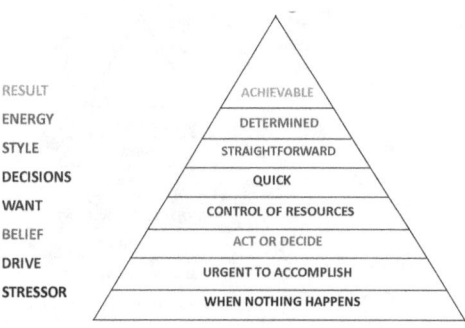

RESULT	ACHIEVABLE
ENERGY	DETERMINED
STYLE	STRAIGHTFORWARD
DECISIONS	QUICK
WANT	CONTROL OF RESOURCES
BELIEF	ACT OR DECIDE
DRIVE	URGENT TO ACCOMPLISH
STRESSOR	WHEN NOTHING HAPPENS

INTERACTION STYLE	IN-CHARGE
Aim	Get an achievable result: what can get done in the time frame
Energy	Determined: direct and relatively single-minded
Style	**Straightforward** • Commanding • Confident • Driven • Social for a Purpose
Pace	Fast: tend to look like they are in a hurry – even when they are not
Decisions	Quick and expedient: the decision can be modified as new information becomes available
Want	Control over resources: to make sure action is taken
Core Belief	It's worth the risk to go ahead and act or decide
Drive	Urgent need to accomplish: feel on edge if actions are not being taken
Stressors	If "things" are out of control or if "the In-Charge person" is not in control Nothing is being accomplished
How to Help	Tell them the reasons Help them see something is being done
Talents	Lead to a goal Execute actions Provide means Mobilize resources

Chapter Five: Visual Fifteen

Chart-the-Course

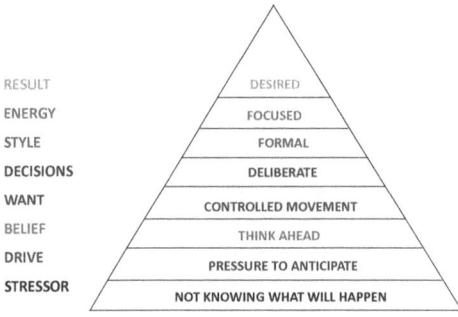

RESULT	DESIRED
ENERGY	FOCUSED
STYLE	FORMAL
DECISIONS	DELIBERATE
WANT	CONTROLLED MOVEMENT
BELIEF	THINK AHEAD
DRIVE	PRESSURE TO ANTICIPATE
STRESSOR	NOT KNOWING WHAT WILL HAPPEN

INTERACTION STYLE	CHART-THE-COURSE
Aim	Get a desired result: what is right for the situation
Energy	Focused: quietly directed toward the goal
Style	**Formal/Self-Contained** • Reserved • Intense • Calm • Composed
Measured	Measured: Step back to think through the steps and potential obstacles
Decisions	Deliberate and purposeful: the decision and approach has been thought through
Want	Directed progress: to make sure the correct action is taken
Core Belief	It's worth the effort to think ahead and reach the goal
Drive	Pressing need to anticipate: feel on edge if they do not have the time to reflect
Stressors	Not knowing what is likely to happen Don't see progress
How to Help	Be calm and direct Let them know what to expect
Talents	See end result Monitor progress Devise a plan Give guidance

Chapter Five: Visual Sixteen

Get-Things-Going

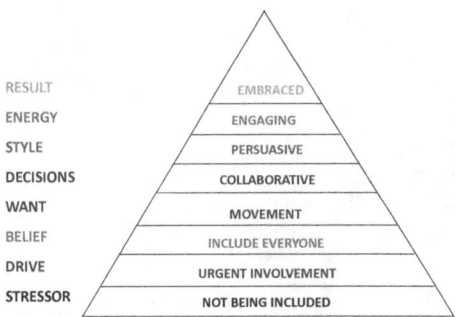

RESULT	EMBRACED
ENERGY	ENGAGING
STYLE	PERSUASIVE
DECISIONS	COLLABORATIVE
WANT	MOVEMENT
BELIEF	INCLUDE EVERYONE
DRIVE	URGENT INVOLVEMENT
STRESSOR	NOT BEING INCLUDED

INTERACTION STYLE	GET-THINGS-GOING
Aim	Get an embraced result: with others really believing in the outcome
Engaging	Enthusiastic: animated, upbeat and buoyant
Style	**Persuasive** • Active • Welcoming • Casual • Expressive
Pace	Energetic: bouncy and lively
Decisions	Collaborative and engaged: the decision has everyone working toward the same goal
Want	Collective movement: seeing progress is occurring as the group is engaged
Core Belief	It's worth the energy to involve everyone and get them to want to participate to achieve the goal
Drive	Urgent need to involve: feel on edge if others are not engaging with the idea or process
Stressors	Not being involved in what is going on Feel unliked or unaccepted
How to Help	Listen as they talk things out Encourage their active participation
Talents	Explore options Share insights Facilitate Brainstorm ideas

Chapter Five: Visual Seventeen

Behind-the-Scenes

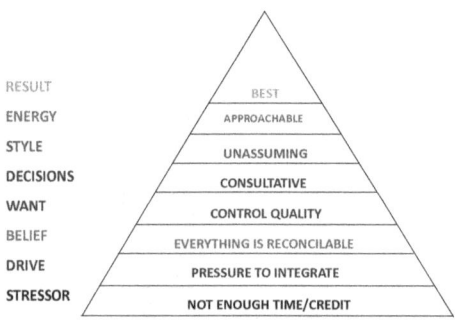

INTERACTION STYLE	BEHIND-THE-SCENES
Aim	Get the best result possible: with access to as many resources as are relevant
Energy	Approachable: relaxed and open
Style	**Unassuming** • Agreeable • Gentle • Patient • Supportive
Pace	Considered: comfortable exploring as much pertinent data as possible
Decisions	Consultative and integrated: the decision involves gathering information one-on-one; then the individual makes the decision or pushes for the decision they want, if they are not the sole decision maker
Want	Control over excellence: checking the quality against the ideal outcome
Core Belief	It's worth the time to integrate and reconcile many inputs
Drive	Pressing need to "connect the dots": feel on edge if ideas or solutions haven't incorporated as much relevant input as possible
Stressors	Not enough data or credit Being pressed to decide too quickly
How to help	Be friendly but not too expressive Give time to reflect and integrate
Talents	Support others achieve a result that has the widest possible support Reconcile inconsistencies Encourage participation Sustain efforts

EXERCISE 5.5: IDENTIFYING YOUR INTERACTION STYLE

- Review the key attributes of each Interaction Style.
- Pick out the aspects of each style that you identify with most.
- Try to focus on your innate style rather than the characteristics that are required in your current work role.
- Which Interaction Style appears like the best fit for you?

TRY IT ON! IDENTIFYING YOUR INTERACTION STYLE

In-Charge

_____

_____

Chart-the-Course

_____

_____

Get-Things-Going

_____

_____

Behind-the-Scenes

_____

_____

Best Fit

_____

_____

If you are struggling with identifying your best-fit Interaction Style, there are several options:

- Continue reading the additional data in this chapter.
- Review some of the resources in the Appendix.
- Check out web sites such as www.type-academy.com and www.lindaberens.com

COACHING POINT: INTERACTION STYLE

Understanding Interaction Style has many benefits in teaching and learning:

- As a Facilitator to understand your strengths and challenges.
- To identify how to flex your style to build rapport with different types.
- To choose which style to use when facilitating different sections of a workshop.

Strengths and Challenges

> "Be yourself, but always your better self."
>
> *Karl G Maeser*

As you can see from this quotation, each Interaction Style inherently tends to possess some strengths and potential blind spots. As a Facilitator, if we understand both our strengths and potential challenges, we can raise our interaction effectiveness and improve relationships with our participants.

COACHING POINT

Remember when facilitating learning, it is really important to consider your Interaction Style. This will influence the energy, pace and movement you use in the workshop!

Here are a few sample ideas for strengths and challenges of each Interaction Style as a Facilitator.

IN-CHARGE STRENGTHS	IN-CHARGE POTENTIAL BLIND SPOTS
Strong focus on achievable results: able to cover a lot of content in a short period of time	May try to include too much content and overwhelm those who need more time to absorb information
Can give clear directives when setting up activities, clarifying learning points or keeping a session on track	May be too abrupt, appear bossy and shut down audience participation
Can make rapid decisions with confidence: will know quickly how to adapt content to differing audience needs.	May not take others' emotions into account when under a time pressure
Responsive, quick thinking and willing to change direction if the content requires it	May not take the time to listen to the participants' input or cut them off mid-sentence

CHART-THE-COURSE STRENGTHS	CHART-THE-COURSE POTENTIAL BLIND SPOTS
Strong focus on the goal for the workshop and the logical process to achieve the desired result	May not be able to adapt, or may need more time to adapt, if the course needs to be restructured in the moment based on participant needs
Follow a thought-through development methodology	Could be more time consuming than necessary
Focused and calm approach: plot and consider the options before acting	Effort mapping out response to the audience might be perceived as lack of engagement
Constantly track progress towards learning goal	May not be tuned in to non-task activities

GET-THINGS-GOING STRENGTHS	GET-THINGS-GOING POTENTIAL BLIND SPOTS
Enthusiastic and expressive in delivering workshops with positive feedback	May get discouraged if the audience does not demonstrate enthusiasm
Naturally reaches out to find options and possibilities that the group can commit to	May talk too much, or too quickly, in the drive to raise the energy and commitment of the group
Positive energy and sense of fun can motivate participants to be engaged and involved	Positive energy may overwhelm some styles
Open communication style allows the group to explore ideas and possibilities	May struggle with staying focused and/or sticking to the schedule.

BEHIND-THE-SCENES STRENGTHS	BEHIND-THE-SCENES POTENTIAL BLIND SPOTS
Helps participants to think through all relevant information, ideas and approaches	Approach may appear too laborious for the other three styles
Good at listening to audience needs	May not direct the workshop to get back on track when needed
Focus on the quality of the end result means willing to stick with topics until learning has occurred.	May feel some conflict between the time frame for meaningful learning and bottom line considerations
Willing to provide support as needed to achieve the goal: comfortable stepping back to allow the group to explore important subjects	May feel uncomfortable asking challenging questions

EXERCISE 5.6: YOUR STRENGTHS AND POTENTIAL CHALLENGES

- Based on your Interaction Style assessment, what do you identify as your 2-3 strengths as a Facilitator?
- What could be your potential challenges?

TRY IT ON: YOUR STRENGTHS AND POTENTIAL CHALLENGES

Write your ideas here...

Strengths as a Facilitator?

_____

_____

_____

Potential Challenges?

_____

_____

_____

Flexing Interaction Style

There are two key elements in flexing Interaction Style:

1. When interacting one-on-one with participants – either answering questions or discussing subject material.
2. Adapting your style to the type of learning that you are facilitating.

In this section, we will explore how to improve one-on-one interactions. In the next section, we will discuss the importance of using different energies for varying components of the workshop. What makes the role of the Facilitator so complex is that the Facilitator may experience a constant drive to engage with the audience in his/her preferred style, combined with the need to balance one-on-one interaction and rapport building, along with the importance of varying delivery approach according to course context.

> ## "The only person's behavior you can directly impact is your own"
> *Source unknown*

FOUL!

It can be easy to assume you can directly influence your students to change their behavior. In reality, a Facilitator can only directly change their own behavior in the hope that this will influence participants to change theirs.

Below are some high-level ideas for how to adapt your style one-on-one to participants' energy.

Interacting with In-Charge

- Demonstrate that you are sensitive to time pressure
- Talk about the achievable goal for the learning event
- Utilize humor to disarm them
- Make sure you know where you are in the agenda so they can see movement towards the end result
- If necessary, push back and be assertive with them
- Ask challenging questions
- Use a fast pace and direct eye contact
- Apply a firm tone of voice

Interacting with Chart-the-Course

- Think things through – don't jump in with an immediate response
- Talk about the desired goal and the process the workshop is following to achieve this goal

- Be calm and direct
- Make sure you emphasize key milestones and any potential roadblocks in achieving the workshop goals
- Slow down and listen to their input
- Be matter of fact in your communication style
- Stay focused in any conversation – don't get side tracked
- Give distance to digest and don't be surprised if no emotion is demonstrated

Interacting with Get-Things-Going

- Listen and demonstrate interest, using open body language
- Talk about the importance of an engaged goal and the evolving process of building involvement
- Use enthusiasm and energy to show you are interested
- Make sure you put a positive spin on any ideas you are sharing
- Deliver information using an up-beat tone of voice
- Highlight the benefits of one or two options
- Use personal examples and an up-beat pace
- Reinforce ideas with positive comments to show you appreciate their exploration process

Interacting with Behind-the-Scenes

- Allow pauses and time for the other to speak
- Talk about the importance of a quality goal and the need for integrating as much relevant data as possible
- Use an open and unassuming approach: approachable body language and gentle tone
- Make sure you allow time to process key information
- Build in thinking time either before or after the interaction
- Offer choices and suggest pros and cons of different choices
- Don't pressure to make a decision immediately – they will dig in their heels!
- Manage your pace by asking questions and listening carefully to the answer

EXERCISE 5.7: FLEXING YOUR ENERGY

- Think of a time when you felt some stress, where it seemed something in the interpersonal dynamic was not working.
- How might this have related to Interaction Style? Yours? Theirs?
- What might you do differently in the future to improve the effectiveness of this conversation?

TRY IT ON – FLEXING YOUR ENERGY

My Best Fit Interaction Style is…

_____

_____

_____

My Assessment of the other person's Interaction Style is…

_____

_____

_____

Sources of Stress?

_____

_____

_____

Improve conversation by…

_____

_____

_____

FOUL!

When we describe flexing energy, the analogy we use is like building up a muscle. The more we flex, the better our ability becomes to "match" the other person's style in a more natural manner. We are not talking about manipulating the other person – there has to be a genuine desire to create rapport.

As you can see, our Interaction Style can influence the dynamic when we are interacting one-on-one with students. This can cause us either to feel "at ease" with a participant, or create a sense of tension in the relationship. If we can flex our energy, we will be able to hold more effective one-on-one conversations with our audience members.

Four Interaction Styles and TEACH

In this section, we will explore how to adapt our style and approach to different course elements.

FOUL!

There can be a misconception that the "best" facilitation style is Get-Things-Going because this energy focuses on audience engagement – a key element in Active Learning. In fact, flexing our energy to the type of content is a more effective way of facilitating effective sessions.

Let's review some ideas below for when each style might be appropriate to use when facilitating. For each suggestion, we will explain in what stage of the T.E.A.C.H. process each might occur. As a reminder, here are the steps in T.E.A.C.H.:

T	**Topic and Hook:** State the subject
E	**Engage the Audience:** Conduct an activity in order to enlist the group in learning and to identify what they already know
A	**Abstract Information:** Introduce concepts, theories, models, information, techniques, and skills
C	**Concrete Application:** Use examples, exercises and activities to cement learning
H	**How to: apply** Encourage learners to take responsibility to implement learning.

It can be effective to use Chart-the-Course energy when....	**It can be effective to use Behind-the-Scenes energy when....**
• Defining learning objectives (Introduction) • Listing the agenda (Introduction) • Anticipating barriers to learning (Introduction/any module) • Setting up the purpose of exercises (Primarily E and C) • Giving instructions (Primarily E and C) • Previewing and reviewing modules (T-Hook) • Reviewing key learning points (any module) and/or deciding key action steps (Any module)	• Surfacing important issues (Introduction/any module) • The group has key input on a subject (E, A and C) • When subjects arise that are not directly related to the content and yet are important for learning to occur (Any module) • If there is a tough discussion that needs to be guided (Any module) • To encourage individuals to contribute (Any module) • When the audience has content knowledge and you do not (Any module) • When a change has to be made to achieve the best quality result (Any module)
It can be effective to use In-Charge energy when....	**It can be effective to use Get-Things-Going energy when....**
• The group needs to get back on track (Any module) • The energy has dropped (Any module) • In the background to achieve the learning goal (Any module) • To be clear about status and options (Any module) • To edit content to achieve a learning goal (Any module) • To "protect" a participant in order to maintain a safe learning environment (Any module) (see more on Directive Facilitation in Chapter Three) • To make/reinforce key learning points	• At the beginning to engage the group (Introduction and T-Hook) • In setting audience expectations to ensure involvement (Introduction and T-Hook) • During activities to reinforce positive learning (E and C) • To lighten the mood – provide a sense of fun (Any module) • In large group discussions to encourage contributions (Any module) • When the audience participation is dropping (Any module) • At the end of the workshop to leave the group feeling positive. (Summary)

As you can see, it can be hard to be "Prescriptive" with when to use each Interaction Style, as learning can be so contextual – what you think should happen, might or might not! Therefore, this means a Flawless Facilitator remains tuned into the group dynamic at all times, recognizes their innate response to any situation, and then chooses the most appropriate style to maintain learning.

EXERCISE 5.8: INTERACTION STYLE AND LEARNING

What have been your insights about the style of energy needed for different contexts? What might you do differently as a result?

<hr>

TRY IT ON – INTERACTION STYLE AND LEARNING

Insights?

_____

_____

_____

Do Differently?

_____

_____

_____

Combining Temperament and Interaction Style: 16 Types

TIMEOUT! TEMPERAMENT TO INTERACTION STYLE

As described earlier, there are four versions of each Temperament. While the core needs, values, and talents are similar for all four versions of the Temperament, the way they interact with others can be very different based on Interaction Style – the "How" lens.

There are four ways that the **Improviser** tends to engage with others:

- **In-Charge** tends to be direct, with a fast use of time and focus on internal logical analysis.
- **Chart-the-Course** tends to be direct, more thoughtful with an ability to figure out the best course of action.
- **Get-Things-Going** tends to be more playful, enthusiastic and values-based.
- **Behind-the-Scenes** tends to be more reflective, caring and easy-going.

There are four ways that the **Stabilizer** tends to engage with others:

- **In-Charge** tends to be direct, reality based with a strong drive to systematically organize the external world.
- **Chart-the-Course** tends to be direct, more thoughtful with an ability to use past experience as the basis for logical actions.
- **Get-Things-Going** tends to be more enthusiastic, people-focused and desiring of harmony/consensus.
- **Behind-the-Scenes** tends to be more reflective, loyal and hard-working in support of the team.

There are four ways that the **Theorist** tends to engage with others:

- **In-Charge** tends to be direct, with a strong future vision and a strong drive to systematically organize the external world.

- **Chart-the-Course** tends to be direct, with an ability to reflect and then articulate new concepts or models.
- **Get-Things-Going** tends to be more animated, possibilities-focused and desiring of new mental frameworks.
- **Behind-the-Scenes** tends to be intensely analytical, in the quest for intellectual purity and accuracy.

There are four ways that the **Catalyst** tends to engage with others:

- **In-Charge** tends to be direct, with a strong future vision and a strong drive to engage others in pursuit of this vision.
- **Chart-the-Course** tends to be empathetic with an ability to effortlessly integrate people and systems.
- **Get-Things-Going** tends to be enthusiastic, possibilities-focused and desiring of helping people and teams develop to their potential.
- **Behind-the-Scenes** tends to be intensely values-based, tolerant and driven to align external behaviors with internal beliefs.

Chapter Five:
Visual Eighteen

Get-Things-Going	Behind-the-Scenes	Get-Things-Going	Behind-the-Scenes
Catalyst		**Improviser**	
In-Charge	Chart-the-Course	In-Charge	Chart-the-Course
Get-Things-Going	Behind-the-Scenes	Get-Things-Going	Behind-the-Scenes
Stabilizer		**Theorist**	
In-Charge	Chart-the-Course	In-Charge	Chart-the-Course

TIMEOUT! INTERACTION STYLE TO TEMPERAMENT

As described earlier, there are four versions of each Interaction Style: while the outward behaviors may look similar, the motivation to act may be different. The differences within each Interaction Style may relate to "Why we do what we do" – our core Temperament.

There are four ways that the **In-Charge** style tends to show up:

- Executing actions as required in the current moment (preferred by Improviser).
- Making rapid decisions to organize and structure reality based on past experience (preferred by Stabilizer).
- Mobilizing resources to accomplish a clear future goal (preferred by Theorist).
- Mentoring to achieve developmental goals for people (preferred by Catalyst).

There are four ways that the **Chart-the-Course** style might show up:

- Evaluating the most logical plan of attack, by balancing risk and reward based on the current reality (preferred by Improviser).
- Reviewing previous experience to create the most methodical plan (preferred by Stabilizer).
- Envisioning a future and creating a systematic process to achieve the goal (preferred by Theorist).
- Having insights on future potential and working with an individual to develop talents (preferred by Catalyst).

There are four ways that the **Get-Things-Going** style may show up:

- Using playfulness to help others feel valued and involved (preferred by Improviser).
- Arranging tasks to make life harmonious and easier (preferred by Stabilizer).
- Brainstorming possibilities to engage people in multiple points of view (preferred by Theorist).
- Imagining options to advocate a cause and help people develop (preferred by Catalyst).

There are four ways that the **Behind-the-Scenes** style may show up:

- Supporting those they care about through their actions (preferred by Improviser).
- Reviewing previous experience to support the team in the most realistic way (preferred by Stabilizer).
- Analyzing and integrating multiple models to originate new concepts (preferred by Theorist).
- Valuing diversity and highlighting opportunities for developing others. (preferred by Catalyst).

In the next Chapter, we will review these 16 types in more detail.

Chapter Summary

For a Facilitator to be effective, they need to recognize the strengths and challenges of their personal Temperament and Interaction Style when leading workshops. In addition, they have to be able to adapt one-on-one and to different learning subjects. In this Chapter, we have reviewed two different "type" theories, Temperament and Interaction Style,

Temperament is important to understand because it gives insights into core needs, talents, values, communication style and potential behaviors. This framework can also be useful for deciding how to design and deliver workshops that appeal to the needs of all four Temperaments, both as adults and as children, to motivate each to learn.

Interaction Style is important because it provides information about drive, energy, potential sources of conflict and ideas for adapting style. It can be helpful for investigating specific strategies for improving one-on-one interaction, while also adjusting style depending on the element and context of the session being covered.

Key Principles Reviewed

- Understanding Temperament and Interaction Style can help us become better facilitators by managing our individual strengths and challenges as well as adapting to appeal to all audiences.
- **Temperament** can help to explain Why we do what we do. The four Temperaments, as named by Linda Berens, are Improviser, Stabilizer, Theorist and Catalyst.
- Identify your innate needs, values and talents as a Facilitator.
- Position the same message in four different ways to appeal to different Temperaments – i.e. Speak Four Languages.
- Watch for clues for Temperament even at a young age.
- Refine course design using the knowledge of Temperament within the T.E.A.C.H. methodology.
- **Interaction Style** can help to explain How we engage with others to get our needs met. The four Interaction Styles, as named by Linda Berens, are In-Charge, Chart-the-Course, Get-Things-Going and Behind-the-Scenes.
- Identify your natural aim, drive, pace and movement as a Facilitator.
- Practice flexing energy in order to create genuine one-on-one rapport.
- Use different styles throughout any workshop based on the course content and group dynamic.
- By combining the two theories of Temperament and Interaction Style, we end up with 16 types.

SCORECARD

- What do you think is your best-fit Temperament? What will you do differently as a result?
- What did you learn about speaking four languages? How will you use this knowledge when designing and/or delivering your content?
- What did you learn about each Temperament as children? What will you do differently as a result?

- What did you learn about causing stress to participants when facilitating? What will you do differently as a result?
- What do you think is your best-fit Interaction Style? What will you do differently as a result?
- How will you begin to practice flexing to different Interaction Styles?
- How will you ensure you remain alert to the group dynamic and adapt your approach if your innate style is not working?

N: NURTURE DIFFERENT THINKING STYLES

In this chapter, we will continue to build on your Flawless Facilitator's toolkit by introducing Cognitive Processes and describing the concept of Whole Type. The reason for doing this is that, in order for a Facilitator to appeal to all types of learners, we need to include four types of information and understand four different preferred patterns for making decisions (the third lens of Whole Type). This information can help from the Facilitator's perspective when designing content. It can also help in catering for different students' learning preferences. Finally, we will use the framework of Whole Type to provide high-level descriptions of each Type Pattern and specific information about each Type's learning preferences.

GAME PLAN

You will learn about:

- The Three Type Lenses: Whole Type
- The Eight Cognitive Processes
- The Eight Cognitive Processes and Learning
- Facilitator Strengths and Challenges
- Learning and Whole Type

The Three Type Lenses: Whole Type

> "Whole Type is a methodology where multiple complementary models (Temperament, Interaction Style and Cognitive Processes) are integrated to provide more in-depth insight into natural preferences, needs, drive and potential behaviors."
>
> *Susan Nash.*

In the previous chapter, we reviewed Facilitator versatility against the backdrop of Temperament (Why we do what we do) and Interaction Style (How we engage with others to meet our Temperament core needs). Now, we will connect these theories with Cognitive Processes – "What" information we naturally select and "What" criteria we naturally use to make decisions – our Thinking Style. When we synthesize these three concepts, we use the phrase Whole Type.

Chapter Six:
Visual One

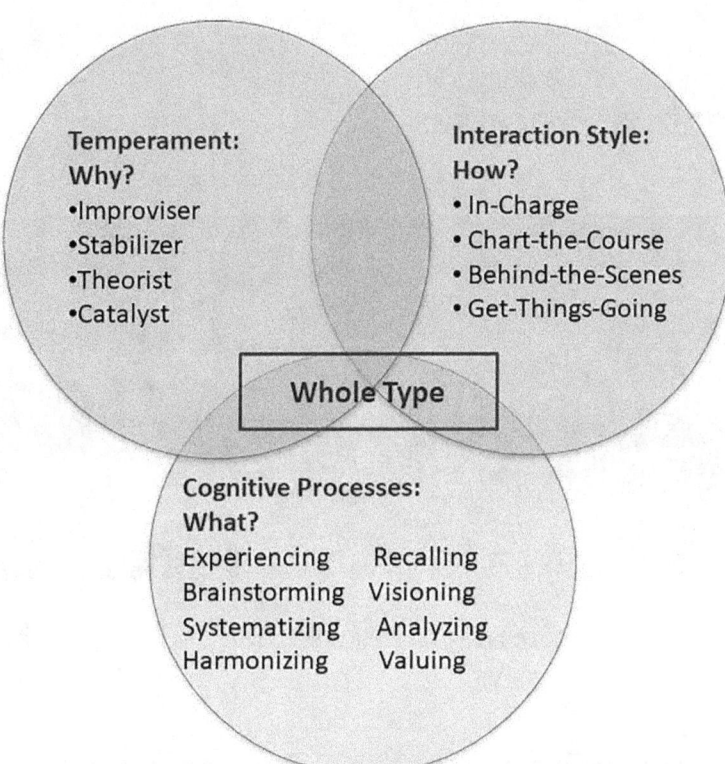

TIMEOUT!

What makes these three separate theories so relevant to Facilitators, is that they can be integrated to enable delivery practices and learning to be reviewed and optimized from three different and yet complementary perspectives.

Before we spend more time exploring Whole Type and learning, let's define the third lens, our Thinking Style, in more detail.

The Eight Cognitive Processes

> "You can't really have a continuing direction for your life until your best liked, most trusted, most preferred kind of perception and your best trusted, most liked and most preferred kind of judgment have agreed on what is to be desired."
>
> *Isabel Briggs-Myers*

The concept of Cognitive Processes originates from Carl Jung in his 1921 book *Psychological Types*.

Jung believed that we spend all our time either **gathering information** using our four Perceiving Cognitive Processes and/or **making decisions** using our four Judging Cognitive Processes.

TIME OUT!

- Cognitive Processes describe the specific ways in which individuals take in and make decisions about information.
- There are eight Cognitive Processes.
- Jung believed that each Type tends to prefer one Cognitive Process to gather information and one Cognitive Process to make decisions.

- He used the word preference to describe how a Cognitive Process is easier to use, takes less energy, is more natural and as a result, more consistently used.
- However, he also recognized that every individual potentially has the capacity to access all eight Cognitive Processes to a greater or lesser extent.

Below are the names of the Eight Cognitive Processes.

INFORMATION GATHERING: PERCEIVING	DECISION MAKING: JUDGING
Experiencing	Systematizing
Recalling	Analyzing
Brainstorming	Harmonizing
Visioning	Valuing

TIMEOUT!

- The way that each person reacts to any given situation is often the result of a complex interaction between multiple Cognitive Processes.
- Rather like a pinball machine, an individual may bounce from using one Cognitive Process to another quickly depending on the situation and his/her comfort with each function.

Cognitive Processes are relevant from both the perspective of the Facilitator (in terms of the information they naturally gravitate towards and the criteria they use to make decisions) as well as in terms of the importance of designing content to appeal to all types of students.

Information Gathering Cognitive Processes (Perceiving)

There are four ways of gathering information from which to make decisions. Every individual can use all four ways, however some are easier for us to use than others, take less conscious thought, and require less energy.

Let's share below an overview of each information gathering Cognitive Process as it may appear when it is preferred.

CHARACTERISTICS	EXPERIENCING	RECALLING	BRAINSTORMING	VISIONING
Definition	This Cognitive Process moves outward for the immediate, acute uptake and exploration of sensory data from the external world through senses such as sight, sound, touch, taste, and smell.	This Cognitive Process moves inward to recall past experiences and compare the present information to a historical data bank of stored sensory data and internal thoughts, feelings, sensations and memories.	This Cognitive Process moves outward for the unrestrained exploration and interpretation of new ideas, patterns and possibilities that are not inherently obvious.	This Cognitive Process moves inward for the unconscious correlation of conceptual ideas, possibilities and symbols that enter consciousness as a whole system or idea.
Description	• Gathering concrete data in the here and now • Seeing options in the moment • Reading sight, sound, smell, taste and body language cues immediately • Being drawn to act on current reality	• Gathering sensory data and using it to compare and contrast with past sensory experiences • Past data can be viewed almost like a videotape • Knowing what's real • Being drawn inwards to reflect on past experience	• Implying patterns and meanings from current information • Reading between the lines to what is not obvious • Thinking out loud and hypothesizing • Being drawn outwards to explore possibilities	• Assimilating data unconsciously • Solution or ideas come into consciousness as a complete picture • Associated with "ahas" and shower solutions • Being drawn inwards to incubate ideas
Time Orientation	Present: What is here and now	Past: What was	Unlimited: What could be	Future: What will be

CHARACTERISTICS	EXPERIENCING	RECALLING	BRAINSTORMING	VISIONING
Possible Signals	• Jumping into action • Reading and commenting on minute changes in body language	• Appearing more cautious as data is processed • Talk about what worked and didn't work in the past	• Appearing positive and upbeat about possibilities • Constantly suggesting "What if…? What if…?"	• Appearing to step back before suggesting the total idea or solution • Will say things such as "I just know"
Advantages as a Facilitator	• Alert to small changes in the environment • Able to seize opportunities • Naturally makes learning active	• Protector of group memory • Prevent the reinvention of the wheel and repeating the same mistakes • Naturally remembers relevant examples?	• Stimulator of new ideas and possibilities • Energy can help achieve breakthroughs • Naturally can connect ideas	• Initiator of innovative solutions • Able to simplify complex models • Naturally able to synthesize and connect ideas
Possible Challenges	• May jump in too quickly without the big picture • May constantly seek new sensory stimuli when bored and deviate from any course plan	• May struggle when beginning new tasks or projects for which they have no experience • May appear negative as they talk about what cannot be done	• May be reluctant to settle on one solution as multiple possibilities emerge • May seek continual change and resist structuring learning	• May be reluctant to accept other's viewpoints • Waiting for the solution to come to mind could delay projects and course design

COACHING POINT

It can be hard to identify your best-fit Cognitive Process because we probably have had exposure to, and practice using, all four Information Gathering processes through our schooling and family background. IN ADDITION, one of these Cognitive Processes will still be more natural for us to access. The Appendix lists other resources that can be used to refine knowledge of Cognitive Processes.

Decision Making Cognitive Processes (Judging)

There are four ways of making decisions from the information gathered. Every individual has the capacity to use all four ways, however some are easier for us to use than others, take less conscious thought and require less energy. Let's share below an overview of each decision making Cognitive Process, as it may appear when it is preferred.

CHARACTERISTICS	SYSTEMATIZING	ANALYZING	BRAINSTORMING	VISIONING
Definition	This Cognitive Process makes decisions using logical, objective criteria to structure the external world in the most efficient way to achieve the end goal. The output can appear as a structured plan.	This Cognitive Process makes decisions where the information gathered is categorized and evaluated against a model using internal logical criteria. The output can appear as a new frame of reference.	This Cognitive Process makes decisions using subjective criteria to optimize interpersonal harmony considering what is appropriate. The output can appear as a supportive and safe environment.	This Cognitive Process makes decisions based on subjective internal values and a belief system to support individual differences. The output can appear as a fair and unbiased environment.
Description	• Making decisions using logical criteria to sequence and organize resources to achieve goals in the external world • Using causal effect logic	• Making decisions where information gathered is evaluated and sorted against an internal mental model • Analyzing data for what is logical	• Making decisions using subjective criteria to optimize interpersonal harmony and achieve consensus decisions • Understanding what is appropriate in a situation	• Making decisions based on subjective values and an internal beliefs system to be tolerant of differences • Comprehending what is fair in a situation
Possible Signals	• Push for closure • Clear boundaries in actions: who is responsible for what and when	• Comfortable with gathering new data • Using questioning of ideas and data to clarify logic	• Push for closure • Demonstrate warmth and openness creating a safe inclusive environment	• Flexible and adaptable • Appear easy going and listen to and value diverse points of view

CHARACTERISTICS	SYSTEMATIZING	ANALYZING	BRAINSTORMING	VISIONING
Advantages as a Facilitator	• Organized and able to plan and prioritize work output • Assertive and to the point	• Able to disengage and ask questions to clarify logic in a given situation • Ability to repackage and reframe models and thoughts	• Able to recognize group dynamics & ensure all team members are involved in decisions • Create psychological safety through genuine connecting	• Act as the conscience of the group • Tolerant and supportive of individual differences – work well with all types
Possible Challenges	• May push for closure too quickly and want to control too many decisions • May appear too rigid or blunt	• May be difficult to change their mind – "Not Invented Here" syndrome – want to win in debate • Internal decisions may be difficult to quantify	• May show all the emotions on face and in their body language: sudden outbursts of emotion • Find it hard to function when there is severe conflict present	• When values are crossed may appear stubborn. • May lose enthusiasm for work when values are disappointed
Aim is to	• Accomplish goals in a structured manner	• Improve a system or theory	• Make everyone comfortable and achieve consensus	• Achieve alignment between external world and internal beliefs

If you want to learn more about Cognitive Processes, please refer to the Resource Guide in the Appendix.

Look at the table below to see the correlation between different Temperaments and the Cognitive Processes that they tend to naturally access:

Information Gathering (Perceiving)

- All **Improvisers** tend to use **Experiencing** to tune into data in the current context.
- All **Stabilizers** tend to use **Recalling** to access a rich databank of sensory experiences.
- All **Theorists** and **Catalysts** tend to use either **Brainstorming** to explore possibilities, patterns and meanings or **Visioning** to assimilate data unconsciously into a new insight.

Decision Making (Judging)

- Some **Stabilizers** and some **Theorists** tend to use **Systematizing** to create a structured plan to achieve goals in the external world.
- Some **Improvisers** and **Theorists** tend to use **Analyzing** to reframe logical data to create a unique argument or point of view.
- Some **Stabilizers** and **Catalysts** tend to use **Harmonizing** to create cohesion in the external world while knowing what is appropriate.
- Some **Improvisers** and **Catalysts** tend to use **Valuing** to act as a group conscience and to tolerate and encourage individual differences.

Chapter Six:
Visual Two

Get-Things-Going Brainstorming Valuing	**Behind-the-Scenes** Valuing Brainstorming	**Get-Things-Going** Experiencing Valuing	**Behind-the-Scenes** Valuing Experiencing
	Catalyst		**Improviser**
In-Charge Harmonizing Visioning	**Chart-the-Course** Visioning Harmonizing	**In-Charge** Experiencing Analyzing	**Chart-the-Course** Analyzing Experiencing
Get-Things-Going Harmonizing Recalling	**Behind-the-Scenes** Recalling Harmonizing	**Get-Things-Going** Brainstorming Analyzing	**Behind-the-Scenes** Analyzing Brainstorming
	Stabilizer		**Theorist**
In-Charge Systematizing Recalling	**Chart-the-Course** Recalling Systematizing	**In-Charge** Systematizing Visioning	**Chart-the-Course** Visioning Systematizing

EXERCISE 6.1: YOUR COGNITIVE PROCESSES

Looking at the descriptions of the Cognitive Processes:

- Think back to Chapter Five where you selected your best-fit Temperament and Interaction Style.
- Look at the previous table, to what extent do you recognize the Information Gathering Process that your Type prefers to access?
- To what extent do you recognize the Decision Making Process that your Type prefers to access?
- What are your learning points from this information?

TRY IT ON!

Recognize Information Gathering Process?

_____

_____

_____

Recognize Decision Making Process?

_____

_____

_____

Learning Points?

_____

_____

_____

The Eight Cognitive Processes and Learning

While it is almost impossible to assess the type pattern of every student in your workshops, a Flawless Facilitator can appeal to all types by ensuring course design appeals to all four Information Gathering Cognitive Processes and considers all four Decision Making criteria. Below are some guidelines to aid in course design.

Perceiving Processes

Experiencing	Recalling
• Provide/encourage sensory experiences: touch, see, hearing, movement, and smell to create a stimulating environment.	• Provide structured clear instructions: what to do, how long, who does what and what is the goal to make the exercise "real".
• Make ideas meaningful with relevant context, sensory details, and physical tools.	• Provide time to review experiences to get in the zone and ground new learnings in context.
• Don't rely only on metaphor.	• Ensure you provide step-by-step approaches to developing skill and provide a roadmap to track progress.
• Focus on challenges, and allow for resourceful responses to crises.	• Give opportunities to learn by observing a skillful role model and then practicing that with correction.
• Give lots of activities and vary tasks – do not stay in Abstract data too long without physical experience.	• Provide practice time in low-distraction environments.
• Talk about what is happening here and now.	• Talk about examples from the past.

Brainstorming	Visioning
• Provide an opportunity to draw upon diverse inputs for brainstorming to generate ideas, possible solutions and creative options. • Give lots of varied input and expect them to "connect the dots". • Encourage role-playing and acting "as if". • Allow time for goals/meanings to coalesce from inputs rather than pushing linear process. • Focus on meanings and relationships between ideas, starting perhaps with metaphors and analogies. Allow time to explore connections. • Talk about possibilities, ideas and concepts in a positive way.	• Provide an opportunity to step back and reflect on goals, purpose, outcomes or concepts. • Give opportunities for future scenario planning and holistic problem solving. • Try to balance interactive learning with time away from external stimulation to enable access to rich internal processes; "rest" means "psyche is free from inputs." • May need help communicating the factors they considered as they developed solutions to problems. • Provide sensory input to use when Visioning isn't working and they need to act quickly. Use physical action to focus the mind. • Talk about the future outcome or theme.

As you can see, techniques that work for one Information-gathering process may not work for another. So varying style and approaches while considering the needs for all four can help to ensure all types have some time when they can use their innate preference.

Judging Processes

Systematizing	Analyzing
• Map out action plans assessing priorities, time lines and responsibilities. • Be clear and organized when you are explaining concepts and models. • Use facts and figures, preferably using visual/spatial formats like grids. • Be clear in word choice, as this process tends to be attentive to the specific words used. • Do not mistake their confidence and speed for competence – invest time in defining areas of strength. • Encourage them to take time to consider responses more thoroughly.	• Allow time for critical questions as data is integrated to support "deep" and "detached" decision-making. • Give time to shift course or backtrack as this process makes and corrects mistakes/inconsistencies. • Expect a pursuit for intellectual purity as they strive for high accuracy before implementing. • Rely on sophisticated, complex reasoning using multiple reasoning methods so allow time/process for this. • Can there be assignments between sessions, to allow for assimilation and reframing? • Make time for questioning as they evaluate data using their complex reasoning.

Harmonizing (Fe) Extroverted Feeling	Valuing (Fi) Introverted Feeling
• Make sure there are good "meet and greet" activities to establish a positive group dynamic.	• Check task and group process elements are balanced for fairness and equality.
• Use ground rules and manage the group dynamic to set and manage a safe learning environment.	• Provide flexibility to "opt out" if elements of the training cross values.
• Protect their responses, as they tend to be easily embarrassed.	• Watch out for any strong response to words that might indicate values have been crossed.
• Be authentic because they will be monitoring how you express yourself.	• Speak thoughtfully – take time and don't rush.
• Tend to attend to you, your words, and how you may be evaluating them. Even when they physically show no outward response to your reactions, their brains are likely registering your behavior and responding internally or verbally.	• Remember they are listening intently to you, especially for your tone of voice.
	• Speak to their values, especially positively felt values, as this will increase attention.
	• Strong gradations of importance but may give circumstantial reasons (dislike vs. don't know).
• Considerations of justice/injustice and moral/ethical choices/failings are salient to them	• Withholding feedback arouses their attention; otherwise they are hard to faze.
• Tend to use and respond to value-laden language. They focus on word choice more than their tone of voice.	• Expect a strong response if values are crossed.

By considering the four types of information and four decision-making processes, you are more likely, as a Facilitator, to meet the learning needs of all types.

EXERCISE 6.2: LEARNING AND THE COGNITIVE PROCESSES

- What have been your "Aha's" about Learning and the Cognitive Processes?
- What will you do differently as a result?

TRY IT ON!

Aha's about Learning and Cognitive Processes

_____

_____

_____

What will you do differently as a result?

_____

_____

_____

For more information on type preferences and the MBTI® assessment methodology, please review the information in the Appendix: The Four Preferences.

Facilitator Strengths and Challenges

One of the most important applications of Whole Type is for the Facilitator to gain an understanding of their innate Talents (in order to be able to capitalize on them) and their potential blind spots (to try to void or overcome them). Below are some high-level type descriptions for each of the 16 types listing their Whole Type, Temperament, Interaction Style and preferred Information Gathering and Decision Making Cognitive Process with some examples of their potential strengths and weaknesses as a Facilitator. Resources for more in-depth type descriptions are listed in the Appendix.

COACHING POINT

This section represents a high-level overview of Whole Type Theory – the Appendix lists more resources to study these models in more depth.

TIMEOUT!

We use the term "Adult" Cognitive Process to describe the Cognitive Process that, for this type pattern, is the easiest to use, tends to develop first, and in which area the Type innately has the most comfort.

We use the term "Parent" Cognitive process to describe the Cognitive Process that, for this type pattern, provides balance and support to the "Adult". Understanding the origins of the theory is not essential at this point – understanding the Talents and Blind Spots of each Whole Type is more important.

Improvisers

WHOLE TYPE	IN-CHARGE IMPROVISER
Overall Description	**In-Charge Improvisers** tend to be high-energy, action-oriented, quick-thinking, objective decision-makers. Their focus on making things happen can make them appear impatient with slow-moving, theoretical discussion and concepts. They are direct and their word choice focuses on "netting it out" or getting to the point. They normally possess intense observation skills, can tune in to what's happening in the moment, are acutely aware of non-verbal cues and then respond as needed. Their minds move so rapidly that often their words are left behind, as they push on for a result or to make an impact. They constantly find new ways of doing things. Although they may be perceived occasionally as uncaring by others, they nonetheless protect the people who are important to them.
Temperament	**Improviser** Need to act in the moment, be impressive and produce immediate concrete tangible results.
Interaction Style	**In-Charge** • Like to move quickly towards a goal. • Maneuver rapidly to take action in the now moment. • Tend to appear quick moving, confident and determined.

WHOLE TYPE	IN-CHARGE IMPROVISER
Adult Function	**Experiencing** Rapid uptake of and drive to act on sensory data in the now moment from the external world. Acute awareness of specifics and realities in the world around them.
Parent Function	**Analyzing** Make decisions using internal logical criteria and principles. Analyze how and why things work.
Possible Strengths as a Facilitator	• Focus is on action that can instantly be applied from learning. • Tend to excel at thinking on their feet. • Tend to make learning "as much like the real world" as possible. • Action oriented implementers.
Potential Challenges as a Facilitator	• May resist structuring workshops – prefer to act in the moment according to what the group needs. • Humor may occasionally be a "little on the edge". • May neglect relevant theories if they are viewed as a "waste of time". • May be unwilling to talk things through with those participants who require more time for reflection and/or have more in-depth questions.

WHOLE TYPE	CHART-THE-COURSE IMPROVISER
Overall Description	**Chart-the-Course Improvisers** live in the present and act in the moment to get to the root cause, and solve problems. They are the most analytical of the Improvisers, enjoying theoretical constructs with practical reasoning. They can absorb large amounts of facts and data with a high affiliation with numbers. They thrive on variety and focus on doing what needs to be done with the least amount of fuss to mitigate risk, balance risk and reward, and work around obstacles. They will change direction readily as additional information becomes available and manoeuver systems to meet their ends. They are adept with tools and are able to reason impersonally and objectively. They may alienate others with their tendency to "work a system", as almost any interaction can be viewed as a game to them.
Temperament	**Improviser** Need to act in the moment, be impressive, and produce immediate concrete tangible results.

WHOLE TYPE	CHART-THE-COURSE IMPROVISER
Interaction Style	**Chart-the-Course** • Like to think ahead to predict the goal. • Evaluate the most logical plan of attack based on the current reality and perceived obstacles. • Tend to appear calm, self-contained and focused.
Adult Function	**Analyzing** Make decisions using their internal logical criteria and principles. Analyze how and why things work. Always approach data from an independent perspective, with their own logical point of view.
Parent Function	**Experiencing** Have a rapid uptake of sensory data in the now moment from the external world. Possess an acute awareness of specifics with an ability to act on realities in the world around them.
Possible Strengths as a Facilitator	• Like to make learning tangible and real: focus on realistic short-term goals. • Highly analytical with ability to access relevant data. • Naturally adept with tools and numbers. • Use economy of effort – don't like to waste energy.
Potential Challenges as a Facilitator	• May appear overly critical and cynical when questioning to clarify logic. • May lack long-term vision and an understanding of how their behavior affects others. • May appear indifferent to students' needs. • Could be uncomfortable with more subjective elements or demonstration of emotions.

WHOLE TYPE	GET-THINGS-GOING IMPROVISERS
Overall Description	**Get-Things-Going Improvisers** are colorful, free-spirited, and people-focused. Using their acute sensory inputs, they make decisions based on what is in alignment with their internal values system. They are interested in people and new experiences, as they live in the moment. They are generous of spirit, active, talkative and flexible. Their natural exuberance attracts others as they get the task done with the maximum amount of fun and minimum amount of fuss. They find enjoyment in food, clothes, animals, the natural world, and activities. They work best in a flexible, unstructured environment. Their tendency to perform in groups and see the light-hearted side may make others perceive them as frivolous.
Temperament	**Improviser** Need the freedom to act in the moment, be impressive, and produce immediate, concrete, and tangible results.
Interaction Style	**Get-Things-Going** • Like to facilitate involvement from the group. • Use playfulness to help others feel valued and involved. • Tend to appear expressive, upbeat and casual.
Adult Function	**Experiencing** Rapid uptake of, and need to act on, sensory data in the now moment from the external world. Acute awareness of specifics and realities in the world around them. Able to read sensory data in the moment.
Parent Function	**Valuing** Make decisions quietly, but firmly based on their own internal beliefs system. Guided by strong inner values and wish life to be in congruence with those beliefs. Tolerant of differences and adaptable until the values system is crossed- then can appear rigid.
Possible Strengths as a Facilitator	• Focus on making learning real while intensely interested in and supportive of human differences. • Friendly, energetic, generous and people focused. • Able to interact easily with, and flex to, different types of students. • Excellent at stimulating involvement through fun and activities.

WHOLE TYPE	GET-THINGS-GOING IMPROVISERS
Potential Challenges as a Facilitator	• May resist planning lessons as they prefer to be able to engage the audience and respond in the moment. • May appear to be too playful and not serious about learning. • May go "off track" and get diverted by audience discussion. • May neglect more abstract models or theories.

WHOLE TYPE	BEHIND-THE-SCENES IMPROVISER
Overall Description	**Behind-the-Scenes Improvisers** live in the present and prize the freedom to follow their own course. They are faithful at fulfilling obligations to people and things that are important to them. They often appear as unassuming, easy-going, gentle, and soft-spoken. They will provide help in concrete tangible ways, and with their observation skills, have a gift for expressing abstract things concretely. Their playful sense of humor may not be seen until they are comfortable with you. They will adapt well to new situations, and approach life from a "Don't worry be happy" perspective. In workshops, their tendency to have a laid-back approach could be viewed as lack of interest or direction.
Temperament	**Improviser** Need the freedom to act in the moment, be impressive, and produce immediate concrete tangible results.
Interaction Style	**Behind-the-Scenes** • Like to take the time to reconcile many inputs. • Support those that they care about through their actions. • Tend to appear approachable, friendly and patient.
Adult Function	**Valuing** Makes decisions quietly, but firmly based on their own internal beliefs system. Guided by strong inner values and wish life to be in congruence with those beliefs. Tolerant of individual differences and easy going until those values are challenged.
Parent Function	**Experiencing** Rapid uptake of and ability to act on sensory data in the now moment from the external world. Acute awareness of specifics and realities in the world around them.

WHOLE TYPE	BEHIND-THE-SCENES IMPROVISER
Possible Strengths as a Facilitator	• Focus on quality of learning in a tolerant, ethical way. • Humane, with the ability to persuade others in a non-confrontational way. • Easy going but with the ability to provide sensible learning linked to practical problems. • Teaches by doing rather than telling.
Potential Challenges as a Facilitator	• May become overwhelmed with the constant need to engage with others when teaching. • May not speak up about what he or she wants, or intervene if a workshop is going off track. • May withdraw from students due to anger and tension and not address the core issue. • If values are crossed, may move from avoidance to confrontation.

Stabilizers

WHOLE TYPE	IN-CHARGE STABILIZER
Overall Description	**In-Charge Stabilizers** are detail-oriented, high-energy decision-makers. They drive for closure with the aim of organizing, planning and structuring the external environment. The most "driven" of the Stabilizers, they take action to get things done, in a systematic and consistent way. They take an objective approach to problem solving and can be tough when the situation demands. They enjoy activity that produces concrete tangible results and are adept at creating systems that assign responsibilities and allocate resources. They enjoy interacting with others, especially around games and team activities. As Facilitators, they set high standards and have a clear sense of what is "right and wrong", and what is "fair".
Temperament	**Stabilizer** Need to be part of a group or a team, fulfil responsibilities, and make a contribution therein.
Interaction Style	**In-Charge** • Like to move quickly towards an attainable goal. • Make rapid decisions to organize and structure learning. • Tend to appear quick moving, confident and determined.

WHOLE TYPE	IN-CHARGE STABILIZER
Adult Function	**Systematizing** Make decisions to achieve learning goals using logical criteria to plan and organize logistics and events in the external world. Adept at sequencing tasks and resources to achieve an end goal. Strong push for closure. Very action oriented.
Parent Function	**Recalling** Gather information by referring back to a rich databank of past sensory experiences that are compared and contrasted to the present. Able to bring the best of the past into the future. Monitors and evaluates for reality.
Possible Strengths as a Facilitator	• Focus on learning that can help improve "current reality" in a tangible, practical way. • Organized and structured with clear sequential lesson plans. • Sees the right way to complete learning assignments with a drive for timely completion. • Sets up systems and procedures for managing learning.
Potential Challenges as a Facilitator	• May dismiss content or approaches that they perceive to be impractical. • May appear too driven for closure and uncomfortable with ambiguity. • May appear to ignore students' feelings in their push to complete the learning. • May rely too much on their authority and be reluctant to involve students sufficiently.

WHOLE TYPE	CHART-THE-COURSE STABILIZER
Overall Description	**Chart-the-Course Stabilizers** are logical, practical, organized, and thorough. They rely on historic experience from which to create concrete lesson plans. They will create processes and procedures to smooth learning, eliminate redundancy and achieve economy of effort. They are loyal and dutiful, and work with steady energy to ensure commitments are met on time. They tend to prefer to have time alone and may appear serious and orderly. They trust facts, are task-oriented and can manage extensive detail. They work hard at their role and, once a skill is learned, they perform it with competence. As Facilitators, they are dedicated and committed and may frustrate their colleagues in their sequential approach combined with reluctance to change without a practical reason.
Temperament	**Stabilizer** Need to be part of a group or a team, fulfil responsibilities, and make a contribution therein.
Interaction Style	**Chart-the-Course** • Like to think ahead, anticipate obstacles and predict the goal. • Review previous experience to think through the most systematic learning approach. • Tend to appear calm, self-contained and focused.
Adult Function	**Recalling** Gather information by referring to a rich databank of past sensory experiences to compare and contrast this information to the present. Able to bring the best of the past to the future and audit the reality of any given situation.
Parent Function	**Systematizing** Make decisions using logical criteria to plan and organize logistics and events in the external world. Sequence events and resources to achieve goals in a timely manner.
Possible Strengths as a Facilitator	• Focus on building learning to a desired result while anticipating how to overcome any barriers to learning. • Quiet. Serious, dedicated and organized: great follow through skills. • No nonsense, hard-working Facilitators who deliver on responsibilities given clearly defined roles. • Meticulous attention to detail and aims for perfection.

WHOLE TYPE	CHART-THE-COURSE STABILIZER
Potential Challenges as a Facilitator	• May appear rigid about time schedules and rules: go by the book. • Instead of delegating , may get bogged down in details. • May neglect the big picture and/or students' emotions when focused on task completion. • May be reluctant to change learning environment as necessary.

WHOLE TYPE	GET-THINGS-GOING STABILIZER
Overall Description	**Get-Things-Going Stabilizers** are warm, personable, and outgoing. They enjoy harmonious learning environments, working within that structure to ensure that organization is established and learning goals are met. They are conscientious and loyal, and value security and stability. They use information from their extensive databank of past sensory experiences to apply in their concrete, people-focused work. They are energized by being with others and are genuinely interested in others' lives and concerns. They enjoy participating in committees and are good at organizing celebrations and preserving traditions. As Facilitators, they will tend to be the organizer of all team and work-shop celebrations, yet may sometimes overload themselves with responsibilities.
Temperament	**Stabilizer** Need to be part of a group or a team, fulfil responsibilities, and make a contribution therein.
Interaction Style	**Get-Things-Going** • Like to facilitate involvement from the group. • Organize tasks to make workshops harmonious and easier. • Tend to appear expressive, upbeat and casual.
Adult Function	**Harmonizing** Make decisions using subjective criteria to optimize group harmony and know what is appropriate to ensure psychological safety. Sensitive to participants' wants and needs. Self discloses to connect, and yet may show emotions on face when stressed.
Parent Function	**Recalling** Gather information by referring to a rich databank of past sensory expe-riences in order to compare and contrast this data to the present. Able to audit workshops, content and data for reality.

WHOLE TYPE	GET-THINGS-GOING STABILIZER
Possible Strengths as a Facilitator	• Focus on group engagement to build an embraced development goal. • Have an energetic, enthusiastic and warm energy – create a safe learning environment. • Aware of and cater to participants' needs. • Responsible and focus on building workshop cohesiveness.
Potential Challenges as a Facilitator	• May let go of the structure in order to meet the group's needs. • May avoid conflict or struggle with meeting workshop time requirements (with the need for group involvement.) • May get demoralized/stressed if participants do not seem engaged in learning. • May seem too talkative as they involve others in team activities.

WHOLE TYPE	BEHIND-THE-SCENES STABILIZER
Overall Description	**Behind-the-Scenes Stabilizers** are stable, supportive, empathetic Facilitators who work tirelessly unobtrusively to achieve learning goals. They are concrete, task-focused, and value tangible products and economy of resources. Valuing traditions and historic experience, they make decisions that will meet the needs of the group. When communicating, they follow a detailed, sequential, step-by-step thought process and tend to establish orderly procedures. They enjoy helping others, are dependable and considerate, and gravitate to roles that involve service to others. Maintaining the cohesiveness of the class and living up to their responsibilities are fundamental to the way they operate. They excel at presenting relevant examples to make learning realistic. As Facilitators, they have to be careful that they are not taken advantage of, because they will do tasks for others in such an unassuming way, the effort can go unnoticed.
Temperament	**Stabilizer** Need to be part of a group or a team, fulfil responsibilities, and make a contribution therein.

WHOLE TYPE	BEHIND-THE-SCENES STABILIZER
Interaction Style	**Behind-the-Scenes** • Like to take the time to reconcile many inputs. • Integrate previous experience to support the learning in the most economical way. • Tend to appear approachable, friendly and patient.
Adult Function	**Recalling** Gather information by referring to a rich databank of past sensory experiences in order to compare and contrast these to the present. Able to bring to the current content/workshop an accurate assessment of what is real.
Parent Function	**Harmonizing** Make decisions using subjective criteria to optimize group harmony. Sensitive to and considerate of participant's feelings.
Possible Strengths as a Facilitator	• Focus on planning content and examples to achieve the best quality result considering the audience involved. • Conscientious: will probably go above and beyond in preparing course material. • Look after students in the group with an established structure and supportive energy. • Good at contingency planning – what might go wrong and how could they avoid this?
Potential Challenges as a Facilitator	• May worry too much about content and participants. • May burden themselves with "over-preparation" and be reluctant to ask to help. • May not assert their own needs: instead may become resentful. • May be uncomfortable with confrontation in the workshop.

Theorists

WHOLE TYPE	IN-CHARGE THEORISTS
Overall Description	**In-Charge Theorists** are direct, organized and possess a strong desire to make their inner visions into new innovative workshops. They are quick thinking, strategic, logical decision-makers, possessing a drive for closure. They value intelligence or competence in their students and abhor inefficiency. They conceptualize and theorize readily and possess the innate ability to take charge and make things happen. They exude confidence and appear energetic and driven. They are aware of intricate connections that they can explain to groups with logical models. As Facilitators, they will want to ensure that the audience is working efficiently to produce results, and may appear uncomfortable with too many emotional issues.
Temperament	**Theorist** Need to be competent, knowledgeable and understand the universal operating principles in order to develop mastery and create their own destiny.
Interaction Style	**In-Charge** • Believe that it is worth taking a risk to decide and correcting later. • Make rapid decisions to accomplish a clear future goal. • Tend to appear quick moving, confident and determined.
Adult Function	**Systematizing** Making decisions using logical criteria to achieve goals by planning and organizing logistics and events in the external world. Adept at marshalling resources to achieve goals in the most expedient manner. Strong push for closure.
Parent Function	**Visioning** Gather information by creating their complete idea or future direction. Able to step back and assimilate data into a complete model.

WHOLE TYPE	IN-CHARGE THEORISTS
Possible Strengths as a Facilitator	• Focus on systems, theories and models to achieve an attainable learning objective or solve a development problem. • Create an organized systematic approach to lesson plans and learning outcomes. • Decisive, clear, direct and assertive in their communication with the group. • Assemble resources and drive the group to participate.
Potential Challenges as a Facilitator	• May be perceived as lacking empathy as they push to achieve closure. • May negate the importance of practical applications or steps. • May be reluctant to allow the group to be "the expert" – may struggle with wanting to answer all questions to reaffirm their individual competence. • May appear cold/impersonal and somewhat oblivious to interpersonal interaction.

WHOLE TYPE	CHART-THE-COURSE THEORIST
Overall Description	**Chart-the-Course Theorists** approach learning with an independent-minded, long-term vision coming from their internal world of possibilities. While they develop abstract models, they put concrete action plans in place to make development goals happen. They can always offer a detached, objective perspective with the propensity for original thought as they see patterns in external events. With their ability to categorize data, they are confident in their ideas and their ability to achieve their goals. They can appear determined as they strive to achieve their high standards of performance. As Facilitators, they may not reveal their inner emotions, yet they can be strongly loyal to the group and adept at providing a neutral independent opinion.
Temperament	**Theorist** Need to be competent, knowledgeable and understand universal operating principles in order to develop mastery and create their own destiny.

WHOLE TYPE	CHART-THE-COURSE THEORIST
Interaction Style	**Chart the Course** • Like to think ahead, anticipate obstacles and predict the goal. • Envision a future by creating a systematic plan to achieve the required learning. • Tend to appear calm, self-contained and focused.
Adult Function	**Visioning** Gather information by creating their complete idea or future direction. Gather data, step back to incubate and then are often able to suggest breakthrough learning models and approaches.
Parent Function	**Systematizing** Make decisions using logical criteria to achieve learning goals by planning and organizing content and events in the external world. When their future picture is complete, adept at organizing resources to achieve the desired result.
Possible Strengths as a Facilitator	• Focus on providing an innovative, independent and original perspective towards a desired learning goal. • Conceptual long-range thinkers with an ability to relate the parts to the overall big picture. • Encourage independence of thought and action in students. • Calm, objective, logical approach to learning with an ability to be tough with poor performance.
Potential Challenges as a Facilitator	• May appear tough, aloof or intense when providing feedback to students. • May appear disengaged when thinking through obstacles and/or changes to lesson approach. • May not be explicit in the link between content and reality and/or neglect practice activities that may be required to build skills. • May constantly redesign content and neglect the tried and true in the pursuit of innovative learning.

WHOLE TYPE	GET-THINGS-GOING THEORISTS
Overall Description	**Get-Things-Going Theorists** are normally quick thinking, verbally expressive and focused on future opportunities. They thrive on looking at concepts and possibilities from multiple angles and then arguing their own philosophy or hypothesis. They are optimistic, gregarious and social. They enjoy debate and can be very persuasive. They naturally generate options and then are able to analyze them strategically, which makes them creative, abstract problem solvers. They are enterprising and resourceful, however they may not always be realistic in structuring plans. As Facilitators, they will tend to be upbeat and enthusiastic, although occasionally their need to take center stage and challenge participant's viewpoints could wear down students and be viewed as confrontational.
Temperament	**Theorist** Need to be competent, knowledgeable and understand universal operating principles in order to develop mastery and create their own destiny.
Interaction Style	**Get-Things-Going** • Like to facilitate involvement from the group. • Brainstorm possibilities to originate new models or points of view. • Tend to appear expressive, upbeat and casual.
Adult Function	**Brainstorming** Constant external exploration of future possibilities, new theories or models, patterns and meanings. Read between the lines with the ability to look at situations from fresh new angles. Tendency to bounce ideas around and be optimistic.
Parent Function	**Analyzing** Make decisions using internal logical criteria and principles. Analyze how and why things work. Evaluate and sort against a mental model to achieve improvements in learning design. Possess a clear "point of view" which they are able to defend against differing perspectives.

WHOLE TYPE	GET-THINGS-GOING THEORISTS
Possible Strengths as a Facilitator	• Focus on the pursuit of innovative learning concepts and approaches while involving students to achieve an embraced learning objective. • Great at providing energy and thrust to new learning approaches, models, and ideas: a stimulating and entertaining Facilitator. • Look beyond the conventional learning solution and challenge participants to believe the impossible is achievable. • Self-confident and assertive, with an ability to argue both sides of an issue.
Potential Challenges as a Facilitator	• May talk too much to externally process ideas and possibilities: may not allow time for the group to speak. • May overwhelm participants with data and/or possibilities. • May appear arrogant as they hold center stage to present their viewpoint. • May dismiss as irrelevant questions about concrete reality and practical concerns.

WHOLE TYPE	BEHIND-THE-SCENES THEORISTS
Overall Description	**Behind-the-Scenes Theorists** spend their learning lives in a quest for logical purity and accuracy. Using abstract data from ideas, future possibilities, and meanings, they analyze this information to align with their internal models. They possess an insight into complex theories and constantly search for patterns and systems to internally categorize data. They often function autonomously as they absorb themselves in mastering and perfecting their theories. They possess a unique ability to dissect the complex and comprehend conceptual subtleties. They enjoy creating intangible solutions and then may struggle with their implementation, as they live in their rich inner world. As Facilitators, they may appear distanced from the "real world" and intense although they can prove to be excellent strategists.
Temperament	**Theorist** Need to be competent, knowledgeable and understand universal operating principles in order to develop mastery and create their own destiny.

WHOLE TYPE	BEHIND-THE-SCENES THEORISTS
Interaction Style	**Behind-the-Scenes** • Like to take the time to reconcile many inputs. • Analyze and integrate multiple models to define new concepts. • Tend to appear approachable, friendly and patient.
Adult Function	**Analyzing** Make decisions using internal logical criteria and principles. Analyze how and why things work. Evaluate and sort against a mental model to improve the operation of the system. Ability to dissect arguments and data, to assess validity, and to come up with a completely different logical perspective.
Parent Function	**Brainstorming** Ability to explore future possibilities, patterns, and meanings and to infer to what is occurring but not stated.
Possible Strengths as a Facilitator	• Focus on contributing an alternative, logical , detached perspective in order to raise the quality of the learning outcome. • Use precision in communication – exactly the right word and nuance for any given situation can help to refine thought processes of students. • Constantly challenges the status quo: naturally create innovative, theoretical systems to explain how and why things work. • Great researchers as they integrate new and complex data into their unique complex model.
Potential Challenges as a Facilitator	• May not provide sufficient structure and process, as they expect students to take responsibility for their own learning. • May overwhelm students with complex theoretical explanations with limited examples or no explicit link to current reality. • May appear overly critical when using questions to clarify resilience of students' thought processes and ideas. • The requirement to be with people throughout a learning experience could overwhelm them as they need significant time alone to reflect.

Catalysts

WHOLE TYPE	IN-CHARGE CATALYST
Overall Description	**In-Charge Catalysts** are outgoing, empathetic, expressive developers of people. They have a remarkable gift for seeing human potential and want to help others "be all that they can be". With their long-term focus, they like closure in their lives as they work to make their visions a reality. They are gifted communicators whether one-on-one, where they are able to get almost anyone to open up to them, or in front of a group, where they are able to stimulate positive enthusiasm. They are highly attuned to the moods and emotions of any audience, and work to create a harmonious environment. As Facilitators, they focus on meaningful content within the learning environment and drive to create genuine interactions with participants. However, their focus on driving through substantial content could detract from achieving team harmony.
Temperament	**Catalyst** Need to have a purpose, be special and make a meaningful contribution to the greater good; helping people to develop.
Interaction Style	**In-Charge** • Like to make expedient, quick decisions. • Move forward quickly to achieve development goals for people. • Tend to appear quick moving, confident and determined.
Adult Function	**Harmonizing** Making decisions using subjective criteria to optimize group interaction. Sensitive to the group's wants and needs, with an ability to self-disclose to connect and establish psychological safety. When stressed may show emotions on their face.
Parent Function	**Visioning** Gather information by creating their own complete idea or future direction. Step back in order to assimilate data. Trust own intuitive insights.

WHOLE TYPE	IN-CHARGE CATALYST
Possible Strengths as a Facilitator	• Focus on uniting the group, while seeing potential in individuals, to achieve a developmental goal. • Fluent verbal skills in uniting disparate views to achieve consensus and develop others. • Create a positive and safe communication climate with warmth and connections. • Adept at drawing out the ideas and thoughts from participants to raise engagement and build a learning culture.
Potential Challenges as a Facilitator	• May get stressed when the need for involvement clashes with the time pressure to achieve the learning goal. • May overly focus on one participant who appears disengaged and neglect the majority of the group who are involved and committed to learning. • May show emotions under stress, particularly when there is a perceived conflict in the workshop. • May include too much content.

WHOLE TYPE	CHART-THE-COURES CATALYST
Overall Description	**Chart-the-Course Catalysts** are quietly insightful individuals who are constantly searching for deeper meanings and the coming into consciousness of their inner visions. They empathetically understand the feelings and motivations of others and are loyal to people and institutions. As tactful, thoughtful, and concerned individuals, they demonstrate interest in the development of others. They are very private people; they quietly exert an influence over participants. They use language that is full of imagery as they structure the external world to work towards their inner picture of the future. As Facilitators, they will be sensitive to participant's emotional issues on their constant quest to make their vision of learning a reality. However, their drive to achieve their development vision may not be balanced with sufficient practical data.
Temperament	**Catalyst** Need to be special. Have a purpose and make a meaningful contribution to the greater good: helping people to develop.

WHOLE TYPE	CHART-THE-COURES CATALYST
Interaction Style	**Chart-the-Course** • Like to think ahead, anticipate obstacles and predict the goal. • Have insights on future potential and work with a group to develop potential. • Tend to appear calm, balanced and focused.
Adult Function	**Visioning** Gather information by creating their individual complete idea of future direction. Need time to step back in order to assimilate data. Confident in suggesting innovative solutions.
Parent Function	**Harmonizing** Make decisions using subjective criteria to optimize group interaction. Sensitive to team dynamics and participant wants and needs.
Possible Strengths as a Facilitator	• Focus on meeting group needs while working towards a desired goal. • Creative, conceptual learning approach with good follow through skills. • Sensitive, compassionate and empathetic with participants: students feel safe and validated. • Integrate people and systems effortlessly in the learning journey.
Potential Challenges as a Facilitator	• Can be unclear in articulating vision for students in such a way as to make it concrete and real. • May forget to apply reason to their insights or include practical steps to achieve the learning goals. • May become single-minded in pursuit of their vision and make arbitrary decisions. • May struggle if the learning environment goes against their beliefs about people and/or what they perceive as a lot of political maneuvering.

WHOLE TYPE	GET-THINGS-GOJNG CATALYST
Overall Description	**Get-Things-Going Catalysts** are energetic, spontaneous, warm-hearted individuals who constantly generate creative, ingenious options for future personal development. They see endless possibilities that relate to the people around them. They love abstract concepts and are able to see beyond the obvious to the hidden meanings and patterns. Their strong inner values guide their decision-making, as they readily give appreciation and support to participants. They are empathetic and engaging, keenly perceptive of others, and use their verbal fluency to persuade and influence those around them. As Facilitators, they are enthusiastic and committed to the relationships with the students, although they sometimes may frustrate others with their lack of concrete focus and seemingly impractical ideas.
Temperament	**Catalyst** Need to have a purpose and make a meaningful contribution to the greater good: helping people to develop.
Interaction Style	**Get-Things-Going** • Like to facilitate involvement from the group. • Brainstorm possibilities to advocate a cause and help people develop. • Tend to appear enthusiastic, buoyant and casual.
Adult Function	**Brainstorming** Constant external exploration of future possibilities, patterns, and meanings. Verbal discussion of possibilities and an ability to read between the lines to the hidden meaning below. Appear endlessly positive and upbeat.
Parent Function	**Valuing** Makes decisions quietly, but firmly based on their own internal beliefs system. Guided by strong inner values and wish life to be in congruence with those. Will appear tolerant of differences until those values are crossed then they can appear rigid in those beliefs.
Possible Strengths as a Facilitator	• Concentrated focus on group engagement, involvement and commitment to subject. • Quick thinking and verbally expressive in exploring new ideas. • Zest for life and enthusiasm for the subject, content or approach. • Act as a catalyst or crusader for new ideas, models and theories as they pertain to people development.

WHOLE TYPE	GET-THINGS-GOJNG CATALYST
Potential Challenges as a Facilitator	• May appear scattered and/or disorganized as they explore possibilities in models and theories. • May get discouraged if they perceive a lack of engagement from the group and "turn up the volume" of their energy. • May struggle with time limitations as they build group engagement and may neglect the "task" element of the session as a result. • May miss detailed implementation steps and fail to follow through on ideas.

WHOLE TYPE	BEHIND-THE-SCENES CATALYST
Overall Description	**Behind-the-Scenes Catalysts** are quiet pursuers of their life's quest as they strive to live according to their strongly held internal values. Not wanting to take center stage, they can appear reserved and somewhat aloof until their internal belief system is "bumped up against" when they can react strongly in its defense. With a moral commitment to the fundamental worth of unique identity, they celebrate individual differences and want a purpose beyond a paycheck. They are adaptable, and enjoy opportunities to explore the complexities of human personality. They value relationships based on authenticity and true connection. However, they may frustrate their students with their neglect of reality and their constant push to live life according to their own internal ideals.
Temperament	**Catalyst** Need to have a purpose and make a meaningful contribution to the greater good: helping people to develop.
Interaction Style	**Behind-the-Scenes** • Like to take the time to reconcile many inputs. • Analyze and integrate multiple models to define new concepts. • Tend to appear approachable, friendly and patient.
Adult Function	**Valuing** Make decisions quietly, but firmly based on their own internal beliefs system. Guided by strong inner values and wish life to be in congruence with those. Tolerant of differences until external behavior is not in alignment with internal values.
Parent Function	**Brainstorming** Enjoy external exploration of future possibilities, patterns, and meanings. Can read between the lines and identify themes.

WHOLE TYPE	BEHIND-THE-SCENES CATALYST
Possible Strengths as a Facilitator	• Focus on In-depth exploration and development of participants' potential. • Excellent listeners, with an ability to tune in to what is important to participants. • Reflect and produce intuitive insights and concepts, particularly in written form. • Possess an authentic, genuine interest in participants and are willing to invest time to achieve the quality, relevant result.
Potential Challenges as a Facilitator	• May find it difficult to teach what is perceived as "meaningless" subject material. • May find it difficult to develop and follow through on detailed lesson plans. • May react strongly when values are crossed. • May struggle with the demands of excessive classroom time with limited reflection time.

EXERCISE 6-3: WHOLE TYPE

- Look at the descriptions for the sixteen types and your assessment of your best-fit Whole Type pattern.
- What do you think your strengths might be as a Facilitator?
- What might be your challenges?

TRY IT ON: WHOLE TYPE

Write your ideas here…

Your Strengths as a Facilitator?

_____

_____

_____

Your Challenges as a Facilitator?

_____

_____

_____

Learning and Whole Type

Improvisers

The snapshots below express the four variations of the Improviser temperament in terms of learning. The first section of each snapshot lists tips for Facilitators. The second section expresses student's learning preferences in their own words.

* Comments from the Type Trilogy Card set authored by Sue Blair and Susan Nash

Get-Things-Going Improviser

- Incorporate movement and hands-on projects
- Communicate using concrete informal language
- Use audio-visuals and tools for learning
- Utilize group projects, team learning, class reports
- Give variety and change in pace to keep the group engaged
- Provide practical relevant goals

As a student: I learn best through discussion, activity and practice. I pick up a lot by watching, show me clearly what to do and I can do it. Once I feel I have mastered something I like to move on before I get bored. I tend to complete work close to the deadline. A friendly atmosphere is very important. *

Behind-the-Scenes Improviser

- Focus on present concrete data
- Give direct experience and an opportunity to try things out
- Provide well-defined goals and a fair learning environment
- Use audio-visuals, practical tests
- Build in time for working alone
- Be aware of their needs for a sensitive teacher

As a student: I love to learn in a stress free environment that has many hands-on activities that are engaging and fun. I don't mind working on my own but I may tune out with too much theory or lack of movement. It's hard to focus if I can't see the relevance to my life. I like to feel valued and supported by the Facilitator. *

In-Charge Improviser

- Incorporate activities and hands-on projects
- Be clear on why you are doing something
- Use group projects, class reports, team competition
- Provide an opportunity to try out ideas in their own way
- Utilize audio-visuals and tools for learning
- Give freedom of choice where possible

As a student: I learn best by doing, show me how something works and I can do it. Tell me what is most important so I can focus. I thrive on active, lively and relevant tasks; without this, I am easily de-motivated. I get the energy to complete my work just before the deadline; this worries some people but is fine with me. *

Chart-the-Course Improviser

- Explain why you are doing an activity
- Provide direct practical application and high-level structure
- Be clear about what is in it for them
- Build in time for working alone
- Provide an opportunity for independent thought and physical exploration
- Give logical facts and data and efficient materials

As a student: I love to learn by doing, enjoy freedom to follow my natural curiosity and study what interests me in depth. I can do most things if I am clearly shown how and I understand how it can be applied in life. I like time to think but sitting still for too long is a challenge. *

Stabilizers

The snapshots below express the four variations of the Stabilizer temperament in terms of learning. The first section of each snapshot lists tips for Facilitators. The second section expresses student's learning preferences in their own words.

* Comments from the Type Trilogy Card set authored by Sue Blair and Susan Nash

Get-Things-Going Stabilizer	Behind-the-Scenes Stabilizer
• Understand they tend to be linear learners with a strong need for structure • Make sure activities are realistic and practical • Concentrate on the relationship between the Facilitator and students which is important • Provide well defined goals • Use harmonious group projects, team working, class reports • Make sure you provide direct experience that builds on prior knowledge **As a student:** I like to learn in an active and structured environment. I work best when I have a good relationship with the Facilitator, am given clear instructions; I can practice to be perfect and can measure progress. Learning with friends is great. *	• Link learning directly to past experience and historical data • Provide an opportunity to listen to lectures and observe audio-visuals • Explore how they could work in a support role to the team • Ensure information provided is practical and real • Give opportunities for repetition and watching role models as this is how they learn best • Understand they tend to be linear learners with a strong need for structure **As a student:** I like an environment that is quiet and structured where teaching is patient and methodical. I like to know what is expected and will work hard to please a Facilitator, especially when I know I am liked and valued. I like rules to be clear and followed and for learning to have a purpose. *

In-Charge Stabilizer	Chart-the-Course Stabilizer
• Make sure linear learning is clear as they have a strong need for organization • Emphasize why before doing something • Provide direct experience and enable using previous knowledge • Use group projects, class reports, team working and competition • Give clear information about specifics of lessons, objectives and timelines • Utilize facts and figures, clear bar charts, and grids **As a student:** I like to have the point of the lesson clearly explained, an environment that is lively and organized, instructions that are specific and clear, and where my successes are recognized and rewarded. I need to respect the teacher's knowledge and expertise. *	• Make sure linear learning is clear as they have a strong need for organization • Make sure you refer to direct experience and historical data • Provide audio-visuals and lectures • Incorporate the opportunity for working alone • Ensure well-defined goals • Utilize practical tests **As a student:** I enjoy learning in a calm and structured environment where I have sequential, clear instructions and my Facilitator's competence is proven. I can memorise fairly easily and I like to have time to perfect my skills. I like to understand and demonstrate proficiency in one thing before moving on to the next. *

Theorists

The snapshots below express the four variations of the Theorist temperament in terms of learning. The first section of each snapshot lists tips for Facilitators. The second section expresses student's learning preferences in their own words.

* Comments from the Type Trilogy Card set authored by Sue Blair and Susan Nash

Get-Things-Going Theorist	**Behind-the-Scenes Theorist**
• A Global learner: so provide an opportunity to explore ideas and concepts	• As a Global learner: provide an opportunity to analyse and reframe logical data to create a new frame of reference
• Give autonomy and intellectual independence	• Incorporate reading, listening and going "deeper" into subjects and models
• Incorporate elements of intellectual debate, and/or group work for interaction and challenge	• Introduce and position theory, and then move to applications
• Introduce and position theory, and then move to applications	• Make sure you include the What and the Why?
• Focus on relevant data, sources of information and logical analysis	• Use precise language and provide an opportunity to refine and develop new concepts
• Offer open-ended instructions and opportunities to be creative with knowledge	• Offer autonomy and intellectual independence
As a student: I like to learn what I want to learn, when and how I want to learn it. This is not often possible. I am naturally curious and have bursts of energy for things that inspire me. It helps to start with an overview. I thrive when learning is fun, lively, challenging, and unpredictable and I value discussion and debate. I may act out or tune out if bored. *	**As a student:** I enjoy learning that is thought provoking and challenging, where exploratory digressions are a welcome break from the routine and I can opt to extend my studies if I wish. I can be frustrated if my learning is restricted. The teachers must earn my respect by their expertise.*

In-Charge Theorist	Chart-the-Course Theorist
• Introduce and explore the theory, then the applications • Use precise language and coherent reasoning • Incorporate group projects, class reports, team competition • Provide relevant data, sources of information and logical analysis • Give clear expectations and deadlines • Encourage independent thought and implementation. **As a student:** I enjoy learning when it is varied, creative, stimulating and challenging. I like structure but also want to follow my own path. I like Facilitators who think we are equal partners in achieving success. I may ask many questions, I like answers that give me more food for thought.*	• Provide a clear learning objective with structured deliverables • Introduce and explore the theory first, then the applications • Give opportunities for working alone and exploring innovative solutions and options • Encourage intellectual independence and give feedback accuracy of their "insights" • Supply relevant exact data and sources of models and theories. • Plan time for reflection and absorption of models. **As a student:** I love to learn independently, at my own pace, in an environment where I am challenged. I value the Facilitator's expertise and when there is respect and order. I like to ask questions and I like answers to be reliable and thought provoking. Opportunities to be artistic and imaginative are welcome.*

Catalysts

The snapshots below express the four variations of the Catalyst temperament in terms of learning. The first section of each snapshot lists tips for Facilitators. The second section expresses student's learning preferences in their own words.

* *Comments from the Type Trilogy Card set authored by Sue Blair and Susan Nash*

Get-Things-Going Catalyst	Behind-the-Scenes Catalyst
• As a Global learner, provide flexibility and an opportunity to explore creative solutions • Use harmonious group projects, team learning and interaction • Give an opportunity to be involved in activities and help the group to connect • Ensure there is a purpose for each lesson–is this important? • Show appreciation and provide genuine positive feedback • Encourage expression of ideas and interest in their point of view.	• As a Global learner, provide flexibility and an opportunity to explore creative solutions • Use reading and opportunities for active listening • Introduce the theory first, then the applications • Give a purpose to link content to a broader perspective • Show genuine positive feedback and appreciation • Use analogies, metaphors, concepts and models to stimulate new ideas
As a student: I like an environment full of energy and enthusiasm. I thrive when different options to learn are available; projects are creative, inspiring and fun and where my natural curiosity is respected. I want to be free to make mistakes and learn from them. It helps if I am reminded about the deadlines. *	**As a student:** I like to understand the reason for learning and am inspired by work I see will make a difference in the world and is meaningful to me. I thrive when I can be creative, imaginative and have time to think. I like working on my own, following my own curiosity. Too much structure, detail and analysis of facts is hard to take. *

In-Charge Catalyst	Chart-the-Course Catalyst
• Incorporate harmonious group projects, team learning and engagement • Introduce the theory first, then applications • Ensure you establish a safe learning environment • Build an authentic relationship with the student, as this is important for learning. • Give them an opportunity to develop others in the classroom • Be careful about any potential embarrassment	• Ensure there is a clear purpose, goal and process for learning • Introduce the theory first, then applications • Manage the group dynamic so there is harmony • Intervene positively if there is a conflict present • Use images, stories, metaphors and symbols to stimulate their imagination • Offer opportunities to for future-focused problem solving
As a student: I like learning that is lively, welcomes creativity, self-expression, and value co-operation over competition. I like to look beyond what is obvious and create new ideas. A good relationship with my teacher is very important; I need to feel valued and accepted. *	**As a student:** I enjoy learning that is creative, imaginative, inspiring and planful. I like my originality to be appreciated, supportive guidance when things get difficult and an understanding of the purpose to keep me motivated. A peaceful setting is essential. *

Having some knowledge of each individual's type pattern can help a Facilitator understand the best approach to use with each student, as well as understanding potential "roadblocks" each learner might face.

EXERCISE 6.4: LEARNING AND WHOLE TYPE

- What have been your key insights about Learning and Whole Type?
- What will you do differently as a result?

TRY IT ON: LEARNING AND WHOLE TYPE

Write your ideas here...

Key Insights?

_____

_____

_____

Do Differently?

_____

_____

_____

Chapter Summary

To be a Flawless Facilitator, it is important to design learning events to appeal to all four Information Gathering processes (Experiencing, Recalling, Brainstorming and Visioning) as well as the four Decision Making processes (Systematizing, Analyzing, Harmonizing and Valuing). In addition, a Facilitator can improve performance if they understand their innate Talents and potential Blind Spots by utilizing the Whole Type concept. Whole Type integrates Temperament, Interaction Style and preferred Cognitive Processes. Finally, we reviewed briefly how to use this knowledge to understand the learning needs of each type. The key insights are listed below.

- Temperament and Interaction style connect with preferred Cognitive Processes in a concept called Whole Type.
- Jung originated the concept of Cognitive Processes or Thinking Style as he believed we spend our lives gathering information and making decisions.

- There are four Cognitive Processes we might use to Gather Information (or Perceive data) and four we might use to Make Decisions (or Judge criteria). We can use all eight processes but individuals normally prefer using one Information Gathering function and one Decision Making function.
- Design learning events to provide opportunities to use all four Information-Gathering processes and cater for all four Decision Making processes, in order to meet the learning needs of different students.
- Use the framework of Whole Type to build self-knowledge and personal development plans.
- Consider how to approach different students and anticipate what learning challenges each might face.

SCORECARD

- What were your key learning points about Cognitive Processes and what do you think you will do differently to appeal to all eight Cognitive Processes?
- What were your learning points about your Whole Type as a Facilitator? What will you do differently as a result?
- What were your learning points about different Types' learning styles? What will you do differently as a result?

SUMMARY AND NEXT STEPS

I hope you have enjoyed and picked up some useful tips for your Flawless Facilitation Toolkit in this publication.

In the Summary.......

We will briefly review the key elements of the Flawless Facilitation. approach and share ideas for next steps.

GAME PLAN

You will review:

- The T.E.A.C.H Methodology.
- L: Leverage Active Learning Principles.
- E: Engage your Learners.
- A: Apply Experiential Learning.
- R: Recognize Different Learning Styles.
- N: Nurture Different Thinking Styles.
- Possible Next Steps.

Too often, individuals assume that presenting and facilitating use the same skill set. In reality, a Facilitator's "Tool Kit" is vastly different and more complex than merely teaching information, knowledge, skills, concepts or ideas.

Flawless Facilitators possess the ability to:

- Design effective learning events.
- Understand how adults learn.
- Facilitate a two-way conversation in real time to engage the group and maintain a safe learning environment.
- Present data clearly using words, delivery, body language and visual aids.
- Constantly evaluate in the moment how and when to focus on Task or Group Process.
- Customize and run relevant activities to cement learning.
- Self-monitor their performance in terms of Whole Type (Temperament, Interaction Style and Cognitive Processes).
- Recognize different Types and adapt their style and approach to maximize learning.

In this book, we have provided detailed "How To" tips and techniques in all of the above areas.

TIMEOUT!

T.E.A.C.H. to L.E.A.R.N.
We used the acronym T.E.A.C.H. as the "anchoring" course/program development methodology. If any program design follows these core principles, then Facilitators are perceived to be more effective.

We have used the acronym L.E.A.R.N. to explain in more detail why and how to develop and apply facilitation skills that appeal to multiple types, generations and cultures.

The T.E.A.C.H. Methodology

The goal for this chapter was to introduce the basic principles of course design that underlie Flawless Facilitation. Without effective course design, it is difficult for Facilitators to create and maintain an active learning environment. We described **The T.E.A.C.H. Methodology** as a way for the Facilitator to integrate and balance Task (What to learn) with Group Process (How to engage the Learners) in a learning experience. The acronym TEACH stands for:

> T: State the Topic
> E: Engage the Audience
> A: Share Abstract data
> C: Provide Concrete Experience
> H: Decide How to Implement ideas

We shared the overall design structure of any workshop including the Introduction, main content and summary. We finally reviewed how to prioritize content so that there is time to incorporate learner engagement.

L: Leverage Active Learning Principles

In this chapter, the goal was to provide the theoretical foundation and validation for the rest of the skills and techniques presented later in the book. We reviewed the principles of Andragogy (Adult to Adult) and Pedagogy (Parent to Child) as a way of understanding Active Learning. We reviewed how current neuroscience research suggests four areas of the brain that correlate with different stages in the Learning Cycle: **Data Gathering, Reflection, Creating Meaning** and **Active Testing**. We reviewed the benefits of social learning and showed how using The T.E.A.C.H. methodology facilitates both these elements. We then introduced the Development Process as a model to understand how the brain operates when trying to implement a new skill or habit, or enhance an existing talent or skill. The purpose of this section is to provide the Facilitator with some key background knowledge about the relevance of Active Learning, and the importance of being as specific as possible in the Development Process.

E: Engage the Audience

This goal for this chapter was to define and describe in detail the facilitation skills that create a conversational learning climate and stimulate positive participant feedback. We explored the complexity of sharing information between one facilitator and more than one receiver by referencing the Communication Process. We described the specific Involving Facilitation skills of asking open and closed questions, pausing, actively listening, repeating, asking follow up questions, paraphrasing and reinforcing participants' answers to create a safe learning environment. We then contrasted the attributes of Directive Facilitation, when the Facilitator tends to be more straightforward in either "teaching mode" or when it is necessary to restore the learning environment. We reviewed some simple guidelines for using Visual Aids such as slides, flip charts and handouts more effectively. We outlined techniques to manage situational challenging situations. Finally, we summarized how these skills integrate with The T.E.A.C.H. Methodology.

A: Apply Experiential Learning

The goal for this chapter was to help the Facilitator select and use a wide variety of learning activities based on the context and group needs. We described some of the variety of learning activities that a Facilitator can use to build credibility, cement learning, build involvement and apply the content introduced. We described the general principles for using any activity to make sure learning is enhanced and not denigrated, We also provided detailed guidelines for how and when each activity might be managed and explored which activities could be used at different stages of the Learning Cycle. As customized activities tend to be more relevant and engaging, we introduced simple principles for doing this. Finally, we reviewed how activities could fit within The T.E.A.C.H. Methodology.

R: Recognize Different Learning Styles

The goal for this chapter was to begin the process of demonstrating how to use knowledge of individual differences to build facilitation expertise. By understanding innate Talents and potential Blind Spots a Facilitator can maximize their expertise. We explored how to make learning relevant for different Types of Learners by reviewing the lenses of Temperament and Interaction Style. First, we described what might motivate different types to learn, using the theory of Temperament originally articulated for the modern world by David Keirsey. We introduced how to vary our language to appeal to different Temperaments, and which learning approaches tend to work for each Type. We also looked at the different energies associated with facilitating learning using the Linda Berens Interaction Styles framework. We discussed the importance of adapting energy and approach to different individuals and content areas in order to maximize engagement and retention. Finally, we reviewed how Temperament and Interaction style integrate with The T.E.A.C.H. Methodology.

N: Nurture Different Thinking Styles

The goal for this chapter was to demonstrate how we could appeal to different Thinking Styles by including a diversity of data gathering approaches and considering different judging criteria. We reviewed in detail the eight "Cognitive Processes", originally articulated by Carl Jung, to show how to apply this knowledge in program design. We integrated Temperament, Interaction Style and Cognitive Processes within the concept called Whole Type. We provided high-level descriptions for each Whole Type profile so that Facilitators could use this knowledge to understand their innate Talents and possible Blind Spots. We finally summarized with some specific techniques for teaching each Type. Facilitators can become more versatile using the knowledge of Whole Type for self-awareness as well as understanding different Types' learning needs.

Possible Next Steps

As you have seen, Flawless Facilitation requires many skills and techniques. Learning and behavior change will not occur without practice, so here are a few simple ideas for what you can do next.

- Review the courses you design. To what extent do they use The T.E.A.C.H. Methodology? How can you incorporate more Hooks and activities?
- Consider the stages in the Learning Cycle. To what extent do you include Data Gathering, Reflection, Creating Meaning and Active Testing? How could you change your approach to incorporate all four elements?
- Video yourself facilitating learning. Use the Facilitation Skills checklist in the appendix to observe your skills. To what extent did you use open questions, pausing and repeating to create a safe learning environment? How Involving were your Skills versus Directive? To what extent did you avoid the "Expert Trap"?
- Which activities do you use frequently? What are some new activities you could use? How will you make sure you customize these activities to the audience and learning objectives?

- How could you learn more about Temperament and Interaction Style? How could you use this knowledge to become a more versatile Facilitator? How can you motivate different Types to learn? To what extent do you tend to use one fixed style when facilitating versus flexing to the context?
- How can you learn more about Whole Type? How can you use this information to build on your innate Talents and manage potential weaknesses? How could you become more effective at facilitating learning for all types? (Check out the additional resources in the Appendix).

What Else?

Good luck using these skills, principles, knowledge and techniques to become a Flawless Facilitator!

APPENDIX

GAME PLAN

You will learn about:

- The Four Preferences (MBTI® Approach)
- Reference Sources
- Facilitation Skills Checklist

The Four Preferences (MBTI® Approach)

> "Personality type is what you prefer when you are using your mind or focusing your attention. There are no right or wrong patterns... Studies and experience have shown that there are consistent patterns for each person."
>
> *Myers Briggs Foundation*

Most people who use Psychological Type use the Myers-Briggs Type Indicator assessment tool and methodology. The purpose of this section is to show how this framework connects with Temperament, Interaction Style and Cognitive Processes to create Whole Type.

TIMEOUT!

The Myers Briggs Type Indicator (MBTI®) was designed to try to assess which of Jung's Cognitive Processes we use most easily and then in what sequence we tend to naturally access them. Myers and Briggs defined four preferences- Extroverting and Introverting (E/I), Sensing and iNutuiting (S/N), Thinking and Feeling (T/F) and Judging and Perceiving (J/P).

This framework provides a four-letter code (e.g. ESTJ) which in essence, acts as a license plate to broadly describe how an individual might approach the world and the typical thinking patterns that they might demonstrate.

FOUL!

- Preference is not the same as Prediction! It does not mean we are predisposed to ONLY use this preference. Situational factors, such as education, context, culture, etc. may also influence behavior.
- No matter what our Type Pattern, we can have the capacity to access other preferences.
- A preference is simply something that we may find easier and gravitate towards first.

Below is a simplified explanation for each of these preferences.

DIRECTION OF ENERGY	
EXTROVERTING (E)	**INTROVERTING (I)**
In what direction does your energy naturally flow?	
If you have an Extroverting preference, energy naturally flows out first to the external world of people and events. More time is spent initiating and externally processing before internal reflection.	If you have an Introverting preference, energy naturally flows inward first to thoughts and reflections. More time is spent receiving and reflecting before external processing.
PERCEIVING FUNCTION (GATHERING DATA)	
SENSING (S)	**INTUITING (N)**
What type of information do you perceive from the world?	

If you have a Sensing preference, you tend to naturally gather information through your five senses, through what you see, hear, smell, touch, and feel. These observations can be in the moment (Experiencing) or remembered from the past (Recalling) . Some who use the Sensing preference are incredibly aware of their immediate environment (Experiencing), while others can replay the sights, sounds and sensations of the past like a videotape (Recalling).	If you have an iNtuiting preference, you naturally gather information through concepts, ideas and inferred meaning. These observations can appear as the unrestrained exploration of ideas (Brainstorming) or as a total picture (Visioning). Some who use the iNtuiting preference excel in seeing patterns in the moment (Brainstorming) and reading between the lines, while others are able to manifest a complete vision, such as an "aha" or shower solution (Visioning).
Those with a Sensing preference tend to trust experience (past or present) and need more specifics in order to believe any information provided. They also tend to be more practical and realistic, and gravitate more towards examples and similes.	Those with an iNtuiting preference tend to trust inspiration and hunches and need to see the big picture when information is provided. They also tend to enjoy exploring possibilities, tend to be less practical, and enjoy metaphors and analogies.

JUDGING FUNCTION (MAKING DECISIONS)	
THINKING (T)	**FEELING (F)**
What criteria do you use to make decisions or judgments?	
If you make decisions using a Thinking preference, you tend to prefer objective, logical criteria such as facts and principles. This can look like systematic structuring and organization of logical data (Systematizing), or categorization of data and examination of principles and models (Analyzing).	If you make decisions using a Feeling preference, you tend to prefer subjective criteria such as personal values or a harmonious result. This can look like an expressive demonstration of empathy and appropriate communication (Harmonzing) or tolerance of differences and fairness (Valuing).
Those with a Thinking preference tend to view data in a more detached way, with more focus on fairness and consistency. They tend to see the flaws, require proof, and may give constructive criticism rather than positive feedback.	Those with a Feeling preference tend to view data with more of a people focus, with more emphasis on personal convictions. They tend to see the positives, value relationships, and give more positive feedback rather than constructive criticism.

FUNCTION IN EXTERNAL WORLD	
JUDGING (J)	**PERCEIVING (P)**
How do you prefer to function in the external world?	

People with a Judging Preference usually prefer closure and tend to push to make decisions. They tend to naturally make plans and structure outcomes. Time is viewed as more fixed and finite.	People with a Perceiving preference either make decisions and change them easily, or postpone making a decision at all. They tend to be more spontaneous and adaptable. Time is viewed as more flexible and/or infinite.

By selecting our innate preference from each of these four dichotomies above, we can identify a four-letter "code". Below is a little more detail on each preference.

Extroverting and Introverting

Many analysts of personality think of Extroverting and Introverting in terms of where you get your energy: from the outer world (Extroverting) or the inner world (Introverting), but this is not how Jung originally described the two terms. His description of the two terms is listed below.

TIMEOUT!

Extroverting is defined as when your energy naturally first flows outward to the external world of people and events before moving inwards to the world of ideas and thoughts.

Introverting is defined as when your energy naturally first flows inwards to the world of ideas and thoughts before moving outwards to the world of people and events.

Using the framework of Interaction Style can often help here.

- All those who share the In-Charge and Get-Things-GoIng styles share the Extroverting preference: they naturally tend to Initiate (take the first move in interactions) and have a quicker use of time (tend to have a faster pace).
- All those who share the Chart-the-Course and Behind-the-Scenes styles share the Introverting preference: they naturally tend to Respond (wait for others to take the

first move in interactions and decide if they want to engage or not) and have a more sustained use of time (tend to be more reflective and thoughtful).

FOUL!

- We have to live in both worlds!
- Just because an individual has an Extroverting preference does not mean that they never reflect and allow their energy to move inwards.
- In the same way, just because an individual has an Introverting preference does not mean that they never come out to interact!
- It is a matter of where your energy flows FIRST most naturally.

We have listed the more detailed behaviors that **TEND TO BE** associated with the Extroverting and Introverting preference below.

FOUL!

- These descriptions reflect preferences and not traits – you MAY see these signals.
- The behaviors tend to be situational.

EXTROVERTING (E)	INTROVERTING (I)
Energy naturally flows outward to process and interact	Energy flows inward to process and reflect
Act first, then think (initiate)	Think first, then act (respond)
Process information in the external world; talk things over	Process information in the internal world; think things through
Are easier to "read": Self-disclose readily	Are harder to "read": Share personal information with a few close people
May talk more than listen	May listen more than talk
May communicate with enthusiasm	May keep enthusiasm to self
Use more expressive body language	Use more reserved body language

EXTROVERTING (E)	INTROVERTING (I)
Respond quickly; verbal stream of consciousness	Respond after taking the time to think; more deliberate speaking
Lots of diverse relationships	Smaller number of in-depth relationships

Sensing and iNtuiting

Jung identified two main ways that we tend to gather or perceive information: Sensing and iNtuiting.

TIMEOUT!

- Individuals who prefer the **Sensing** process, tend to primarily gather information through their senses such as sight, sound, smell, touch and taste. They tend to trust whatever can be measured or documented and what is real and tangible. They tend to use more concrete language that contains specific words and real-life examples. They prefer to use either Experiencing or Recalling.
- Individuals who prefer the **iNtuiting** process, tend to primarily gather information through ideas, patterns, possibilities hypotheses, and inferred meanings. They also tend to trust concepts, models, theories, and potential, minimizing the importance of concrete evidence. They tend to use more abstract language that contains more general and metaphorical words. They prefer to use either Brainstorming or Visioning.

The more detailed behaviors that **MAY BE** associated with a Sensing and iNtuiting orientation are listed in the chart below.

SENSING (S)	INTUITING (N)
Tend to trust what is concrete—see, hear, touch, feel, taste, etc.	Tend to trust what is abstract—concepts, theories, etc.
May value realism and common sense	May value imagination and innovation

SENSING (S)	INTUITING (N)
Trust what is measured and documented; rely on data	Trust theories and impressions
Like new ideas if they have practical application	Like new ideas and models for their own sake
May create new approaches from past experience or from what is happening in the moment	May create new approaches from thoughts and hypotheses
Present information sequentially step by step or briefly and to the point	Present information organized around a conceptual framework or metaphor
Tend to be more practical	Tend to be more conceptual
Move from specific to general: start with the steps and move to the end result	Move from general to specific: start with the end result and then build up the steps
Use concrete language	Use abstract language
Notice specific details like changes in someone's appearance; can be frustrated when others are oblivious to the concrete environment	Notice and interpret what's between the lines in communication; can be frustrated when others take things literally
At their best are realistic but may at times appear too focused on the details	At their best are visionary but may at times appear impractical

Thinking and Feeling

Jung identified two main ways that we tend to make decisions or judge events: Thinking and Feeling. Both are rational decision-making processes, they simply use different criteria.

TIMEOUT!

- Individuals who make decisions primarily based on a **Thinking** preference, tend to be more interested in objective criteria such as what is logical and what will service the bottom line. They may see criteria as black and white while making sure criteria are consistently applied. They tend to view situations with a sense of detachment. They prefer to use either Systematizing or Analyzing.

• Individuals who make decisions primarily based on a **Feeling** preference, tend to be more interested in subjective criteria such as personal values and the people involved. They may see criteria as more like shades of grey and consider special circumstances. They tend to view situations from a more involved perspective. They prefer to use either Harmonizing or Valuing.

Listed below are some of the characteristic behaviors that **MAY BE** associated with a Thinking and Feeling preference.

THINKING (T)	FEELING (F)
Use objective criteria	Use subjective criteria
Focus on facts, logic, truth and underlying principles	Focus on human values, needs, people and harmony
Analyze the problem without personalizing it	Consider the effect on others or what it means to them
Weigh the pros and cons objectively	Measure importance to self and others
Goal = justice and fairness, standards	Goal = harmony and integrity, see the exception to the rule
Tend to be task-focused	Tend to be relationship focused
May appear critical	May appear illogical
Truth over tact	Tact over truth
Feelings are valid if logical: they need to be understood to be truly felt	Feelings are always valid: they are felt and difficult to explain
Conflict can be energizing	Conflict can be gut wrenching
Need to be in control of their emotions	Need to consider or express their emotions
Remember numbers and figures more easily	Remember faces and names more easily
Others say I sometimes appear cold insensitive, and uncaring	Others say I sometimes appear overemotional, illogical and weak

Judging and Perceiving

The final preference, the Judging and Perceiving Preference, was added to Jung's typology by Myers and Briggs to help to explain whether individuals used the Judging (Thinking/ Feeling) or Perceiving (Sensing/iNtuiting) Function in the **external world.**

FOUL!

Judging in this context means how we make decisions or bring our world to closure.

This is not the same as being judgmental!

TIMEOUT!

- Individuals with a **Judging preference** naturally use a Judging Function (Thinking or Feeling) in the external world (Systematizing or Harmonizing). As a result, they tend to prefer to achieve closure. They tend to make plans either by organizing resources to achieve an end goal (Systematizing), or by pushing for conclusion to achieve group congruence (Harmonizing). Therefore, individuals with a Judging preference tend to like to either have a structured plan or push for consensus.
- Individuals with a **Perceiving preference** naturally use a Perceiving Function (Sensing or iNtuiting) in the external world. As a result, they tend to prefer to remain flexible. They tend to be open to possibilities either by exploring options from current concrete data (Experiencing), or by generating possibilities and reading future patterns (Brainstorming). Therefore, individuals with a Perceiving preference either make decisions and change them easily, or postpone making a decision as they explore ideas.

Listed below are some of the characteristic behaviors that **MAY BE** associated with a Judging and Perceiving Preference

JUDGING (J)	PERCEIVING (P)
More comfortable with a decision made	More comfortable leaving options open
Prefer to adhere to their decision	Prefer to change a decision if circumstances change
Set goals and push to achieve them on time	Change goals as information becomes available
Prefer knowing what to expect	Enjoy adapting to new situations
Derive satisfaction from finishing a project and marking the achievement	Derive satisfaction from starting a project and process involved
Deadlines are serious: time is finite	Deadlines are elastic: time is a renewable resource
Prefer working with structure	Prefer going with the flow
Tend to schedule time, plan and organize	Tend to be more spontaneous
Fixed milestones and process	Emergent process

The following diagram depicts these relationships, provides the terms for each, and "expands" the traditional MBTI® diagram.

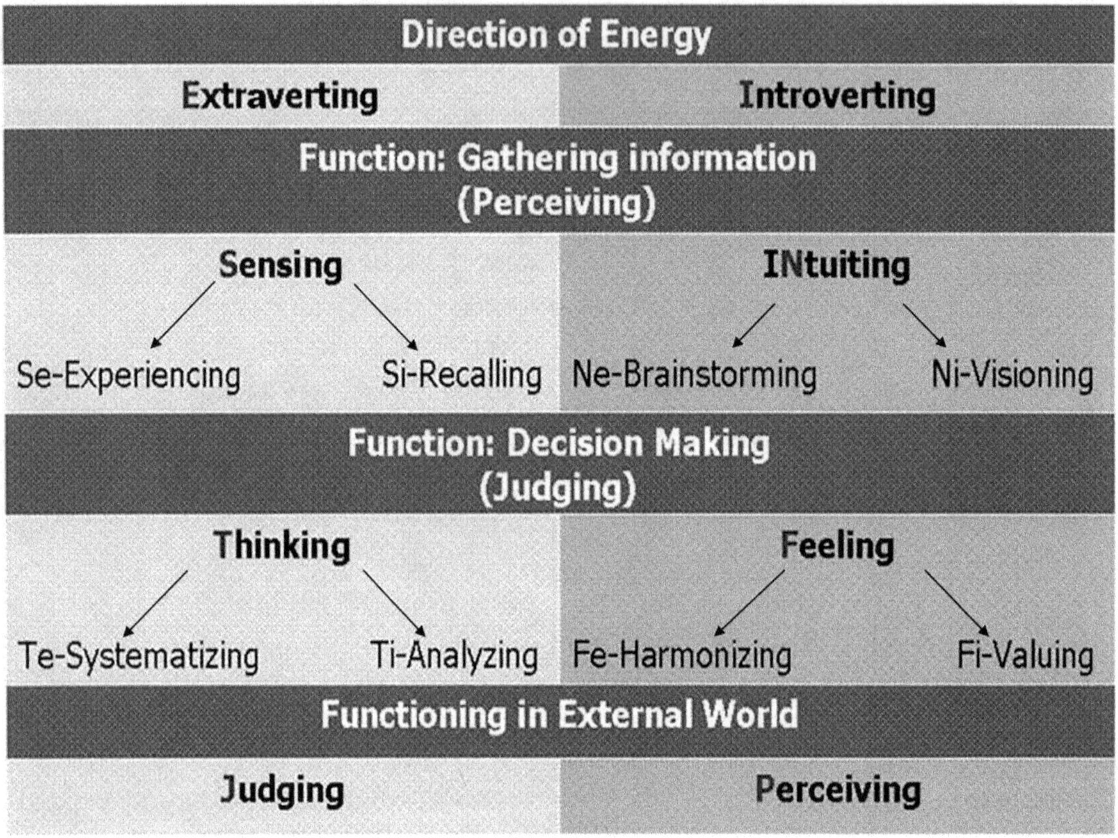

Direction of Energy	
Extraverting	**Introverting**
Function: Gathering information (Perceiving)	
Sensing	**INtuiting**
Se-Experiencing Si-Recalling	Ne-Brainstorming Ni-Visioning
Function: Decision Making (Judging)	
Thinking	**Feeling**
Te-Systematizing Ti-Analyzing	Fe-Harmonizing Fi-Valuing
Functioning in External World	
Judging	**Perceiving**

Four-Letter Type Pattern

By selecting a preference from the four outlined by Myers and Briggs, you can identify with a "Best-Fit" Type Pattern. There are 16 Whole Type Patterns using this methodology.

TIMEOUT!

We use the term "Best-Fit" because no one description will fit a person completely. There will always be elements that individuals do not identify with.

EXERCISE A-1: YOUR PREFERENCES

Looking at the descriptions of the four preferences:-

What did you most identify with? Extroverting or Introverting and Why?-

What did you most identify with? Sensing or iNtuiting and Why?-

What did you most identify with? Thinking or Feeling and Why?-

What did you most identify with? Judging or Perceiving and Why?

TRY IT ON: YOUR PREFERENCES

Write your ideas here...

Extroverting (E) or Introverting (I) and Why?

_____

_____

Sensing (S) or iNtuiting (N) and Why?

_____

_____

Thinking (T) or Feeling (F) and Why?

_____

_____

Judging (J) or Perceiving (P) and Why?

_____

_____

Appendix:
Visual Two

Based on this review your best-fit type is:

_____

E or I   S or N   T or F   J or P

_____

As you can see from the following diagram, each Temperament and Interaction Style correlates with certain preferences from the MBTI type profile e.g. Improvisers all share the S and P preferences. In the same way, each Interaction Style correlates with two sets of preferences e.g. all In-Charge styles share either EN-J preferences or EST_ preferences.

FOUL!

Although Temperament and Interaction Style SHARE certain type preferences, each theory is separate and more comprehensive than simply "combining the letters".

Below is a Type Table that links Temperament, Interaction Style and Type (The Cognitive Processes associated with each type are in the previous Chapter).

Appendix:
Visual Three

Get-Things-Going **ENFP**	Behind-the-Scenes **INFP**	Get-Things-Going **ESFP**	Behind-the-Scenes **ISFP**
	Catalyst		Improviser
In-Charge **ENFJ**	Chart-the-Course **INFJ**	In-Charge **ESTP**	Chart-the-Course **ISTP**
Get-Things-Going **ESFJ**	Behind-the-Scenes **ISFJ**	Get-Things-Going **ENTP**	Behind-the-Scenes **INTP**
	Stabilizer		Theorist
In-Charge **ESTJ**	Chart-the-Course **ISTJ**	In-Charge **ENTJ**	Chart-the-Course **INTJ**

By utilizing the concepts of Temperament, Interaction Style, Cognitive Processes and Type, we have access to a rich reference source into what motivates each Type (Temperament), how each Type engages with others (Interaction Style) and how each type thinks about their current reality (Cognitive Processes). All of these elements can help Facilitators to both understand their strengths and potential challenges, and also to better design and deliver workshops that meet the needs of all types.

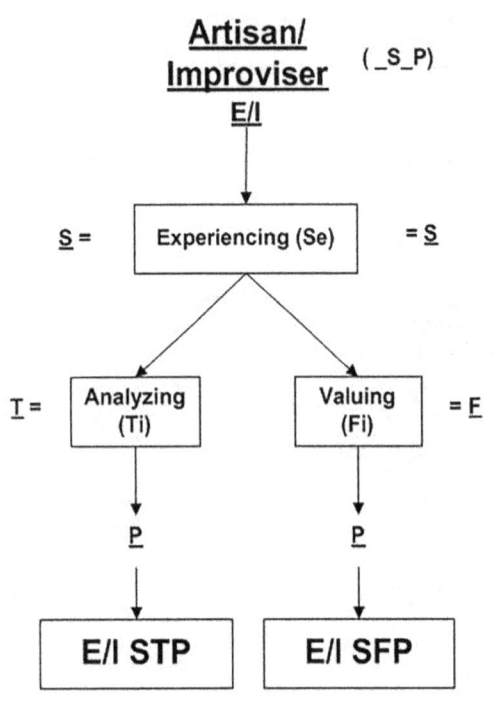

Artisan/ Improviser (_S_P)

E/I

S = Experiencing (Se) = S

T = Analyzing (Ti)   Valuing (Fi) = F

P   P

E/I STP   E/I SFP

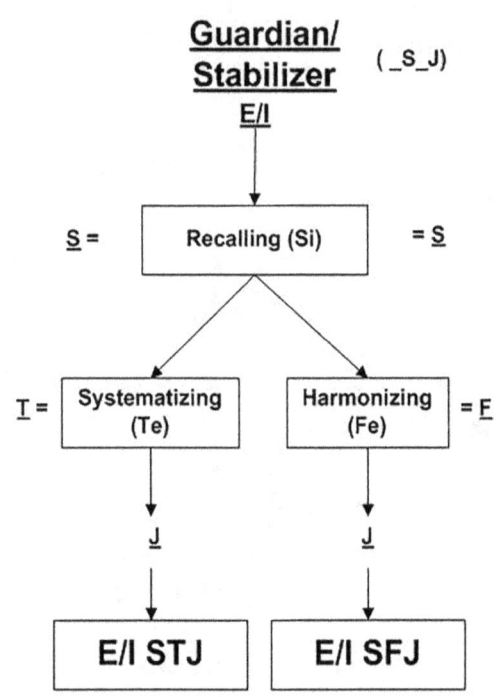

Guardian/ Stabilizer (_S_J)

E/I

S = Recalling (Si) = S

T = Systematizing (Te)   Harmonizing (Fe) = F

J   J

E/I STJ   E/I SFJ

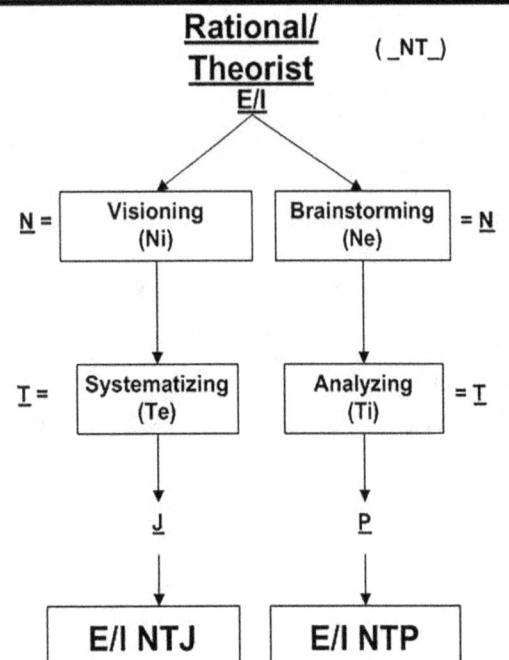

Rational/ Theorist (_NT_)

E/I

N = Visioning (Ni)   Brainstorming (Ne) = N

T = Systematizing (Te)   Analyzing (Ti) = T

J   P

E/I NTJ   E/I NTP

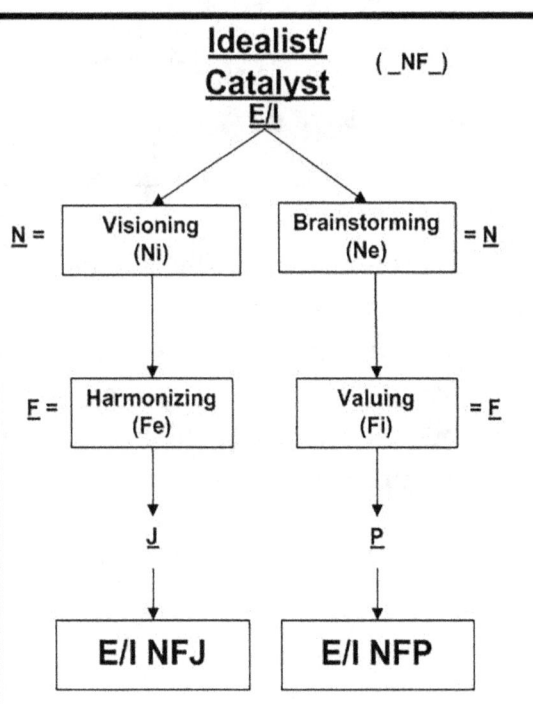

Idealist/ Catalyst (_NF_)

E/I

N = Visioning (Ni)   Brainstorming (Ne) = N

F = Harmonizing (Fe)   Valuing (Fi) = F

J   P

E/I NFJ   E/I NFP

Reference Sources

Temperament

Berens, Linda. V. *Understanding Yourself and Others: An Introduction to Temperament-4.0*. 2008

Delunas, E. *Survival Games Personalities Play*. 1992

Keirsey, D. *Please Understand Me II*. 1998

Keirsey, D, and Bates, M. *Please Understand Me*. 1978

Nash, S. *Turning Team Performance Inside Out*. 1999

Nash, S. *Dating, Mating and Relating* 2013

Nash, S. and Nash D. *Delivering Outstanding Service* 2002

Nash, S. and Bolin, C *Teamwork from the Inside Out Field Book* 2003

Nash S. *Starting and Running Your Own Consultancy Business*. 2007

Tieger, P. D., and Barron-Tieger, B. *Do What You Are*. 2014

Tieger, P. D., and Barron-Tieger, B. *Nurture by Nature*. 2001

Interaction Style

Berens, Linda. V. *Interaction Essentials: 3 Keys to Effective Relationships in the Workplace and Beyond*. 2011

Berens, Linda. V. And Gerke Susan K. *Quick Guide to Interaction Style and Time Dynamics*. 2003

Berens, Linda. V. And Gerke Susan K. *Quick Guide to Interaction Style and Working Remotely*. 2003

Berens, Linda. V. *Understanding Yourself and Others: An Introduction to Interaction Style 3.0*. 2008

Nash, S. *Contextual Coaching*. 2011

Stothart, C. *How to Get On with Anyone*. 2018

Cognitive Processes

Berens, Linda. V., Nardi, Dario. *Understanding Yourself and Others: An Introduction to the Personality Type Code Radiance House*. 1999

Berens, Linda. V. et al, *Quick Guide to Personality Types in Organizations*. 2002

Hartzler, G and Hartzler, M *Facets of Type: Activities to Develop the Type Preferences*. 2004

Hartzler, G and Hartzler, M *Functions of Type: Activities to Develop the Eight Jungian Functions*. 2005

Haas, Leona and Hunziker, Mark *Building Blocks of Personality Type*. 2014

Myers, Isabel Briggs and Peter B. Myers. *Gifts Differing*. 1995

Myers, Katherine D. and Kirby, Linda K. *Introduction to Type Dynamics and Development*. 1994

Nardi, Dario *8 Keys to Self Leadership* Unite 2005

Nardi, Dario PHD *Neuroscience of Personality* . 2011

Thompson, H. L. *Jung's Function-Attitudes Explained*. 1996.

Whole Type

Berens, Linda. V., Nardi, Dario. *The 16 Personality Types: Descriptions for Self-Discovery*. 1999.

Berens, Linda. V. et al, *Quick Guide to Personality Types in Organizations*. 2002.

Blair, S. *Personality Puzzle Cards and Guidebook* 2011

Blair, S. *Type for Teens Cards and Guidebook* 2013

Blair, S. *Learning Puzzle* 2017

Brownsword, Alan W. *It Takes All Types*. 1994

Mc Guiness, M, *You've Got Personality*. 2016

Nash, S and Blair, S *Type Trilogy Card Set and Complete Guidebook* 2015

Nash, S. *Let's Split the Difference*. 2009.

Segal, Marci *Creativity and Personality Type*. 2001.

Archetypes

Beebe, J. Energies and Patterns in Psychological Type. 2017

Hunzinger, M. *Depth Typology: C. G. Jung, Isabel Myers, John Beebe and The Guide Map to Becoming Who We Are*. 2015

Web Sites

Card sets and Guidebook:
https://www.personalitydynamics.co.nz/testimonials/personality-puzzle/
https://type-academy.co.uk/

Whole Type Reference Materials
http://www.radiancehouse.com/
https://www.lindaberens.com/

On-line assessments
http://www.type-coach.com

Facilitation Skills Checklist

USE FACILITATION SKILLS TO ENGAGE	NOTES
• Asking open questions • Asking closed questions • Managing the pause • Repeating answers word-for-word • Asking follow-up questions • Asking leading questions • Using names • Giving genuine positive feedback • Asking permission to paraphrase • Repeating every question asked • Using Ping Pong as necessary • Refer back to what individuals have said earlier using their name • Use positive body language to validate input	
Use of Slides • Use the clicker effectively • Click and question per bullet • Correct slide at all times • Pacing of slides	
Use of Flip Chart • Use of Color • Pre-preparing Flip Charts • Love your FC • Writing word-for-word on flip chart – not your words • Asking questions if words are not clear • Use of a partner to write flip chart • Paraphrasing for partner • Managing pace with a partner	
Use of Participant Guide • Referring to correct page • Holding up PG/Love your PG	

USE FACILITATION SKILLS TO ENGAGE	NOTES
Use of Video • Set up and debrief	
Sending the Message • Use of humor • Clarity of voice tone • Appropriate and varied pace • Word choice – use of simple yet clear words • Specific gestures • Use of movement • Varying facial expression • Making eye contact • Adding personal examples and stories as appropriate	
Handouts • Preparation of handouts • Distribution and management	
Use of Experiential Learning • Using a variety of exercises • Clarity in instructions • Dividing the group • Clear set up/Prime the Pump • Defining the purpose of the exercise • Monitoring exercise • Managing the debrief • Emphasizing key learning points: what, so what, now what • Frequency of activities	

USE FACILITATION SKILLS TO ENGAGE	NOTES
Overall • Set up and preparation • Timing • Comfort with materials • Using transition points • Managing stress or nerves • Frequency of involvement • Awareness of group process • Ability to make the learning personalized	

CPSIA information can be obtained
at www.ICGtesting.com
Printed in the USA
FSHW022226160919
62079FS

9 781733 822503